THE COOK IS IN THE PARLOR

The Cook
Is in the Parlor

by

Marguerite Gilbert McCarthy

Gramercy Publishing Company

New York

Introduction

This is my own personal cook book. It is not intended for those who need to learn how to cook, but it will, I believe, be helpful to those who can cook and who wish to serve more imaginative and delectable food. It grew out of my own experience in arranging menus, in supervising the preparation of food, and in cooking food. It has really been written for the many friends who have said they enjoyed the food which they have shared with me in my city home and at my ranch.

There is actually no such thing as a book of entirely new and original recipes, since cooking has been going on in the world since Eve presumably first found that the fat from a roasted calf improved the taste of edible roots and grains, and since Charles Lamb's hero discovered that crisped pig was delicious. The fact that earlier generations enjoyed certain combinations of food is no reason for scorning them, but certainly they often may be improved in flavor and in nutriment, or prepared more easily than formerly.

Some combinations of ingredients were contrived in the spirit of the moment, and although immediately jotted down, never seemed afterwards to produce quite the fine flavor of my initial attempt. The real reason for the deviation may be that we rarely have exactly the same leftovers in the refrigerator. I recall one dish, highly approved when I served it, compounded of left-over fried rice, turkey dressing and gravy, bits of the turkey meat, soup meat with the soup stock, and some creamed onions — all "odds and ends" I found in the refrigerator. Probably I added Worcestershire sauce, a little Tabasco, and one of the many herbs always to be found in my kitchen. This mixture was tucked in a casserole, covered, and left to simmer gently until someone suggested it was time to eat. One of my sons-in-law mixed a green salad, someone else toasted French bread, and that, with some fruit, was all. But you can realize the difficulty of giving a measured recipe that would insure the same flavor as the mixture we had that night.

There is, of course, one ingredient needed for all recipes that only the cook can give. That is her interest in preparing food that will add to the enjoyment of her family and friends. A real love for what one is doing underlies all successful achievement, and especially the creation of delectable food.

Contents

PART I

MAKING THE MOST OF EVERYTHING

Making the Most of Everything

Food need not be expensive to be delicious. In fact, you are more likely to become known as an authority on delectable food if, instead of serving the traditional "party food," you serve something less expensive which is delicious because of the way it is cooked. A seasoning of herbs or a unique blending of flavors may add a distinctive touch. It may take courage on your part to serve your friends a cheap cut of meat. But don't be afraid to experiment, and when you become an expert in preparing the less popular foods, you will probably find yourself regarded as an epicure.

Pot roast can become a great delicacy when served crisp and brown with a deliciously flavored gravy that it has acquired from being soaked in wine for several days. Or maybe the addition of a few ginger snaps crumbled in the gravy has added that certain touch which intrigues the palate.

Many a housewife passes by the flank steak, that is delicious when stuffed with well-seasoned bread crumbs, because she does not know how to prepare it. She also disregards the brisket of beef that she might have served with a bitey horse-radish sauce. Her husband might have been thrilled had he been served a meal of short ribs with a savory brown gravy poured over the accompanying carrots, onions, and boiled or mashed potatoes.

When I was first married, our budget allowed just five dollars a week from which to provide our meals, as well as to pay for the laundry, carfare, and incidentals. The many uses to which I could put a soupbone helped make the money go further. First, I would buy a shinbone with marrow in the center and the rim of good beef around the outside. At the same time, if I felt affluent, I would buy a veal knuckle. I always asked the butcher to add a few chicken feet, which he was glad to give me as no one else wanted them. The chicken feet would furnish the gelatine substance so necessary in broth.

Next, I would buy a variety of soup vegetables, which in those days were inexpensive. I usually shopped at the end of the day when the grocer was glad to sell his leftovers cheap rather than have them spoil.

By adding a head of lettuce, some spaghetti, a bit of cheese, and a loaf of French bread, I was well supplied for the next few days.

On sorting over the vegetables, I usually found more than I needed for soup. First, the ripe tomato was carefully set aside. The soup didn't need the tomato, and it would provide a salad when combined with the lettuce. The leaves from the celery were put away to be used in the salad or dried for future seasoning.

Next, the soupbones, plus the onion and celery, were put to simmer with a few herbs, which an Italian neighbor had suggested that I grow in little pots in my kitchen window. Then, when the soup had simmered long enough, I carefully removed the marrow from the center of the bone and put it away to serve later, reheated on a piece of toast, as a nutritious appetizer for dinner. The stock was strained and put aside to cool, the soup meat removed and saved for future use.

In the meantime, my soup vegetables had been put to boil. I always saved the potato to add later to the soup meat for making hash, or sometimes I ground the meat and added it to the spaghetti along with a bit of cheese, to be served for the next day's dinner. Some of the cooked vegetables I mixed with a cream sauce, covered them with bread crumbs, and baked as an addition to the meal.

As dried beans were cheap, I always had a dish of them boiled and ready to add to the remains of the soup for minestrone or to mash and mix with milk for bean soup. For a salad, I added chopped green onion tops to the beans before mixing in the sharply seasoned dressing. Being of New England extraction, I also baked beans with salt pork, which was cheap, adding a trickle of molasses for extra flavor. With the addition of cole-slaw, made perhaps from part of the soup cabbage, I could provide another meal.

Another economy was the use of substitutes for butter. I used margarine where a butter-like flavor was necessary (all recipes in this book except those for hot soup will respond equally well with either butter or a substitute), but my real economy was in the use of meat fats. The fat from the top of the soup stock, with its flavor of herbs and other seasonings, I used for browning meats. It added an elusive combination of flavors that delighted and baffled my friends. Whenever the obliging butcher added a bit of chicken fat to my purchases, I rendered it to be used later when making mock-chicken stew. This was made by browning a cheap cut of veal stew meat in some of the chicken fat and cooking it in chicken broth, which at that time could be bought very cheaply from a tamale factory. (You can use chicken cubes.) The rest of the fat I used for dumplings; it not only enhanced the flavor but also increased the illusion that there was chicken in the stew.

Other meat fats, such as that from lamb breast or salt pork, I saved for frying potatoes or hash. But the choicest of all fats was that from bacon or ham. This was obtained cheaply by buying pieces of rind, which I fried slowly until all the fat was extracted; the leftover rind was cooked with spinach or string beans to give them additional flavor. Not being able to afford bacon except as a rare treat, I sometimes sautéed slices of bread until brown in the fat from the rind and when the bread was covered with a poached egg, it made a good substitute for the bacon itself. The fat could also be used in place of butter in making biscuits as well as in cream sauce.

Making the most of everything can become an exciting game. Each carcass of meat has certain parts that, although appetizing when properly prepared, are inexpensive. These cuts usually require longer cooking, but that only gives them more chance to assimilate the richness of whatever seasonings you have added.

They also improve when reheated, so may be cooked far ahead of the time of serving.

Breast of lamb is delicious when prepared as a stew, or it may be spread with sausage meat or bread stuffing, then rolled, tied, and roasted in the oven. Next time you are preparing a barbecue, try roast lamb breast. Trim off some of the fat, rub the lamb well with crushed garlic, and season with salt, pepper, and herbs. Let it roast slowly until tender, then cut it in pieces and let your friends eat it with their fingers.

Roast lamb shoulder has more flavor than the leg and is twice as juicy. It may be roasted whole, or else boned and rolled, or may have a pocket cut and stuffed with a number of different fillings. However it is prepared, surround it with vegetables so that your entire dinner is cooked at one time with only the roasting pan to wash. Lamb shanks are also delicious when well-seasoned and roasted slowly. In fact, they taste very much like turkey. And lamb kidneys may be cooked in a chafing dish and flavored with red wine or a combination of dry mustard and lemon.

Pork, too, offers opportunities to economize. Try spareribs and sauerkraut prepared by my special recipe. Take some along as your contribution the next time you are invited to a picnic. Have it already cooked and hot, and wrap the roaster in newspapers to keep in the heat.

Many people say that pork does not agree with them, and probably the reason is that it has not been properly cooked. Test your meat with a meat thermometer to see that it is cooked sufficiently. Boiling the pork with herbs and a little garlic before it is roasted will not only keep the meat juicy but will add to the flavor as well.

In order to gain the pleasure that you should from your experiments, you need a collection of herbs and seasonings. A beginner need not purchase every herb in the market, for mixed dried herbs are now packaged to season different types of food. They come labeled so that there is no guesswork; some are for fish, some for salad or soup, and others to be used generally. "Use sparingly" is the watchword as far as herbs are concerned.

They should *suggest* flavor, not *declare* it. A "pinch" of herbs is the right amount at any time.

On one shelf or in a box to themselves, it is well to gather seasonings that are good for salads. These may also be used to flavor vegetables and cream sauce, and to add a new tang to egg dishes. I suggest Maggi's Seasoning, dry mustard or mustard sauce, as well as anchovies or anchovy paste. And most certainly, Tabasco sauce, paprika, cayenne, and Worcestershire sauce.

Don't forget the wine vinegars and always save every bit of wine left after dining. If it is properly corked, it will keep indefinitely in your refrigerator. Most cooking is improved by the addition of a little wine, or wine extract if you prefer.

Kitchen Bouquet will darken your gravy as well as enrich it, and for a combination of flavors add Bell's Poultry Seasoning. For emergencies, you should keep on hand liquid seasonings, such as onion, garlic, green pepper, and parsley. They can take the place of fresh ingredients if necessary.

Meat-flavored cubes and chicken cubes should hold an important place on your shelf. They may be added to soup, gravy, vegetables, and meat to enhance the flavor and give it richness.

So, using these suggestions, try out a few of the less expensive cuts of meat and save on your budget. If, during the day, you are not able to give the time for their long cooking, then plan your meals further ahead. Have tomorrow's dinner cooking the evening before while you darn your husband's socks.

Sunday Morning Breakfast

Sunday morning offers an opportunity to entertain economically and with very little effort. The unhurried feeling about this particular morning immediately brings forth a desire for relaxation.

You will probably decide to serve breakfast around noon, thus combining two meals in one. Your party may be large or small, elaborate or simple, but no matter which, it should be fun. Everything should be so well organized that neither you nor your guests are compelled to dash around at the last minute. Nor should you keep your guests waiting while you putter around trying to cook breakfast.

In everything there is a key to efficiency, a short cut to success. One of the secrets to a successful party is service, and to give good service in a servantless home requires a system. Trays have often solved this problem for me. By using trays the food may be served from the buffet or right from the kitchen stove with little effort and everyone receives his food while it is still hot. These trays should be of lightweight composition, arranged attractively, and need not involve any great expense.

Here is one place where you can add that original touch to make your party different. If your home calls for Early American, use red and white checked gingham for doilies and napkins, and fringe the edges. For china, buy reproductions of milk glass, which can be found in the five and ten cent store. Or you might use unbleached muslin, dye it with bright colors — the doilies and napkins contrasting — and use Mexican pottery and glassware.

The china I use at my ranch I bought in Honolulu at a Chinese grocery store. The plates are decorated with an orange and black rooster, looking very silly under a large green cabbage leaf. As no cups came with the set, I found some made of clay in a glorious warm yellow. With that as a start, I collected animal salts and peppers as well as sugars and creamers. You can imagine the chuckles of my guests as they examine their trays on Sunday morning and pour cream from the mouth of a fish and shake salt from the topknot of a bird.

If you prefer to seat your guests at one large table, you can still keep everything gay. Use plenty of color, if only in your decorations. Bowls of flowers may pick up the color of your tablecloth and carry it on to the water glasses and compotes filled with jelly. Or fill a decorative piece of pottery with a combination of fruit and green leaves to give your room that needed spot of gaiety.

Sunday morning is one time when you really have leisure to enjoy your garden, so what more attractive place could you find to serve breakfast? Here you may use trays so that each person may seek out the particular spot that appeals to him, or you may decide to use the table that you have thoughtfully arranged beneath a large shady tree.

If the weather is too chilly for the garden, why not gather in the living room in front of the fireplace?

As for the food that you serve for your breakfast, some people find they can entertain more easily if they perfect one or two menus and stick to them. There is nothing wrong with that idea as long as you add a touch of originality to the perfection of the cooking. Far better to offer your guests well-cooked ham and eggs, displayed on amusing china, than to attempt an elaborate menu too complicated to be served with ease and satisfaction.

Perhaps your husband is the type who likes to help with the cooking. If he makes waffles — most men seem to make them better than their wives — suggest that he serve "Mystery Syrup" with them; it will keep everyone guessing all during breakfast. If he makes hot cakes, little thin ones, fill them with creamed chicken or creamed chipped beef.

You might like to show your skill to your admiring guests.

Then why not give a kitchen party? I find, regardless of age or wealth or dignity, there is something fascinating to everyone about being in someone else's kitchen. It is such a friendly place, that is if the hostess is fairly orderly and has made her plans beforehand. Men always drift back to our kitchen, in town or at the ranch. After all, the kitchen, where good food is prepared, is the foundation of life, good health, and happiness.

So, whether you serve breakfast from a tray or from a table, whether in the garden or in the kitchen, whether your husband or you are the chef, make breakfast on Sunday morning a festive occasion — something to look forward to during the week.

Menu

TROPICAL COCKTAIL

OMELET WITH MUSHROOMS

BAKED POTATO BALLS

DELICIOUS MUFFINS

FIG JAM WITH LEMON AND NUTS

TROPICAL COCKTAIL

Mix equal proportions of orange and pineapple juice.

OMELET WITH MUSHROOMS

Sauté ½ pound of chopped mushrooms in 3 tablespoons of butter until brown and cooked through. Keep hot while your omelet is cooking. Beat together, with a fork, 10 eggs and 3 tablespoons of cream. Pour this mixture through a sieve covered with a cloth. Rub the surface of an iron frying pan with salt until smooth. Rinse. Melt 3 tablespoons of butter in the pan and then pour in the beaten eggs. Have the fire hot and, as the eggs start to cook on the bottom, lift the edges with a spatula, allowing the uncooked portion to flow down into the pan. When cooked, put the mushrooms on one half and fold over the other half. Serve on a hot platter and sprinkle with chopped parsley. Serves 6.

BAKED POTATO BALLS

Mash boiled white potatoes, season, add milk and butter, making a stiff mixture. Shape into balls and roll in melted butter, then in crushed corn flakes. These may be made the day before and stored in the refrigerator. About ½ hour before they are to be served, remove from the refrigerator, place in a buttered pan, and heat through in a moderate oven.

DELICIOUS MUFFINS

Sift together 1 cup of flour, 2 teaspoons of baking powder, 2 tablespoons of sugar, and ¼ teaspoon of salt. Add 2 tablespoons of soft butter and mix well with the tips of your fingers. Then add ½ cup of cream and 1 beaten egg. Beat well together, put in greased muffin tins and bake in a moderate oven (350°) for about 25 minutes. Makes 8 to 12 muffins.

FIG JAM WITH LEMON AND NUTS

Peel black figs and cut into pieces. Measure cup for cup of figs and sugar. For 1 quart of figs, add 2 lemons, sliced thin, leaving the skin on. Boil until the syrup drops in clots from the side of the spoon. Add 1 cup of chopped walnut meats. Seal in sterilized jars.

```
┌─────────────────────────────────────────┐
│                                         │
│              Menu                       │
│                                         │
│         APPLES IN WHITE WINE            │
│                                         │
│      MILLBROOK EGGS EN CASSEROLE        │
│                                         │
│            CORN DODGERS                 │
│                                         │
│            TANGERINE JAM                │
│                                         │
└─────────────────────────────────────────┘
```

APPLES IN WHITE WINE

Pare, core, and quarter 6 apples. Boil in a syrup of 1 cup each of white wine, water, and sugar, with ½ teaspoon of cinnamon. When the apples are tender, pour into a serving dish and chill.

MILLBROOK EGGS EN CASSEROLE

Cover the bottom of individual casseroles with round slices of toast spread with any of the following: liverwurst or deviled ham, mashed and thinned with a little mayonnaise; chopped cooked bacon; a slice of boiled ham; or any fish, such as lobster, shrimp, tuna, or crab. Break 1 egg carefully on top of each slice of toast and then pour over Millbrook Sauce. Bake in a moderate oven (350°) until nearly set; then brown under the broiler.

Millbrook Sauce. — Blend ½ cup of mayonnaise with 1 large-sized can of evaporated milk. Add ½ teaspoon of anchovy paste and 1 teaspoon of Worcestershire sauce.

CORN DODGERS

Stir together 2 cups of white corn meal (water-ground, if possible), 1 tablespoon of flour, ½ teaspoon of soda, 1 teaspoon of baking powder, 1 teaspoon of sugar, and ⅛ teaspoon of salt. Add 1 cup of buttermilk and 4 tablespoons of bacon fat. If not thin enough for shaping, add a little water. Take in your hands

by tablespoonfuls and shape in ovals. Bake on a greased pan.
Serves 6.

TANGERINE JAM

Grate 1 teaspoon of tangerine rind. Remove the skin and
seeds from the tangerines and cut up the pulp. To 2 cups of
tangerine pulp and juice, add 1½ cups of sugar, 1 teaspoon of
grated tangerine rind, and the pulp and juice of 1 lemon. Boil
until syrupy, about 10 minutes, cool, and seal in sterilized jars.
(This jam is delicious when heated and poured over vanilla ice
cream.)

Menu

BROILED GRAPEFRUIT

BACON AND POTATO OMELET

BUTTERY MELBA TOAST

ORANGE MARMALADE

BROILED GRAPEFRUIT

The evening before the grapefruit is to be served, cut it in
half, loosen segments, and sprinkle brown sugar over the top.
Pour over a little sherry and cover the fruit with waxed paper.
Next morning, dot with butter just before broiling.

BACON AND POTATO OMELET

Allow 1 slice of bacon, cut in small pieces, and half a raw potato,
cubed, for every 2 eggs. Fry bacon until crisp and remove from
fat. Add the potato and fry slowly until done. Beat required
number of eggs, add bacon, and a few sprigs of parsley, chopped
fine. Pour into the pan on top of the potatoes and cook until
the bottom is done. Place under the broiler to cook and brown
the top. Fold over and serve immediately with buttered toast.

BUTTERY MELBA TOAST

Slice white bread thin; butter the loaf each time before slicing. Lay slices on a cookie sheet and place in a moderate oven (350°) until slightly browned. Serve hot from the oven or reheat.

Menu

RUBY-RED APPLE SLICES

HAM POLENTA

CRUMB COFFEE CAKE

RUBY–RED APPLE SLICES

Wash, core, and slice without paring 2 quarts of red apples. Put them in a baking dish and pour 2 cups of sugar over them. Cover the casserole and bake very slowly at 250° for 4 hours. The apples will be red as rubies clear through and are delicious. Cook the day before and either reheat or serve cold with or without cream. Serves 6.

HAM POLENTA

The day before you wish to serve the polenta, bring 4 cups of water to a boil and add 1 teaspoon of salt. Stir in slowly, so as not to stop the boiling, 1 cup of corn meal. Be sure to stir as you pour, so that the corn meal will not lump. Let it boil up, being careful that it does not boil over. Boil for 5 minutes, then transfer to the top of a double boiler and continue cooking over hot water for ½ hour. Stir in ½ to 1 cup of minced, leftover ham, or canned luncheon meat. When thoroughly mixed, pour into a square pan to cool. Set in the refrigerator until the next day. When you are ready to serve it, cut in fingers 3 inches long and 1 inch wide. Dredge in flour and brown in bacon fat until crisp. Serves 4 to 6.

CRUMB COFFEE CAKE

Sift together 1 cup of sugar with 2 cups of flour and ½ teaspoon each of salt, ginger, cinnamon, and nutmeg. Work in with your fingers ½ cup of shortening. Reserve 1 cup of this mixture for the top. Beat together 1 egg and ½ cup of sour milk or buttermilk. Add 1 teaspoon of baking powder and ½ teaspoon of soda. Add to the flour mixture and beat until thoroughly mixed. Add ½ cup each of chopped nuts and raisins. Butter a square pan and put half of the reserved crumbs in the bottom, add the batter, and sprinkle the rest of the crumbs on the top. Bake for 40 minutes in a moderate oven (350°). (This may be reheated.) Serves 6.

Menu

CANNED GRAPEFRUIT JUICE

SAUSAGE PATTIES ON HOMINY GRITS CIRCLES

FRIED APPLE RINGS

WHEAT CAKES

MYSTERY SYRUP

SAUSAGE PATTIES ON HOMINY GRITS CIRCLES

Season bulk sausage with finely chopped chives. Boil hominy grits the day before, cool in a flat pan, and cut with a cookie cutter. Roll in flour. Shape the sausage patty the same size as the hominy grits circle and roll in flour. Fry both until brown. Place each sausage patty on a hominy grits circle. Serve on a platter and decorate with parsley.

FRIED APPLE RINGS

Cut 1 dozen apple slices ½ inch thick, left unpeeled but cored. Soak for 20 minutes or longer in a mixture of 1 tablespoon of lemon juice, 4 tablespoons of brown sugar, and 3 tablespoons of sherry. Drain and dip in flour. Melt ½ cup of butter in a flat pan and lay in the apple slices. Place under the broiler and brown slowly, turning once. Remove from pan and dust lightly with a mixture of cinnamon and sugar. Serves 4 to 6.

WHEAT CAKES
(Wilson's)

While living in my "bandbox" in New York, I helped serve breakfast at the Soldiers' and Sailors' Club, where Wilson, the chef, taught me to flip these pancakes — baked to a mouth-watering brown and fragile as your grandmother's best teacup. But if you serve them, be generous with your melted butter; pour over plenty — an extravagant amount — and add a pitcher of Mystery Syrup to tickle your guests' palates and whet their curiosity.

1 cup milk	1½ cups flour
2 eggs, well beaten	2½ teaspoons baking powder
3 tablespoons melted shortening	3 tablespoons sugar
¼ teaspoon soda	¾ teaspoon salt

Mix well the milk, the melted shortening, and the beaten eggs. Add the dry ingredients; stir until smooth. Cook on not too hot a griddle.

The cakes, as served to the boys in the canteen, were large. If you want a thinner cake, add a little more milk. Serve with Mystery Syrup. Serves 4 to 6.

Mystery Syrup. — We call this Mystery Syrup because whenever we serve it, everyone tries to guess what is in it. The secret is cooking brandy added to hot maple syrup. The amount? Let your conscience be your guide! (Melted butter also may be added.)

Menu

BAKED APPLES

EGGS NEW ORLEANS

FLUFFY COFFEE CAKE

BAKED APPLES
(Aunt Ella's)

In Aunt Ella's kitchen every Saturday morning, spicy, fruity smells seeped out of the oven of the old wood stove where apples baked beside loaves of bread. And every Sunday night, Uncle Jim placed one of the apples neatly in a bowl, added a generous amount of rich Guernsey milk to the thick apple syrup, and crumbled fresh homemade bread evenly over the top. But that is no reason why you should not serve these apples for dessert; just add a sauce of sour cream sweetened with sugar and a suggestion of rum.

Select 4 baking apples without skin blemish, core, leaving blossom end closed. Pare one quarter down from the top. Arrange in a baking dish with lid. Prepare a sauce of ½ cup of maple syrup or white corn syrup, ½ cup of sugar, 1 cup of water, ⅛ teaspoon of cinnamon. Heat until sugar dissolves. Pour over apples and cover the dish. Bake 45 minutes at 350°. Uncover and continue baking, basting often, for 30 minutes. Remove from oven, add 1 tablespoon of butter to hot syrup, and continue basting until the apples are almost cool. Serve warm or cold. Serves 4.

EGGS NEW ORLEANS

Make a medium cream sauce, and for each cup of the sauce add 2 beaten egg yolks, ½ cup of grated cheese, and a wine glass of sherry. (One cup of sauce is enough for 4 eggs.) Season with salt and pepper. Trim and sauté in butter the desired number of pieces of toast; then place on a serving platter and keep hot. Cover each slice of toast with a slice of boiled ham that has been lightly sautéed. Top this with a slice of fried tomato. Poach as many eggs as you have people to serve. When the eggs are done, place one on each toast mound and pour the sauce around them, but do not cover the eggs.

FLUFFY COFFEE CAKE
(Dorothy's)

Sift together 1 cup of flour, 3 teaspoons of baking powder, ¼ teaspoon of salt, and 2 teaspoons of cinnamon. Stir in ½ cup of sugar. Beat 1 egg with ½ cup of milk. Add to the dry ingredients with ¼ cup of melted butter and mix well. Pour into a shallow pan. Cover the top with a mixture of cinnamon and sugar, and sprinkle some finely chopped nuts over all. Bake 30 minutes in a 375° oven. This rises quite high, so allow enough room in your pan. A very light coffee cake! (It may be made the day before and reheated.) Serves 4.

Menu

HONEYDEW MELON WITH LIME

EGG TIMBALES FLAVORED WITH CHEESE

BUTTERSCOTCH BISCUITS

EGG TIMBALES FLAVORED WITH CHEESE

Make a cream sauce with 3 tablespoons of butter, 2 tablespoons of flour, and 1¼ cups of milk. Season with celery salt and ⅛ teaspoon each of white pepper, nutmeg, and thyme. Beat the yolks of 6 eggs and stir gradually into the hot cream sauce. Add ½ cup of freshly grated cheese. Beat the 6 egg whites stiff and add, while beating, 1 teaspoon each of finely chopped parsley and chives. Fold into the yolk mixture and, when blended, pour into 6 buttered custard cups. Set the cups in a pan of hot water, and bake in a moderate oven (350°) for about 30 minutes, or until the eggs are set. Unmold on a hot serving platter and surround with slices of fried bacon. Serves 6.

BUTTERSCOTCH BISCUITS

Use any recipe for baking powder biscuits or use the prepared biscuit mixture put up in packages. Roll the dough to make a long, narrow strip. Cream together ⅔ cup of butter with 1½ cups of brown sugar and spread over the biscuit dough with the long side towards you. Roll up the dough tightly and cut into 2-inch pieces. Drop a dab of butter and a teaspoon of brown sugar in each muffin cup and place a biscuit in each one. Bake 20 minutes in a moderate oven (350°).

Menu

PEACHES AND GRAPE-NUTS PARADISE

LIGHT AND FLUFFY SCRAMBLED EGGS

TOASTED ENGLISH MUFFINS

GOLDEN JAM

PEACHES AND GRAPE–NUTS PARADISE

Pour a serving of Grape-Nuts into individual bowls. Cover with fresh sliced peaches. Serve with liquid honey and cream.

LIGHT AND FLUFFY SCRAMBLED EGGS

Take the desired number of eggs and beat whites and yolks separately. Fold whites into the yolks and put in the buttered top of a double boiler. Do not add seasoning. Stir gently until eggs are the right consistency to be served. Serve on half of an English muffin, toasted and spread with deviled ham thinned with mayonnaise.

GOLDEN JAM

This jam is made with oranges, apricots, and pineapple. Wash 1 pound of dried apricots, cut into pieces, and soak overnight in just enough water to cover the fruit. Add 2 oranges and 1 lemon, peeled, sliced fine, and cut into small pieces. Add a 1-pound can of crushed pineapple, 8 cups of sugar, and ¼ teaspoon of salt. Place on an asbestos mat over a low fire and boil for 50 minutes. Pour the mixture into sterilized jelly glasses, seal with paraffin, and cover.

Menu

STRAWBERRIES AND PINEAPPLE IN ORANGE
JUICE

EGGS À LA GORDON

APPLE MUFFINS

STRAWBERRIES AND PINEAPPLE IN ORANGE JUICE

Wash and hull strawberries and cube fresh or canned pineapple. Place in a glass bowl and pour orange juice over them. Serve ice-cold.

EGGS À LA GORDON

Use 2 slices of bacon, chopped fine, or 4 tablespoons of raw ham, ground. Fry slowly, and when nearly cooked add ½ cup of fresh bread crumbs; continue frying until the meat and bread are light brown, stirring all the time. Beat 4 eggs with ⅓ cup of milk, pour over the crumbs and meat, and stir until the eggs are cooked. Serves 3.

APPLE MUFFINS

Sift 2¼ cups of sifted cake flour with 3½ teaspoons of baking powder, ½ teaspoon of salt, ¼ teaspoon each of nutmeg and cinnamon. Cream together 4 tablespoons of vegetable shortening with ½ cup of sugar and stir in 1 well-beaten egg. Add dry ingredients alternately with 1 cup of milk. Fold in 1 cup of finely chopped, pared apples. Fill muffin tins almost full. Sprinkle with an additional 2 tablespoons of sugar seasoned with ¼ teaspoon each of cinnamon and nutmeg. Bake in a moderate oven (350°). Serves 6.

Menu

PRUNE AND ORANGE JUICE COCKTAIL

CREAMED POTATOES WITH MINCED HAM

FRIED EGGS ANDRE

PECAN MUFFINS

PRUNE AND ORANGE JUICE COCKTAIL

Use bottled prune juice and mix half and half with orange juice. Serve ice-cold in medium-sized glasses.

CREAMED POTATOES WITH MINCED HAM

Prepare creamed potatoes, and add half the amount of cooked ham or canned luncheon meat, minced. Put in a casserole, cover with buttered bread crumbs, and place in the oven to heat through and brown the crumbs.

FRIED EGGS ANDRÉ

Sauté eggs in olive oil until the eggs become crisp and brown around the edges. This also makes a delicious luncheon dish served with a tomato or Spanish sauce.

PECAN MUFFINS

To escape a storm while motoring in Canada, we stopped at a most unpretentious-looking house bearing the sign "Teas." With some misgiving we entered. Within a very few minutes these muffins, freshly baked, were served. The secret? The hostess kept the dry ingredients measured and mixed, the egg and liquid also ready.

Cream ¼ cup of butter with ¼ cup of sugar, and add 2 well-beaten eggs. Sift 2 cups of flour with 4 teaspoons of baking powder and ½ teaspoon of salt; add alternately to the egg mixture with 1 cup of milk. Add ¾ cup of chopped pecans. Bake in buttered muffin pans for 25 minutes in a 400° oven. Serves 4 to 6.

Menu

HONEYDEW MELON WITH FROSTED GRAPES

EGGS AND MUSHROOMS

BUTTERY MELBA TOAST

BREAD-CRUMB PANCAKES

MYSTERY SYRUP

HONEYDEW MELON WITH FROSTED GRAPES

Choose large perfect grapes, and use small bunches of about 6 for each serving. The method of frosting is easy. Use a paint brush or a small piece of brown paper, fringed on the edges. Paint the grapes with unbeaten egg white. Then sprinkle them unevenly with granulated sugar. Allow to dry. Large green, white, or purple grapes may be used. Place a wedge of the melon on a grape leaf and lay the bunch of grapes over it.

EGGS AND MUSHROOMS

2 tablespoons butter
½ pound mushrooms
2 tablespoons flour
2 cups chicken broth
3 tablespoons thick cream or evaporated milk

½ teaspoon chopped onion
1 tablespoon chopped parsley
Salt and pepper
6 eggs

2 tablespoons melted butter ⎱ to be sprinkled over the top
Grated Parmesan cheese ⎰

Melt 2 tablespoons of butter in a pan and sauté the mushrooms. When browned and cooked, stir in the flour and blend well. Add broth, cream, onion, and parsley; season with salt and pepper. Cook until smooth. Pour the sauce into a flat dish and dot the eggs evenly over the surface. Pour the melted butter over the top and sprinkle with the Parmesan cheese. Bake in a 350° oven until the eggs are cooked. Serves 6.

BREAD–CRUMB PANCAKES

Scald 1½ cups of milk and add 2 tablespoons of butter and ½ cup of fresh bread crumbs. Let stand until bread crumbs are soft. Add 2 beaten eggs. Sift 4 level teaspoons of baking powder with ½ cup of flour, ½ teaspoon of salt, and 1 teaspoon of sugar. Add to first mixture. Bake on pancake griddle. Serve with Mystery Syrup (p. 16). Serves 4.

Don't worry if the batter seems thin. These are the most delicate pancakes!

Menu

PINK DREAMS

JULIENNE POTATOES FRIED WITH BACON

SCRAMBLED EGGS

NEVER-FAIL POPOVERS

APRICOT JAM

PINK DREAMS

Combine cranberry juice and fresh orange juice in equal proportions.

JULIENNE POTATOES FRIED WITH BACON

Slice lengthwise 6 medium-sized raw, peeled potatoes and cut into thin strips. Cut 6 strips of bacon into small shreds and fry for a moment in a hot frying pan. Add the potato strips and mix well with the bacon. Flatten with a pancake turner into a tightly packed cake. Cook for about 10 minutes, and then turn like a pancake and cook on the other side very slowly for 15 minutes. Have the frying pan covered, but be careful that the potatoes do not burn. Remove to a hot platter and pour the drippings from the pan over the potatoes. Sprinkle with chopped parsley. Serves 6.

SCRAMBLED EGGS

Beat 6 eggs with 6 tablespoons of cream or evaporated milk. Season with salt and pepper. Melt 3 tablespoons of butter in a skillet over a slow fire. Add 1 tablespoon of grated onion to the butter. When the butter has melted, pour in the eggs and cook over a slow fire, stirring gently as the eggs cook. When the eggs are creamy, remove them from the pan and serve on thin slices of toast spread with anchovy paste thinned with mayonnaise. These eggs may be cooked in a buttered double boiler, if you prefer. Serves 4.

NEVER–FAIL POPOVERS
(Marjorie Rainey's)

The secret of the unfailing success of these popovers lies in having the molds and the oven cold when the baking starts, although most recipes call for them hot.

Sift 1 cup of bread flour with ¼ teaspoon of salt. Beat 2 eggs slightly and stir in 1 cup of milk and 1 teaspoon of melted butter. Add the liquid to the flour and stir until well mixed and smooth. Fill cold, well-greased custard cups a little more than half full of batter. Place cups on a cooky sheet and place in a cold oven. Turn on the heat and set the regulator at 425° and bake for 1 hour. Serves 4.

APRICOT JAM

Wash 1 pound of dried apricots and soak in 6 cups of water overnight. In the morning, add 3 pounds of sugar and 4 tablespoons of lemon juice to the apricots and the water in which they were soaked. Boil for about 2 hours, skimming off the foam as it rises. One-half hour before it is finished cooking, add ½ cup of slivered almonds. Pour in sterilized jelly glasses or jars and seal.

Menu

STRAWBERRIES WITH STRAWBERRY JAM

BACON

EGGS IN MUSTARD SAUCE

APPLE PANCAKES

THE DOCTOR'S SYRUP

STRAWBERRIES WITH STRAWBERRY JAM

Wash and hull strawberries and arrange in a large glass bowl. Dilute strawberry jam by heating it with a small amount of boiling water. Cool the jam and pour over the strawberries. Strawberry jelly may be used in place of the jam.

EGGS IN MUSTARD SAUCE

Mix 1 teaspoon of prepared mustard and ¼ teaspoon of salt with 1 cup of evaporated milk. Add 3 tablespoons of grated cheese. Grease a baking dish (or use individual dishes) and break into it 6 eggs. Cover the eggs with the sauce and sprinkle buttered bread crumbs over the top. Place the dish in a pan of hot water and bake in a 350° oven for about 15 minutes. Serves 4.

APPLE PANCAKES

Add 1 cup of coarsely grated apples to Wheat Cakes (p. 16) recipe. (Be sure to drain the apples well before adding.) Also add enough extra milk to make the right consistency for pouring. Serve with The Doctor's Syrup.

The Doctor's Syrup. — Boil together equal parts of brown and white sugar with enough water to cover. Cook until the syrup spins a thread; then add a lump of butter.

Menu

BAKED ORANGES WITH RUM

FRIED GROUND LIVER WITH BACON

CREAMED POTATOES

SALLY LUNN

BAKED ORANGES WITH RUM

Cut oranges in half, remove the segments, and replace in the cup formed by the orange skin. For each orange, add 1 teaspoon each of sugar, butter, and rum. Bake in a 350° oven for 20 minutes. Brown under the broiler.

FRIED GROUND LIVER WITH BACON

Grind 2 pounds of liver. Soak 2 slices of bread in milk, crumble, and add to the liver. Season to taste with a little grated onion and salt and pepper. Drop by spoonfuls into hot olive oil and brown on both sides. Serve with fried bacon. Serves 6.

SALLY LUNN

Cream 1 cup of sugar with ½ cup of butter. Beat 2 eggs with 2 cups of milk, and add to the sugar and butter. Sift 3½ cups of flour with 6 teaspoons of baking powder and 1 teaspoon of salt. Stir in the egg mixture. Pour in a greased flat pan 9 × 14 inches. Mix ½ cup of sugar and 1 tablespoon of cinnamon. Sprinkle over the top. Bake in a moderate oven (375°) for about 30 to 40 minutes, until the cake is firm. Serves 6.

Sunday Night Supper

Don't lose track of your friends just because you are bogged down with responsibility and work. Ask them to drop in for Sunday night supper. This is not the occasion for getting out the best china and silver; its attraction lies in its complete informality. It is not necessary to set the table. Instead arrange supper on the buffet or dining-room table and let the guests help themselves. Let the guests sit where they wish — on the living-room floor, or out in the garden, or even on the stairs.

But no matter what time or where you plan to serve it, let the supper be simple. Don't fuss. Plan your menu carefully and prepare your food far enough ahead, so that on Monday morning you don't find yourself so tired that your week gets off to a bad start.

As a rule, Sunday night is not the time for late bridge or poker games. Let the warmth of your welcome and the hospitality of your home, coupled with good food and relaxing conversation, be the ingredients that make up this particular party.

If the weather is warm, prepare a molded salad the day before and then at the last moment all you have to do is surround the mold with a variety of vegetables arranged according to color. Here is practically your entire supper. With it you might feature a special bread or a hearty dessert; both of these may also be prepared the day before. Or you might prefer a salad containing fruit; if so, arrange it to look spectacular. Let it be beautiful as well as delicious. There are also salads of molded fish (Use a fish mold and decorate it appropriately.), and when this is accompanied by a variety of vegetables such as cucumbers, tomatoes, and string beans, and served with a piquant sauce, nothing could please your friends more.

Sunday supper on a cold night is a time when the soup kettle may be much in evidence. Perhaps you have an old soup tureen and large soup plates that belonged to Great Aunt Bessie. If so, feature them, especially if you are serving supper at the table. Nothing looks quite as hospitable as the host sitting at the head of his table, ladling out large spoonfuls of rich creamy soup into old-fashioned soup dishes that the guests pass around the table and which, you may be sure, they will return for a second helping. Even soup can make you famous — that is, if you glamorize it.

If you are serving supper from the buffet, invest in one of the pottery soup kettles with alcohol lamp beneath. These are not only decorative, but the small flame keeps the soup hot for second, even third, helpings. Or, if you plan to use individual trays for your guests, buy the little glazed soup bowls with lids; these are conversational pieces as well as practical.

The casserole is a solution for simplifying Sunday supper. With the right amount of ingredients and by cooking everything the day before, your entire supper is ready to serve, without any last-minute fussing and with only one cooking dish to wash.

This Sunday night supper may be the occasion for bringing together a group of your husband's golf friends. If so, you may want to corral all the golf widows in the afternoon. They can help with the supper preparations and at the same time have a chance to catch up on a bit of ladies' chatter before the husbands return. Or you might plan a community supper and have each woman guest contribute her share of the food.

So ask your friends to drop in for Sunday night supper, but be sure to plan and prepare everything far enough ahead so that your party is no effort for you. Remember, to give a successful party, it must be fun for you as well as your guests.

This entire supper may be arranged on the buffet. The soup steaming in a deep pottery kettle over an alcohol burner could be placed at one end. At the other end, arrange the pudding cake with the dessert plates conveniently near, and in the center of the buffet display your salad, surrounded by its colorful arrangement of fruit.

Menu

CORN CHOWDER

CHEESE RING WITH FRUIT SALAD

CRISP BREAD LOAF

PUDDING CAKE WITH CUSTARD FILLING

CORN CHOWDER

Fry 2 ounces of salt pork, chopped fine, and add 2 finely minced onions. Cook slowly. In a kettle heat 1 quart of water and add 2½ cups of canned niblet corn. Add the pork and onion and cook for 10 minutes. Press the contents of 2 cans of potato soup through the purée sieve and add to the corn. Stir in 1 quart of milk and let come to a boil. Season to taste with celery salt, pepper, and a dash of Tabasco sauce. (May be reheated.) Serve with crumbled pilot crackers on top. Serves 6.

CHEESE RING WITH FRUIT SALAD
(Gladys's)

Soak 1 tablespoon of gelatine in 1 tablespoon of cold water. Dissolve in 1 cup of hot milk. Mash 2 3-ounce packages of cream cheese and mix with the hot milk. Add 1 cup of grated American cheese and let cool. Whip 1 cup of cream and fold into the mixture. Pour into a rinsed ring mold. Place in the refrigerator until firm. (Prepare the day before.) Unmold and fill the center with Fruit Salad Dressing and surround with pineapple, pears, and peaches. Decorate with sprigs of mint. Serves 4 to 6.

Fruit Salad Dressing. — Drain 1 large can of sliced pineapple for 2 hours. (Use pineapple slices for salad.) Add 2 tablespoons of vinegar to the juice and let come to a boil. Mix 1½ tablespoons of flour with ½ cup of granulated sugar; add beaten yolks of 2 eggs and combine with the juice. Cook in the top of a double boiler until thick. To retain the flavor, cover while cooling. (Prepare the day before.) When ready to serve, add ½ cup of cream, whipped, or 1 package cream cheese mashed with a little cream.

CRISP BREAD LOAF

Cut all the crust off a loaf of white bread except the bottom. Cut in half lengthwise, but not through the bottom crust. Then cut across in thirds. Butter generously the top and sides, and also inside the cuts. Place in a 275° oven for about 20 minutes until crisp, then brown under the broiler.

PUDDING CAKE WITH CUSTARD FILLING

Cream together well 1 cup of sugar with ⅓ cup of butter. Beat in 3 eggs, one at a time, beating for a few minutes after each egg is added. Then add alternately ½ cup of milk and 2 cups of flour sifted with 2½ teaspoons of baking powder and ½ teaspoon of salt. Add 1 teaspoon of vanilla. Bake in 2 layers in a 400° oven. Remove from pan and cool. Spread Custard Sauce between layers and sprinkle powdered sugar over the top. (May be prepared the day before.) Serves 6.

Custard Sauce. — Beat lightly 3 eggs or 6 egg yolks. Mix ¼ cup of sugar, ⅓ cup of flour, and a pinch of salt. Add to eggs. Heat 1 pint of milk in the top of a double boiler and pour over the egg mixture. Stir well and then pour back into the double boiler. Cook until thick; then cool. Add ½ teaspoon of vanilla and 3 tablespoons of sherry. (Prepare the day before.)

Menu

TOMATOES WITH DEVILED HAM

POTATOES ANNA

ICED CAULIFLOWER SALAD

GINGERBREAD RING

HOT BUTTERSCOTCH SAUCE

TOMATOES WITH DEVILED HAM

Grate 3 small onions; dice ½ green pepper and 2 stalks of celery. Cut the tops off 6 tomatoes and scoop out the pulp. Melt 2 tablespoons of butter in a pan and add the onion, green pepper, celery, and 1 small can of deviled ham. Cook for about 5 minutes, and stir to keep from burning. Add 1 small can of mushrooms, drained. Season with 1 teaspoon of Worcestershire sauce, Tabasco, a pinch of sugar, salt, and black pepper. Add the tomato pulp and cook for 10 minutes. Stir in 2 cups of soft bread crumbs. Cook 5 minutes more. Stuff the tomatoes. Cover the top with buttered crumbs and paprika. (Prepare in the morning.) Bake in a 400° oven for 15 minutes. Serves 6.

POTATOES ANNA

For 6 people, cut 7 medium-sized potatoes into thin slices. Arrange in layers, with the pieces overlapping, in a buttered pie pan, with a little melted butter poured over. Bake in a moderate oven (350°) until they are cooked through and are golden-brown on top. (Peel and slice the potatoes in the morning, cover tightly, and store in refrigerator until time to bake them.)

ICED CAULIFLOWER SALAD

Boil the cauliflower. When done, place in cold water and pick apart into little florets. Place on a towel to dry; then put in the refrigerator to chill. When ready to serve, arrange in a salad bowl, and cover with mayonnaise and French dressing mixed. Sprinkle with chopped parsley.

GINGERBREAD RING

Cream together ½ cup of butter and 1½ cups of brown sugar. Add 1 egg, well beaten. Sift together 1½ cups of flour and 1 teaspoon each of ginger, soda, and cinnamon, ½ teaspoon of ground cloves, and ⅛ teaspoon of salt. Mix ½ cup of molasses with ½ cup of boiling water. Add the dry ingredients alternately with the molasses to the sugar and butter mixture. Bake in a buttered and floured ring mold in a moderate oven (350°) for 30 to 40 minutes.

Unmold and place a bowl of whipped cream in the center. Serve Hot Butterscotch Sauce separately. Vanilla ice cream may be served with this dessert in place of whipped cream. Serves 6.

HOT BUTTERSCOTCH SAUCE
(Maxine's)

1 cup brown sugar	½ cup milk
2 tablespoons flour	½ cup water
⅛ teaspoon salt	2 tablespoons butter
½ teaspoon vanilla	

Blend sugar and flour and add the rest of the ingredients. Cook for 2 minutes, stirring constantly. Serve warm. This is also delicious served hot, poured over ice cream or sponge cake topped with whipped cream. This sauce may be stored in the refrigerator in a glass jar and reheated in the top of a double boiler when needed.

Menu

CASSEROLE OF CURRIED SHRIMPS AND
SPAGHETTI

MIXED FRESH VEGETABLE SALAD

BUTTERY MELBA TOAST

COFFEE SPANISH CREAM

CREAM CHEESE COOKIES

CASSEROLE OF CURRIED SHRIMPS AND SPAGHETTI

Make 3 cups of cream sauce, using 3 cups of milk to 3 table-spoons each of butter and flour. Season to taste and flavor with 1 tablespoon of onion juice. Add curry powder dissolved in a little cold milk — the amount of curry varying with your taste. (Prepare the day before.) Clean 2 small cans of shrimps and add to the cream sauce. Pour into the bottom of a casserole and cover with ½ pound of spaghetti, boiled. Sprinkle with grated cheese. Bake with the lid on in a 275° oven until heated through. Remove the lid and brown under the broiler. Serves 6 to 8.

MIXED FRESH VEGETABLE SALAD

1 cup cooked green peas	1 cup shredded raw cabbage
1 cup cooked fresh Lima beans	2 tomatoes, peeled and quartered
½ cup shredded raw carrots	1 small head lettuce, cut in eighths
1 cucumber, sliced	French dressing

Garlic

Rub salad bowl with clove of garlic cut in half. Put all ingredients in bowl. Pour over enough French dressing to moisten ingredients thoroughly. Toss lightly with a wooden fork and spoon. Serve on a nest of lettuce leaves. (Cook the vegetables the day before.) Serves 6 to 8.

COFFEE SPANISH CREAM

½ cup milk
1 cup strong coffee
2 tablespoons granulated gelatine
¼ teaspoon vanilla

2 eggs
4 tablespoons sugar
⅛ teaspoon salt

Soak the gelatine in 2 tablespoons of water. Scald the milk, add the coffee heated to boiling point and the gelatine, stirring until the gelatine is dissolved. Beat the egg yolks with the sugar and salt, and add to the milk. Cook over hot water, stirring constantly until thickened. Remove from the fire and let cool. Add the egg whites, which have been beaten stiff, and the vanilla. Fold in gently. Dip individual molds in cold water and fill with the mixture. (Prepare the day before.) Unmold and serve with sweetened cream or ice cream. Serves 6.

CREAM CHEESE COOKIES

Cream together 3 ounces of cream cheese with 1 cup of shortening. Add 1 cup of sugar, 1 egg yolk, and ½ teaspoon of vanilla and blend thoroughly. Add 2½ cups of flour and mix until smooth. Put through a cookie press. Bake 15 minutes in a 350° oven. (Prepare the day before.)

Menu

MINESTRONE SOUP

FRENCH BREAD HEATED WITH GARLIC BUTTER

GINGER ALE SALAD-DESSERT

BROWN SUGAR CHEWS

MINESTRONE SOUP

Fry together until brown ¼ pound each of chopped bacon, chopped ham, and chopped Italian sausage. Add 2 peeled, chopped tomatoes, ½ cup of rice, ½ cup of navy beans soaked overnight, ½ cup of chopped celery, and 1½ quarts of soup stock. Simmer until the beans are tender. Cool and skim off fat. Add 1 cup of shredded cabbage and ¼ cup each of fresh peas, Lima beans, and string beans. Simmer until the vegetables are tender. (Canned vegetables may be used.) Taste for seasoning and thin with additional soup stock, if necessary. Serve piping hot, with grated Parmesan cheese. (Prepare the day before.) Serves 6 to 8.

Serve this soup at the table, either from a French pottery soup kettle or from an antique china tureen. Make a "ceremony" of serving it!

FRENCH BREAD HEATED WITH GARLIC BUTTER

Slice French bread in ½-inch slices, but do not cut through the bottom crust. Melt butter and add a crushed clove of garlic. Spread butter between slices with a knife or pastry brush. Wrap in paper and put in the oven to heat. Let the guests break off their own pieces of bread.

GINGER ALE SALAD–DESSERT

Instead of the usual variety of dessert, serve this salad for a change.

Soak 2 tablespoons of gelatine in 2 tablespoons of cold water; then dissolve in ¼ cup of boiling water. If gelatine does not dissolve completely, stir over hot water. Add 1 pint of ginger ale, ½ cup of sugar, and the juice of 1 lemon. Pour a layer of the gelatine mixture into a decorative ring mold and chill until firm. Fill with the rest of the gelatine, then add seedless grapes and chopped bits of preserved ginger. Put in the refrigerator until firm. (Prepare the day before.) Unmold on a large platter. Surround with half slices of pineapple, orange segments, and large cooked prunes filled with cream cheese and chopped nuts. Decorate with mint leaves. Place a bowl of Fruit Salad Dressing (p. 31) in the center of the mold. Serves 6 to 8.

BROWN SUGAR CHEWS
(Mrs. Clark's)

Mix together 2 cups of sifted light brown sugar, ⅛ teaspoon each of salt and soda, and 2 well-beaten eggs. Add 1 cup of chopped nuts. Pour into a buttered pan 9 × 9 inches so cookie mixture will be ½ inch thick. Bake in a slow oven (250°) for 55 minutes. Cut in squares when cool.

Don't get excited because this recipe does not call for flour or baking powder. That is the secret of these delicious chewy cookies.

Menu

SOUTHERN BEAN SOUP

GELATINE AND CHEESE MOLD WITH
VEGETABLE SALAD

QUICK BISCUITS

LEMON CREAM SHERBET

GOLDEN CUP CAKES

SOUTHERN BEAN SOUP

Soak 2 pounds of beans overnight. In the morning drain and put into a soup kettle with 4 quarts of fresh water. Chop fine 2 onions, 3 carrots, 1 stalk of celery, and ½ green pepper. Add to the soup with 3 sprigs of parsley. Add 1 pound of ham or bacon, and let simmer very slowly all day, or until the beans have cooked to a mush. Skim off the fat and strain the mixture through a fine sieve, mashing the beans to a paste. Taste for seasoning.

Peel ½ pound of garlic sausage or frankfurters, and slice thin. Add to the soup and simmer for 15 minutes. Add 1 cup of cream and serve. (Better if prepared ahead of time and reheated.) Serves 6 to 8.

GELATINE AND CHEESE MOLD WITH VEGETABLE SALAD

Dissolve 1 package of lemon gelatine in 1½ cups of boiling water. Add 1 teaspoon of grated onion, 1 teaspoon of horseradish, and 2 teaspoons of tarragon vinegar. Cool. Pour ⅓ of the mixture into a ring mold and chill until firm. Mash 1 cake of cream cheese with a small section of Roquefort cheese and add to the remainder of the gelatine. Pour into the mold and chill until firm. (Prepare the day before.) Serves 6.

When ready to serve, unmold on a round platter, fill the center with a salad of mixed vegetables and surround with sliced cold meat and deviled eggs.

QUICK BISCUITS
(Rosemary's)

A friend of mine makes a specialty of serving assorted hot breads for Sunday morning breakfast. The bread, in miniature sizes, is arranged on an enormous wicker tray — muffins, tiny squares of corn bread, gingerbread, baby biscuits, and tiny rolls. It is an amusing idea — try it.

Use any prepared biscuit flour and add a little more milk than the recipe calls for. Flour a piece of waxed paper, place the biscuit dough on it very gently and sprinkle a little flour over the top. Pat out lightly and leave rather thick. Dip the cutter in flour before cutting out each biscuit. Place in a buttered pan and leave in the refrigerator until ready. Bake in a hot oven (425°). (If you want to make old-fashioned strawberry shortcake, add a little sugar to the dough when mixing.)

LEMON CREAM SHERBET

Grate the rind of 2 lemons and combine with ½ cup of lemon juice and 1½ cups of powdered sugar. Let stand for several hours. Add the lemon mixture to 1 quart of milk or milk and cream mixed. Turn into the tray of an automatic refrigerator and turn the control to the coldest point. Freeze until firm. Remove to a chilled bowl and beat with a rotary beater until smooth and fluffy. Return to the tray and freeze to the right consistency to serve. If the sherbet is to be stored, reset the refrigerator control to its original position. Serves 6.

GOLDEN CUP CAKES

Whip ½ cup of butter until soft. Beat in 1 cup of sugar. Add 2 eggs and beat well after each is added. Add 1 cup of chopped nut meats to ¾ cup of sifted flour. Sift 2 teaspoons of baking powder and ⅛ teaspoon of salt with 1 cup of sifted flour. Add alternately to the sugar mixture, with ½ cup of milk, and beat thoroughly. Stir in the flour and nut mixture, and add 1 teaspoon of vanilla. Butter muffin tins and pour in the mixture. Bake in a 350° oven for 30 minutes.

Menu

CRAB SALAD RING

GRAHAM PRUNE BREAD

SPONGE PUDDING WITH
CURRANT OR CREAMY PUDDING SAUCE

CRAB SALAD RING

Soak 2 tablespoons of gelatine in ½ cup of cold water. Heat 1 can of tomato soup and 1 cup of water until it boils and add the gelatine, stirring until it dissolves. Mash 3 cakes of cream cheese with 2 tablespoons of mayonnaise and add to the tomato soup when cool.

Chop fine 1 peeled cucumber, 1 onion, and 1 stalk of celery. Mix with 3 cups of flaked crab meat, either fresh or canned, and stir into the tomato-cheese mixture. Season with 1 teaspoon of salt and a dash of cayenne. Pour into a greased mold and chill until firm. (Prepare the day before.)

When this Crab Salad Ring is to be used as the main course, surround the mold with stuffed eggs, canned artichoke hearts, mounds of shredded string beans, cooked and chilled, and any other cooked vegetable. Serve with mayonnaise, flavored with horse-radish, or with Green Mayonnaise.

Green Mayonnaise.—Pick over and wash 1 quart of spinach. Put through the grinder, using the fine blade and being sure to catch all the juice. Chop 4 small onions very fine, mince a small bunch of chives, and add with the spinach to 2 cups of mayonnaise. Stir in 2 or 3 tablespoons of tarragon vinegar. Add 2 tablespoons of chopped parsley and taste for seasoning. (Prepare in the morning.)

GRAHAM PRUNE BREAD

Sift together 1½ cups of white flour with 1 cup of sugar, 1 teaspoon of baking powder, ½ teaspoon of soda, and ½ teaspoon of salt. Add ¾ cup of chopped nut meats to 1 cup of graham flour and add to the first mixture. Add 2 tablespoons of melted shortening to 1 cup of sour milk. Mix with the flour and add ½ cup of prune juice and 1 cup of prune pulp. Stir until well mixed; then pour into a greased loaf pan. Bake in a moderate oven (350°) for 1½ hours. (Prepare ahead of time.)

SPONGE PUDDING
(Aunt Ella's)

Mix ¼ cup of sugar, ½ teaspoon of salt, and ½ cup of flour. Blend with ½ cup of cold milk. Stir slowly into 1 pint of hot milk. Cook until thick and smooth. Then add ¼ cup of butter and 1 teaspoon of vanilla. When well blended, stir this mixture into the beaten yolks of 4 eggs; then fold in the stiffly beaten whites. Pour the pudding into a shallow baking dish, place in a pan of hot water, and bake for ½ hour in a hot oven (400°). Serve with Currant or Creamy Pudding Sauce. Serves 6.

Currant Sauce. — Whip 1 glass of currant jelly with a fork until soft. Add ½ teaspoon of grated lemon rind and brandy to taste.

Creamy Pudding Sauce. — Beat ½ cup of butter until light. Add 1 cup of powdered sugar and ½ cup of cream or evaporated milk. Set the dish in a pan of hot water and stir until creamy. Flavor with sherry.

Menu

CHICKEN CURRY SOUP

MOLDED SHRIMP AND TOMATO SALAD

BUTTERY MELBA TOAST

CREAM PUFFS WITH
HOT CHOCOLATE SAUCE

CHICKEN CURRY SOUP

Put 3 cans of chicken and rice soup through a purée sieve. Add 1 large can of evaporated milk and 2 cups of fresh milk. Season with curry powder according to your taste. (Dissolve the powder in a little of the cold milk.) Heat and serve very hot. Serves 6.

This is a very nice soup to serve in individual pottery soup pots with lids. You may also serve this soup ice-cold.

MOLDED SHRIMP AND TOMATO SALAD

Soak 2 tablespoons of gelatine in ½ cup of cold water. Heat 1 can of tomato soup, add the gelatine and 2 cakes of cream cheese. Beat with an egg beater until well blended. Let cool; then add 1 cup of mayonnaise, and season with 2 tablespoons of grated onion and 2 tablespoons of capers. Add 2 cups of whole shrimps, cleaned, and 2 tablespoons of chopped stuffed olives. Pour into a ring mold and chill until set. (Prepare the day before.) Unmold on a platter and fill the center with water cress and surround with halves of green pepper filled with mixed fresh vegetables which have been marinated in French dressing. Serves 6.

CREAM PUFFS WITH HOT CHOCOLATE SAUCE

To 1 cup of boiling water add ½ cup of butter. Let melt. Add 1 cup of all-purpose flour and pour it in all at once. Stir vigorously until the mixture forms a ball in the center of the pan. Cool a little and then add 4 eggs. Beat the flour mixture after the addition of each egg. Drop by tablespoonfuls on a buttered cookie sheet, shaping into mounds. Bake in a moderately hot oven (375°) for about 40 minutes. Fill with Custard Sauce (p. 31) and serve with Hot Chocolate Sauce. Makes 24 small puffs. (Puffs, custard sauce, and chocolate sauce may be prepared the day before and combined later.) Serves 6.

Hot Chocolate Sauce. — Melt 4 squares of chocolate in the top of a double boiler; add 1 cup of cream, 1½ cups of sugar, and 3 tablespoons of butter. Stir until well blended. Remove the top of the boiler, place over a low flame, and boil without stirring for 5 to 7 minutes. Stir in ¼ cup of sherry and 1 teaspoon of vanilla. (The sherry may be omitted.) Prepare ahead of time and reheat in a double boiler. Serves 6.

Menu

LOBSTER BISQUE

LUNCHEON SALAD

GRAPE-NUT BREAD

PINEAPPLE-DATE PUDDING WITH
ORANGE SAUCE

LOBSTER BISQUE

Mix 1 can of mushroom soup, 1 can of tomato soup, and 1 can of flaked lobster meat. Thin with cream or milk and season with paprika and curry powder. Heat in the top of a double boiler until ready to serve. Serves 6.

LUNCHEON SALAD

Mix 3 cups of diced canned beets with 2 cups of diced cold boiled potatoes and marinate with French dressing. Add ½ cup each of shredded boiled ham and Swiss cheese. Toss with pieces of lettuce until well mixed.

GRAPE–NUT BREAD
(Flora's)

Soak 1 cup of Grape-Nuts in 2 cups of sour milk for 1 hour. Add 4 cups of bread flour mixed with 2 teaspoons of soda and ¾ cup of sugar. Mix ¼ cup of melted shortening with 1 cup of sweet milk and add to the flour mixture. Bake in 2 well-greased loaf tins for 1 hour at 350°.

PINEAPPLE–DATE PUDDING

Beat 1 egg; add ½ cup of sugar, ½ teaspoon of salt, 3 tablespoons of melted butter, and 1 cup of pineapple juice. Beat and then add 1 cup of chopped dates, ¼ cup of chopped raisins, ½ cup of chopped nuts, and 1 teaspoon of vanilla.

Sift together 1 teaspoon each of cinnamon and baking powder, ¼ teaspoon of nutmeg, ¾ teaspoon of soda, and 1½ cups of flour. Add to the first mixture. Grease a covered mold, fill two thirds full and steam for 2 hours. Unmold, saturate with brandy, and send to the table lighted. Serve with Orange Sauce.

The pudding may be removed from the mold, cooled, wrapped in waxed paper, and stored in the refrigerator for several weeks.

Orange Sauce. — Mix in the top of a double boiler 1½ cups of granulated sugar, ¼ cup of flour, the grated rind of 1 orange, and ⅛ teaspoon of salt. Add ½ cup of cold water gradually and stir until smooth. Pour in 1½ cups of boiling water and stir constantly until smooth and thick. Cook for 15 minutes. Add the juice of 2 oranges and 1 lemon. (Prepare the day before and reheat.)

```
                        Menu

                CHICKEN  WITH  HERBS

                SCOTCH  MUFFINS

        AVOCADO  SALAD  RING  WITH  VEGETABLES

                CHESTNUT  PUDDING
```

CHICKEN WITH HERBS

Clean 1 chicken weighing about 3½ pounds and place in the cavity 1 anchovy, 1 onion, and a piece of lemon peel. Tie in a small piece of cheesecloth 1 tablespoon of mixed dried herbs or a mixture of bay leaf, marjoram, parsley, rosemary, and sage, and place inside the chicken. Fasten the opening with toothpicks, wrap the chicken in cooking parchment, and tie securely. Simmer in water to cover for 1½ hours.

In another pan place the neck, liver, heart, and gizzard; cook in 2 cups of water with ½ teaspoon of dried mixed herbs, 1 anchovy, 3 peppercorns, and a blade of mace. Simmer for ½ hour. Strain. Add ½ cup of dry white wine and simmer slowly until only ¾ cup of the liquid remains. Add 1 tablespoon of butter and stir in the beaten yolk of 1 egg. Cook slowly, stirring constantly, until thickened.

When the chicken is tender, remove from the kettle and open the paper carefully. Drain the juice which is inside the paper into the wine sauce. Carve the chicken and arrange on a platter. Pour the sauce over the chicken and garnish with slices of crisp bacon. Serves 4.

SCOTCH MUFFINS

In a mixing bowl, sift 1 cup of flour with 2 teaspoons of baking powder, ⅛ teaspoon soda, and ½ teaspoon of salt. Add 1 cup of finely ground oatmeal and ½ cup of granulated sugar. Add ½ cup of ground nuts and 1 cup of chopped dates. Stir 2 tablespoons of melted shortening into 1 cup of sour milk. Add 2 well-beaten eggs and mix with the dry ingredients. Fill greased muffin tins half full. Bake in a 350° oven for about 25 minutes. Serves 6.

AVOCADO SALAD RING WITH VEGETABLES

Dissolve 1 package of lemon gelatine in 1 cup of boiling water. Chill, and when beginning to thicken, whip until light. Mix 1 cup of mayonnaise with 3 tablespoons of lemon juice and 1 teaspoon of salt. Fold into the gelatine.

Mash enough avocado to make 1 cup and add to the gelatine with 1 cup of cream, whipped. Pour into a ring mold rinsed with cold water. Chill until firm. (Prepare the day before.) Unmold and fill the center with cooked vegetables and surround with lettuce. Serves 4.

CHESTNUT PUDDING

Boil 1 pound of chestnuts for about 20 minutes. Peel and remove brown skins. Press through a purée sieve while still hot. Chill. Beat 1 cup of cream until stiff and add gradually the juice of 2 oranges. Sweeten to taste. Add the puréed chestnuts. Serve in a bowl or in individual glasses with bits of currant jelly over the top. Serves 4.

Menu

CHICKEN WITH HAM EN CASSEROLE

SMOTHERED PEAS

HOE CAKE

CHUTNEY MOLD

CHICKEN WITH HAM EN CASSEROLE

Stew 1 chicken or hen in boiling water with onions, celery, and a little parsley. When tender, cool and remove the meat from the bones. Cut into serving pieces. (Prepare the day before.)

Melt ½ cup of butter in a shallow earthenware casserole and add 1 finely chopped onion. Cook but do not brown. Add 1 cup of canned or sautéed fresh mushrooms, and season with ½ teaspoon of salt, 1 tablespoon of paprika, and a dash of nutmeg.

Place 8 slices of thinly sliced boiled ham on top of the onion mixture, and arrange the pieces of chicken on top of the ham. Add enough cream or evaporated milk to cover the meat and simmer gently for about 15 minutes. Remove from the fire and sprinkle with freshly grated Parmesan cheese. Place in a hot oven (400°) until the cheese browns. Serves 6 to 8.

SMOTHERED PEAS
(Honore's)

Shell 2 pounds of peas. Melt 2 tablespoons of butter in a pan and add 4 finely shredded green onions, tops and all, 1 lump of sugar, a sprig of parsley, and salt and pepper. Place the shelled peas on top of the onions and cover with the leaves of a small head of lettuce. Cover and simmer over a very slow fire until the peas are tender. (A pinch of thyme may be added.) Serves 4.

HOE CAKE

Stir 1 cup of yellow corn meal into 1 cup of boiling water, seasoned with ½ teaspoon of salt. Beat in 3 tablespoons of melted butter. Drop by spoonfuls onto a buttered cookie sheet and bake in a hot oven (400°) for 20 minutes, until the edges are brown. Serves 6.

CHUTNEY MOLD

Dissolve 1 package of lime gelatine in 1 cup of boiling water. Mix the juice of 1 lime and 2 lemons with enough water to make ¾ cup and add to the gelatine. Chill. Spread 6 tablespoons of chutney, chopped fine, in the bottom of a ring mold and pour in the chilled gelatine. Place in the refrigerator until firm. (Prepare the day before.) Unmold on a platter and fill the center with Fruit Salad Dressing (p. 30). Surround with assorted fresh and canned fruit. Serves 4 to 6.

Menu

LEFTOVER LAMB IN GELATINE

POTATO PIE

ZUCCHINI WITH CHEESE

CHOCOLATE ICE CREAM

LEFTOVER LAMB IN GELATINE

Soak 1½ tablespoons of gelatine in ¼ cup of cold water, then add ⅔ cup of hot canned bouillon, and stir until dissolved. Mix 3 cups of ground cooked lamb, ½ teaspoon of salt, 2 tablespoons of onion juice, 2 tablespoons of chopped parsley, and a dash of cayenne. Combine lamb mixture with gelatine and, lastly, fold in 1 cup of cream, whipped stiff. Pour into a ring mold dipped in cold water Place in the refrigerator until firm. (Prepare the day before.) Unmold and fill the center with a bowl of mayonnaise which has been seasoned with mustard. Serves 4 to 6.

POTATO PIE

I remember the "ohs" and "ahs" which greeted these potatoes when served by a friend for a buffet dinner. Since then I have served them often, many times with variations. Sometimes I add green pepper or pimiento cut in shreds, or bits of bacon. Other times I use bacon drippings in place of butter to give a different flavor.

Peel the desired number of potatoes and slice about ¼ inch thick. Shred each slice in match-like sticks. (Place in milk to keep from discoloring.)

Butter the bottom and sides of a pie pan and arrange the potato sticks in a crisscross pattern on the bottom. Fill the rest of the pan with the sticks. (It is not necessary to continue the pattern, for it will not show.) Pour over 1 cup of melted butter, seasoned with ½ teaspoon of salt and ⅛ teaspoon of pepper. Cover with a tight lid and bake in a moderate oven (350°) for about ½ hour. Remove the lid and continue baking until the potatoes are done. Turn upside down onto a serving platter and sprinkle over the potatoes chopped parsley or chives, or a mixture of both, and a dusting of freshly ground black pepper.

ZUCCHINI WITH CHEESE

Dice 4 zucchini into small pieces and cook over a moderate flame with as little water as possible. Add ⅛ teaspoon of salt and stir the zucchini occasionally as it cooks. When tender, drain and add 1 tablespoon each of butter and grated cheese, and ¼ cup of cream. Stir while the cheese melts; then take off the fire and add a lightly beaten egg yolk. Turn into a buttered baking dish, grate more cheese over the top, dot with butter, and brown in a 400° oven. Serves 4.

CHOCOLATE ICE CREAM

To 1 beaten egg, add ¾ cup of Hershey's chocolate syrup and fold in ½ pint of cream, whipped. Place in the tray of an automatic refrigerator and freeze 3 hours, or overnight. Serves 4.

Menu

MILLBROOK STEWED HEN WITH NOODLES

CARROTS AND ONIONS

MIXED GREEN SALAD

PEPPERMINT MOUSSE

YELLOW CAKE WITH QUICK CHOCOLATE ICING

MILLBROOK STEWED HEN WITH NOODLES

Cook a stewing hen until tender in boiling salted water seasoned with 2 onions, a clove of garlic, and celery. Remove the skin and bones and cut the hen into serving pieces. (Prepare the day before.) Cook 1 large package of noodles in boiling salted water for 15 minutes. Drain and place in a casserole. Sprinkle with grated Parmesan cheese and dot with butter. Cover with the chicken pieces. Make a gravy from chicken stock and cream (evaporated milk may be used), thicken with flour, and add 6 hard-boiled egg yolks pressed through a sieve. Pour gravy over the noodles and chicken. Cover liberally with Parmesan cheese and brown in a 400° oven. Serves 6 to 8.

CARROTS AND ONIONS
(Maud's)

Put through the food chopper 2 pounds of scraped carrots and ½ pound of peeled onions. Pour over them 2 tablespoons of melted butter, and season with salt, pepper, and a pinch of sugar. Add enough brown gravy or canned bouillon to cover and stew gently until tender. Turn into a hot dish and garnish with minced parsley. (Cook ahead of time and reheat in a double boiler.) Serves 6.

MIXED GREEN SALAD

Mix ice-cold romaine, endive, fresh spinach leaves, chicory, and lettuce. Break the leaves, don't cut them. Add 2 raw zucchini, chopped. (Prepare ahead of time and keep chilled until ready.) Cover with French dressing and toss lightly.

PEPPERMINT MOUSSE

Soak 1 pound of finely crushed peppermint stick candy in 1 pint of milk for several hours. Add 1 pint of cream, whipped, and freeze in the tray of an automatic refrigerator. Serves 6.

YELLOW CAKE
(Aunt Nellie's)

Sift together 3 cups of cake flour, 4 teaspoons of baking powder, and ¼ teaspoon of salt. Cream 1 cup of butter with 2 cups of sugar. (Using your hands secures a better blending than using a spoon.) Beat in 4 eggs, 1 at a time, and then beat vigorously. (If you have an electric mixer, now is the time to use it.) Add the sifted flour mixture alternately with 1 cup of milk until all has been used, beating after each ingredient is added. Add 2 teaspoons of vanilla and pour into greased cake tins. Bake in a moderate oven (350°) for 30 minutes.

Quick Chocolate Icing. — Melt 2 squares of chocolate with 3 tablespoons of butter in the top of a double boiler. Remove from the fire and add 2 cups of powdered sugar and 6 tablespoons of cream. Beat thoroughly; then add 1 teaspoon of vanilla and ½ teaspoon of salt. Spread over the top of the cake and sprinkle with chopped nuts. (Double the recipe if used for 2 layers and sides.)

Menu

DEVILED EGGS IN ASPIC WITH WATER CRESS

SPAGHETTI CONWAY

PULLED BREAD

BAKED ASSORTED FRUIT

DEVILED EGGS IN ASPIC WITH WATER CRESS

To make the aspic jelly, soften 1 envelope of gelatine in 4 tablespoons of cold water. Dissolve in 1¾ cups of hot stock or diluted canned consommé. Put a thin layer in the bottom of a ring mold and set in the refrigerator until firm. Shell 8 hard-boiled eggs and cut in half lengthwise. Remove yolks, mash, and add 1 tablespoon of butter, 1 tablespoon of lemon juice, ½ teaspoon of anchovy paste, and a dash of cayenne. Add enough mayonnaise to make a stiff mixture. Add salt and pepper, and taste for seasoning. Fill the whites with this mixture. Decorate the halves with a slice of stuffed green olive and a tiny sprig of parsley. Lay the eggs cut-side-down in the aspic ring, pour a little aspic over them, and let it become firm; then fill the ring with the remainder. (Prepare the day before.) Unmold on a platter, place a bowl of French dressing in the center, and surround with water cress. Serves 4 to 6.

SPAGHETTI CONWAY

Add 1 pound of spaghetti to boiling salted water and cook for 20 minutes. Pour into a colander and run cold water over the spaghetti until the water is clear. Drain and put into the top of a double boiler. Add olive oil or butter and work it through the spaghetti with your fingers. Mix in 6 slices of crisp bacon, finely chopped, 6 tablespoons of chopped chives or green onion tops, and 2 tablespoons of grated cheese. Reheat over hot water and serve with more grated Parmesan cheese. Serves 4 to 6.

PULLED BREAD

Cut the crusts off a loaf of white bread and pull the bread into pieces. Toast in a very slow oven until brown and crisp.

BAKED ASSORTED FRUIT

Place layers of different kinds of fruit (either freshly cooked or canned) in a baking dish and sprinkle chopped nuts, brown sugar, and bits of butter between the layers. Pour over them ½ cup of cooking brandy or sherry, either separately or mixed. Crumb macaroon cookies and sprinkle over the top. Bake in a slow oven (275°) until heated through, about 30 minutes. (Arrange the fruit ahead of time and bake just before serving.)

Menu

SALMON SALAD IN MOLD WITH VEGETABLES

NOODLES SONIA

BUTTERED RYE BREAD

PECAN PIE

SALMON SALAD IN MOLD WITH VEGETABLES

Dissolve 1 package of salad gelatine in 1 cup of boiling water. Add 1 tablespoon of grated onion and season with salt and pepper. Chill the gelatine until it begins to stiffen and then fold in ¼ cup of mayonnaise. Add 2 cups of cooked salmon, or other fish, ¼ cup of chopped celery, 2 tablespoons of chopped green pepper, and 2 teaspoons of lemon juice. Pour into a fish mold and place in the refrigerator until firm. (Prepare the day before.) When ready to serve, unmold in the center of a platter decorated with thick slices of tomato, marinated in French dressing and crossed with anchovy fillets. Deviled eggs and bunches of cooked marinated string beans may be used also. Serves 6.

NOODLES SONIA

Cook 1 package of noodles in boiling salted water until tender but not mushy. Mix 2 tablespoons of poppy seeds with ¼ cup of chopped nuts (almonds or walnuts). Brown in butter and sprinkle over noodles. (Noodles may be kept hot in top of double boiler until ready to serve.) Serves 4 to 6.

PECAN PIE

Beat 3 eggs and add 1 cup of dark Karo corn syrup, ½ cup of sugar, 1 cup of pecans cut into pieces, ¼ teaspoon of salt, and 1 teaspoon of vanilla. Pour into an unbaked pie shell in a 9-inch pie tin. Bake for 1 hour in a medium oven (350°). Serves 6.

Menu

STUFFED EGGS WITH CUCUMBER SAUCE

SPAGHETTI BAKED WITH CREAM AND CHEESE

ARTICHOKE AND RADISH SALAD

PINEAPPLE SLICES WITH COCOANUT SAUCE

STUFFED EGGS WITH CUCUMBER SAUCE

Hard-boil 10 eggs, cut in half lengthwise, and stuff 8 of them, mixing lemon juice, butter, a little onion juice, prepared mustard, salt and pepper with the mashed yolks. Prepare Never-Fail Hollandaise Sauce (p. 89), and add to it ½ cup of mayonnaise and the juice of 1 lemon. Grate 1 large cucumber and drain. Add to the sauce and pour over the halves of the eggs, arranged on a platter. Press the other 2 eggs through a coarse sieve and sprinkle over the top of the sauce with 2 tablespoons of chopped parsley. Serves 6.

SPAGHETTI BAKED WITH CREAM AND CHEESE

Cook ½ pound of spaghetti in boiling salted water for 20 minutes. Drain and mix with ¾ cup of grated cheese. Place in an earthenware casserole and pour over it thin cream, or evaporated milk diluted with fresh milk, and mixed with 1 tablespoon of prepared mustard. Add enough milk to come to the top of the spaghetti. Sprinkle ¼ cup of grated cheese over the top, dot with butter, and bake in a slow oven (275°) until brown. Sprinkle with paprika. Serves 4.

ARTICHOKE AND RADISH SALAD

Drain a can of baby artichokes, marinate them in French dressing, and chill. (Some artichokes come bottled in French dressing. In that case, just put them in the refrigerator to chill.) Make radish roses, allowing 6 radishes for each person. Place an artichoke in the center of each individual plate, on a bed of endive, and encircle the artichoke with a ring of 6 radish roses. Put a dab of stiff mayonnaise on the artichoke.

PINEAPPLE SLICES WITH COCOANUT SAUCE

Peel and slice a ripe pineapple (Canned pineapple may be used.) and arrange the slices on a round glass platter. Pour a generous amount of rum over the slices and place in the refrigerator to chill. (Prepare in the morning.) Just before serving, spread the slices with Cocoanut Sauce. Decorate the platter with sprigs of fresh mint and serve.

Cocoanut Sauce.—Grate enough fresh cocoanut to make 1 pound. Put the cocoanut milk, the grated meat, and 1 cup of sugar in an enamel saucepan. Place on an asbestos mat over a low fire and simmer for about 3 hours. Skim and place in sterilized jars. Keep in a cool place. It should keep fresh for about 2 months. (This sauce may be purchased in cans from a few specialty shops, but this is an excellent substitute and well worth the trouble to make it.)

Menu

RANCH MEAT BALLS

STUFFED EGGPLANT WITH NUTS

FRENCH BREAD HEATED WITH GARLIC BUTTER

MIXED GREEN SALAD

FRENCH DRESSING

FROZEN BING CHERRIES

RANCH MEAT BALLS

In the morning make meat balls of 1 pound of ground round steak, ½ cup of raw rice, ½ cup of bread crumbs, 1 onion chopped fine, 1 teaspoon of chopped parsley, and 1 teaspoon of salt. Place in an earthenware casserole and cover with waxed paper. An hour before dinner, add 1 No.-2½ can of tomatoes, 1 chopped onion, 1 chopped green pepper, 1 bay leaf, ½ teaspoon of salt, and 1 cup of water, if needed. Simmer slowly on top of the stove for 1 hour. Sprinkle with grated cheese just before serving. Serves 4.

STUFFED EGGPLANT WITH NUTS

Cut a slice lengthwise from 1 large eggplant. Scoop out the pulp, and cook it in boiling salted water until tender. Drain and chop fine. Sauté one small minced onion in butter until soft, but do not brown. Add chopped eggplant, ½ cup of soft bread crumbs, ½ cup of chopped nuts, and 2 well-beaten eggs. Mix well and season to taste. Fill eggplant shell and sprinkle with sifted dried bread crumbs, dot with butter, and bake about 20 minutes in a moderate oven (350°). Serves 4.

FRENCH DRESSING

1 cup olive oil	1 teaspoon dry mustard
¼ cup lemon juice	1 teaspoon grated onion
½ teaspoon salt	1 teaspoon Worcestershire sauce
½ teaspoon paprika	1 clove garlic, cut crosswise

Mix ingredients in a glass jar. Shake well before using.

FROZEN BING CHERRIES

Empty 1 large can of pitted Bing cherries into the freezing tray of an electric refrigerator. Turn up the control and freeze to a mush. Serve in a glass bowl and pass sweetened whipped cream flavored with brandy. (Other fruit, such as apricots or figs, either freshly cooked or canned, may be used in this manner.) Serves 4.

Menu

MINCED CLAM LOAF

BAKED GREEN SUMMER SQUASH

BANANA BREAD

SPONGE CAKE WITH ORANGE FILLING

MINCED CLAM LOAF
(Harriet's)

2 cans minced clams	½ pound hamburger
1 dozen soda crackers, crushed	¼ pound ground pork

Season with salt, pepper, and Worcestershire sauce. Mix all ingredients and moisten with clam broth. Mold in a loaf pan and brush over with white of egg. (Prepare in the morning and store in the refrigerator until later.) Bake 1 hour in a moderate oven (375°). Serves 6.

BAKED GREEN SUMMER SQUASH

Wash squash and slice in rings. Arrange a layer in the bottom of a baking dish and lay rings of sliced onions on top. Dot with butter and sprinkle with salt and pepper. Continue layers until the dish is full. Cover and bake for 30 minutes in a moderate oven (350°). Remove cover, add ½ cup of cream, and continue baking until browned.

BANANA BREAD

Melt ½ cup of butter and add 2 eggs beaten with 5 tablespoons of sour cream. Sift together 1 cup of sugar, 1 teaspoon of soda, ½ teaspoon of salt, and 2 cups of sifted flour. Add to egg mixture. Mash 3 bananas and add with 1 cup of chopped walnuts. Mix well and bake in a greased bread pan in a 325° oven for 1 hour. (Bake the day before.)

SPONGE CAKE WITH ORANGE FILLING

Buy or make a round sponge cake. For the filling mix ¾ cup of sugar with 3 tablespoons of flour and beat in 1 egg. Add the grated rind and juice of 1 orange. Cook in the top of a double boiler until thick. Cool and fold in 1 cup of cream, whipped. Slice the sponge cake in half and spread the filling between the layers. Frost with Butter Orange Frosting.

Butter Orange Frosting. — Beat 1 egg yolk into 2 cups of powdered sugar. Blend in 4 tablespoons of soft butter. Add 1 tablespoon of cream and 2 tablespoons of orange juice. Spread the top and sides of the cake and sprinkle thickly with chopped nuts.

Menu

CHICKEN ASPIC

JELLIED MUSHROOMS

SPAGHETTI WITH BUTTER AND CHEESE

DEVONSHIRE TRIFLE

CHICKEN ASPIC

Dissolve 1 package of lemon gelatine in 1½ cups of boiling water. Add 2 tablespoons of horse-radish and 2 teaspoons of lemon juice. Add 2 cups of sliced celery, 1 cup of diced chicken, and 15 sliced stuffed olives. Arrange in a mold and chill until firm. (Prepare the day before.) Surround with Jellied Mushrooms. Serves 4 to 6.

JELLIED MUSHROOMS

Soak 1 tablespoon of gelatine in ¼ cup of cold water. Dissolve in 1¼ cups of boiling water. Add 1 teaspoon of lemon juice and ½ teaspoon of salt. Drain 1 large can of mushroom pieces. Add ¼ cup of mushroom juice to the gelatine and chill until thickened. Fold in the mushroom pieces and pour into individual molds. Chill until firm. (Prepare the day before.) Serves 4.

SPAGHETTI WITH BUTTER AND CHEESE

Cook 1 pound of spaghetti in boiling salted water for 20 minutes. Rinse in hot water, drain, and toss lightly with ½ cup of melted butter and 2 cups of grated cheese. Place in a serving bowl and sprinkle freshly ground pepper over the top. Serves 6.

DEVONSHIRE TRIFLE

Make boiled custard or use the ready-prepared custard mixture. Let cool. Cut a small sponge cake into slices and place in a serving dish. Spread with raspberry jam. Sprinkle with 1 cup of port wine or sherry. Cover with sliced almonds and pour the custard over the top. Place in the refrigerator for 2 hours or overnight. Cover with whipped cream, if desired.

Menu

SALMON WITH VEGETABLES EN CASSEROLE

MILLBROOK WATER CRESS

BUTTERY MELBA TOAST

APPLES BAKED WITH SHERRY

SALMON WITH VEGETABLES EN CASSEROLE

Melt 1 tablespoon of butter in an earthenware casserole. Drain 1 can of salmon but leave it whole. Place in the center of the casserole and surround it with canned whole kernel corn and green peppers. Drain canned artichoke hearts and place in the corn around the salmon. Sprinkle with salt and pepper. Pour 1 cup or more of sour cream over all and bake uncovered in a 350° oven until the cream is browned. Serves 4 to 6.

MILLBROOK WATER CRESS

Allow 1 bunch of water cress for each person. Remove the coarse stems at the bottom but leave the tender stems and leaves. Wash thoroughly and dry in a towel. Chop fine in a chopping bowl and cook in boiling salted water for about 20 minutes. Flavor with grated onion, adding cracked or coarsely ground black pepper and plenty of butter or olive oil.

APPLES BAKED WITH SHERRY

Remove the cores from 6 tart baking apples and fill the centers with a mixture of ¾ cup of sugar, creamed with ¼ cup of butter and seasoned with a dash of cinnamon. Place in a baking dish and pour ½ cup of sherry around the apples. Cover and bake in a 400° oven for about 25 minutes, basting with the sherry and adding more as necessary. Serves 6.

Menu

SPAGHETTI WITH JOE'S SHRIMP SAUCE

WILTED LETTUCE OR SPINACH

CHEESE BREAD

APRICOTS IN KIRSCH

SPAGHETTI WITH JOE'S SHRIMP SAUCE

Crush 3 cloves of garlic and fry in 1 cup of olive oil with 4 small chili peppers. (Little dried red peppers may be used.) Cook until the garlic is brown; remove it and the peppers from the oil. Add 2 pounds of cleaned fresh or canned shrimp and sauté in the olive oil. Remove the shrimp and set aside until the sauce is ready. In the olive oil sauté 8 sliced medium-sized onions until brown. Add 2 large cans of tomatoes and 4 cans of tomato paste, with 1 cup of water rinsed from the cans of paste. Cook in top of double boiler for 2 hours. Add 1 tablespoon of sugar, 1½ teaspoons of salt, and the shrimp. Simmer for 20 minutes more. Pour over boiled spaghetti and sprinkle with grated Parmesan cheese. For this amount of sauce, cook 1½ pounds of spaghetti. Serves 8.

WILTED LETTUCE OR SPINACH

Wash ½ pound of lettuce (preferably Bibb lettuce) or spinach leaves. Let stand ½ hour in a bowl of ice water. Drain and dry on a towel. Shred into a salad bowl. Add 1 small grated onion, 4 slices of fried bacon chopped fine, and the chopped white of 1 hard-boiled egg. Season with 1 teaspoon of salt and a dash of pepper and cayenne. Mix well, using two forks. Add ⅛ cup of wine vinegar to the bacon fat and the mashed yolk of egg. Let mixture come to a boil and pour over the greens. Serve at once. Serves 4 to 6.

CHEESE BREAD

Scald 1 cup of milk and add ¼ cup of sugar and 1½ teaspoons of salt. Cool to lukewarm and add ½ teaspoon of dry mustard, ¼ teaspoon of paprika and a dash of cayenne. Soften 1 cake of fresh yeast in ¼ cup of lukewarm water. Add the yeast to the warm milk. Stir in 1 well-beaten egg, 2 cups of freshly grated cheese, and as much flour as can be stirred into the dough without kneading. Knead on a well-floured board. Cover the dough with a towel and let stand 10 minutes. Cut in half and form into 2 balls. Place in 2 well-greased loaf pans, cover and let rise in a warm place until double in size. Bake in a slow oven (275°) for 45 minutes. Remove from the pans, brush with melted butter, and cool on a cake rack. Serve fresh from the oven or toasted and spread with melted butter.

APRICOTS IN KIRSCH

Drain 1 large can of chilled apricots. Mix ¼ cup of kirsch with some of the apricot juice and pour over the apricots. Serve with Frozen Cream. Serves 6.

Frozen Cream. — Pour ½ pint of cream into a freezing tray in the refrigerator. Let freeze until crystals form. Place in a bowl and serve with any fruit.

Menu

CHEESE PIE

BAKED POTATOES FILLED WITH SPINACH

ORANGE JELLY RING WITH
ORANGE AND LEMON MAYONNAISE

ORANGE MARMALADE MUFFINS

CHEESE PIE

Line a 9-inch glass pie plate with pastry. Cover with 4 medium-sized onions, chopped fine, and 1 package of processed Swiss cheese, cut in small cubes. Peel and dice 4 tomatoes. Mix with 1 small can of anchovies, minced fine, 1 tablespoon of Worcestershire sauce, and ½ teaspoon of salt. Pour over the cheese. Add 1 cup of cream or evaporated milk diluted with milk. Bake in a slow oven (275°) 1 hour. Serve warm, not hot.

BAKED POTATOES FILLED WITH SPINACH

Drain 1 large can of spinach or equal amount of cooked fresh spinach and chop fine. Season with grated onion, salt, pepper, and celery salt. Wash 3 large baking potatoes and rub the skins with bacon drippings. Bake in a hot oven for 1 hour, or until done. Cut in half lengthwise and scoop out the pulp. Mash and beat until fluffy; add 2 tablespoons of melted butter, ½ cup of hot milk, and season with salt and pepper. Fill the potato shells with spinach; decorate with a border of mashed potato. Cover the spinach with finely chopped bacon. Place in a moderate oven (350°) until the bacon is cooked and the potato is well browned.

ORANGE JELLY RING
(Serve as a dessert with Orange Marmalade Muffins.)

Soak 1 tablespoon of gelatine in ¼ cup of cold water. Dissolve in ½ cup of boiling water. Add 1 cup of orange juice and 1 tablespoon of lemon juice. Stir in ¼ cup of sugar and ⅛ teaspoon of salt and continue stirring until dissolved. Chill. When it begins to thicken, pour a little in the bottom of a ring mold and place in the refrigerator until firm. Add 1 can of grapes, well drained, or fresh grapes, skinned and seeded, 1 cup of chopped nuts; then pour in the rest of the gelatine. Chill until firm. (Prepare the day before.) Unmold on a bed of lettuce and fill the center with a bowl of Orange and Lemon Mayonnaise. Serves 4 to 6.

Orange and Lemon Mayonnaise. — Grate the rind of 1 orange and 1 lemon into 1 cup of mayonnaise. Add ½ cup of whipped cream and 1 teaspoon of lemon juice.

ORANGE MARMALADE MUFFINS
(Lucy's)

Cream together ⅓ cup each of sugar and shortening. Add 2 well-beaten eggs and ½ teaspoon of vanilla. Beat well. Sift together 1¾ cups of flour, ½ teaspoon of salt, and 2 teaspoons of baking powder. Add the flour mixture alternately with ⅓ cup of milk. Beat thoroughly. Fill greased muffin tins half full. Place 1 teaspoon of Marmalade Sauce in each one and fill nearly full with the rest of the batter. Bake in a moderate oven (350°) for 20 minutes.

Marmalade Sauce. — Mix ¼ cup each of brown sugar and flour. Stir in 1 tablespoon of soft butter, 1 teaspoon of cream, and 2 tablespoons of orange marmalade. Mix thoroughly. (Prepare ahead of time.)

Cooking in a Bandbox

Cooking in a small apartment has its own particular problems. The lack of space, the presence of odors from the cooking, and, if you work all day, the question of how to arrange time in which to purchase and to cook your food may all confront you. Yet you may want to entertain your friends or perhaps to impress your beau or new husband with your knowledge of culinary art. Certainly, if you are preparing dinner for your one and only, you don't want to be so involved in last-moment cooking that you cannot stop to greet him, nor do you want him to have to drink his cocktail alone in the living room while you labor over a hot stove in the kitchen.

The use of a casserole will allow you to prepare your meal ahead of time, to dispel unpleasant cooking odors, and to reduce last-minute work. The casserole also lessens the task of dishwashing, as practically your entire meal may be cooked and served in the one container.

Even if you are crowded for space, use one shelf for emergency supplies. If you select them carefully and know the recipes for a few quick dishes, you can whip up a meal for unexpected guests at a moment's notice.

For two months I lived in a bandbox in New York City. It was great fun and a liberal education in conserving space as well as time. Really to know a city, you must actually keep house there; it is not enough just to occupy a room in a hotel. In other words, you need "a kitchen and a latchkey!" Then you face the same problems as the local housewives. You join them in exploring the different food shops. You face situations different from those you meet at the family home. Your visit becomes an interesting adventure. The next time you feel the need of a vacation, rent an apartment in a city in another part of the country and start housekeeping.

In New York, I was entranced with the high, three-wheeled carts loaded with groceries which the delivery boys pushed along Park Avenue. The array of delicious looking salads in the Swedish specialty shop fascinated me. And when I found my way to the grocery department in a large store, I wanted to buy everything I saw. There were so many suggestions for "quickies" or for emergency meals that before I realized it I had yielded to the temptation and bought more supplies than my bandbox of a home could hold.

I found many kinds of fancy soups all ready to be served, canned meats and sausages temptingly displayed, fish put up in large or small containers, ready to be mixed with a little cream sauce, a dash of sherry or herbs. With these and a wide range of canned vegetables, I was ready to plan an emergency meal. Whole fruits, bottled in brandy and looking like a picture in their glass containers, were an impressive addition to my emergency shelf.

I found a little grocery store with an old world atmosphere. The entrance was down three steps, and when I pushed open the door, a bell tinkled. From the rear of the store where he lived, the owner would appear, wiping his hands on his white apron and beaming expectantly. Choice fruit and early tomatoes in their tissue paper coats were unwrapped for my inspection. And as he hovered in the background, I alternately examined my list and asked questions. The whole transaction was "folksy" and intimate, quite different from what I expected to find in such a large city.

Each Tuesday, I stopped at the neighborhood poultry shop and after looking over the fowl, selected what I needed for the week. As soon as I returned to my apartment, I put the chicken neck, the back, the feet, and the tips of the wings on to boil in cold water. I added an onion, dried or fresh celery leaves, and seasoning. Later, a chicken broth cube or two were added to strengthen the flavor and make the quantity go further.

The rest of the chicken I wrapped in paper and put away in the refrigerator in a covered dish. If I planned to fry or roast part of it the first of the week, the remainder, still in its wrapper of paper, was placed in the freezing compartment where the ice cubes belong and left until frozen solid. It was then transferred to the glass tray underneath the freezing unit until needed. The frozen chicken takes a little longer to cook, but tastes just the same as the unfrozen.

Don't forget the chafing dish! It offers another easy way to cook and serve food. If your kitchen is the size of a cubbyhole, you will find that the chafing dish will make entertaining much easier.

If your bandbox home is very small, the serving of a party may be a problem. Nests of tables are one answer. They may be stored one inside of the other when not in use so that three or four will take up no more room than one table. If you have places to put them, set the tables before your guests arrive. Otherwise bring them out later on. Arrange your service on individual trays and place a tray on each table, or place your silver and doilies directly on the table. You may either serve your dinner buffet style, if you have room, or you may place the food upon your guests' plates in the kitchen and let one of them help you pass them.

Menu

INDIVIDUAL MEAT LOAVES WITH
ROASTED POTATOES

BOILED CELERY WITH HORSE-RADISH SAUCE

CORN MEAL MUFFINS

PEACHES WITH RASPBERRIES

INDIVIDUAL MEAT LOAVES WITH ROASTED POTATOES

Mix 4 cups of ground veal or beef with 1 cup of fresh bread crumbs, 1 egg, and 1 cup of milk. Season with 1½ tablespoons of chili sauce, 2 teaspoons of salt, and a dash of pepper, 1 table-spoon of grated onion, and a minced clove of garlic. Mix well and divide into 4 equal portions. Roll each portion around 1 cooked (canned may be used) pork sausage, shaping it into a little individual loaf. Place in a greased baking pan, surround with peeled potatoes cut in quarters, and bake in a moderate oven (350°) for 30 minutes. (The loaves may be prepared ahead of time and baked just before dinner.) Serves 6.

BOILED CELERY WITH HORSE-RADISH SAUCE

Make a cream sauce with 2 cups of milk (or cream and milk mixed) and 2 tablespoons each of butter and flour. Cook 1 large bunch of celery, cut in 1-inch pieces, in boiling salted water un-til tender. Drain. Add 3 tablespoons of horse-radish to the cream sauce, season with salt and pepper, and mix with the celery. Serve hot. (This may be prepared ahead of time and reheated in a double boiler.) Serves 6.

CORN MEAL MUFFINS

Sift together 1 cup of flour, ½ teaspoon of salt, 4 teaspoons of baking powder, 2 tablespoons of sugar, and 1 cup of yellow corn meal. Add 2 eggs beaten with 1 cup of milk. Fry 2 slices of finely shredded bacon and add with 2 tablespoons of the bacon fat to the mixture. Pour into greased muffin tins and bake in a moderate oven (350°) for 25 minutes. (The dry ingredients may be mixed ahead of time, adding the fried bacon at the last moment. Or muffins may be baked ahead of time and warmed in a slow oven.)

PEACHES WITH RASPBERRIES

Peel 6 peaches and dip in equal parts of lemon juice and water to prevent them from turning dark. Cut them in half and place in a glass dish, cut sides up. Mash 2 baskets of raspberries and rub through a sieve. Add a little sherry and sweeten to taste. Mix well and pour over the peaches. Blend 2 cakes of Philadelphia cream cheese with 1 cup of sweet or sour cream. Pour over the fruit. (Raspberry jelly or jam may be dissolved, the sherry added, and used in place of the fresh berries.) Serves 6.

Menu

TUNA EN CASSEROLE

SALAD BOWL

CHEESE MUFFINS

WATERMELON WITH ASSORTED FRUIT

TUNA EN CASSEROLE

Make a cream sauce of 2 tablespoons of butter and 2 table-spoons of flour, 1¼ cups of milk, and ½ cup of evaporated milk. Add ¾ cup of mayonnaise, 1 tablespoon of catsup, and salt and pepper to taste. Beat until thoroughly blended. Drain a 13-ounce can of tuna and cut in cubes. (All of this may be done ahead of time and the tuna and the cream sauce stored in covered dishes in the refrigerator.) Put tuna in the top of a double boiler to heat. Peel 3 large tomatoes and cut into medium-small pieces, discarding the seeds. Cut 3 hard-boiled eggs in quarters length-wise. Chop 2 tablespoons of water cress. Add all to the cream sauce mixture, pour into an earthenware casserole, and heat slowly. Fold in the tuna and serve. Serves 4 to 6.

SALAD BOWL

Line a salad bowl with chicory and romaine broken in pieces. Fill with sliced artichoke bottoms (canned or boiled) and sliced cucumbers mixed with French dressing. Garnish with peeled tomatoes cut into quarters.

CHEESE MUFFINS

Force through a ricer ½ pound of American Cheddar cheese. Sift 2 cups of cake flour with 4 teaspoons of baking powder. (If you started your muffins ahead of time, suspend prepara-tions at this point.) About ½ hour before they are to be served, add the cheese to the flour and mix lightly with 2 forks until well blended. Beat together 1 egg and 1 cup of milk, and add to the flour and cheese mixture. Mix well and add 3 tablespoons of melted butter. Place in greased muffin tins and bake in a moderate oven (350°) for 30 minutes. Serves 6.

WATERMELON WITH ASSORTED FRUIT

Cut a small watermelon in half lengthwise and scoop out the center. Fill each half with assorted fruits — watermelon balls, fresh pineapple cut in cubes, black cherries, and strawberries. Pour 2 tablespoons of kirsch over each half and serve with the watermelon surrounded with bunches of fresh mint.

Menu

CHICKEN ROASTED EN CASSEROLE

RICE BROWNED IN OLIVE OIL

IMPERIAL SALAD

PINEAPPLE FLUFF WITH CUSTARD SAUCE

CHICKEN ROASTED EN CASSEROLE

Cut up a roasting chicken and brown in butter (or bacon fat) in an earthenware casserole. Add salt, pepper, chopped parsley, 1 grated onion, and 1 whole clove of garlic. Sprinkle a tiny bit of water lightly over the chicken. Put the lid on the casserole and cook in a slow oven (275°) until the chicken is tender. Remove chicken from the casserole but keep it warm. Add 1 can of mushrooms to the juice in the casserole and heat through. Remove garlic clove. Add 1 tablespoon of sherry and 1 large can of evaporated milk diluted with 1 cup of fresh milk. Stir while it bubbles up. Put the chicken back in the casserole, arranging it attractively, cover again and keep warm until ready to serve.

RICE BROWNED IN OLIVE OIL

1½ tablespoons olive oil   1 cup raw rice
2 cups boiling bouillon or chicken stock   Salt to taste

Put olive oil or drippings in an earthenware casserole. When
hot, add rice (1 cup will serve 4 people) and stir with a long-
pronged fork over a slow fire until the rice is browned. Add
enough hot broth (or water) to cover well, put on lid, and
place in a moderate oven (350°) until the rice is soft. Add more
stock as needed, being sure it is boiling when it is added. This
may be prepared the day before, placed in the refrigerator, and
later reheated in the top of a double boiler, adding more stock
or bouillon if too dry. In fact, I have reheated the same rice many
times over, then finally added the remainder to a few scraps
of chicken and some gravy, and baked it in a casserole with
bread crumbs on the top, making one of those delicious dishes
for which there is neither name nor recipe. Serves 4.

IMPERIAL SALAD

Put 1 tablespoon of very finely minced onion in the bottom
of a big salad bowl. Fill it two thirds full of escarole or romaine,
broken coarsely. Slice over the top 6 canned beets or boiled fresh
beets, 1 hard-boiled egg, and some pieces of anchovy fillet. Add
French dressing and toss lightly.

PINEAPPLE FLUFF

Soak 1 package of gelatine in ½ cup of cold water and dissolve over boiling water. Beat 4 egg whites very stiff and add
slowly ½ cup of sugar. Beat in the gelatine gradually. Stir in 1
teaspoon of vanilla and ½ cup of grated pineapple. Pour into a
melon mold rinsed in cold water. Place in the refrigerator until
firm. (Prepare the day before.) Unmold and serve with Custard
Sauce (p. 31). Serves 4 to 6.

Menu

NOODLE AND CHEESE CASSEROLE

VEGETABLE SALAD PLATTER

BAKED APPLES WITH SOUR CREAM RUM SAUCE

This was one of those situations which remain in your memory like a horrible nightmare. One Monday, I casually asked a few friends to stop by for supper on "next Thursday," meaning "next week Thursday." You can imagine my embarrassment when my guests arrived on the *first* Thursday night just as I was about to sit down to a meager supper of tomato soup, frankfurters, cauliflower, and a baked apple. There was nothing for me to do but admit my mistake, invite my guests into the kitchen, and put them to work. With the addition of canned vegetables and some leftovers from the refrigerator, I created this menu to stretch my supper to feed 6.

NOODLE AND CHEESE CASSEROLE

Cook 1 5-ounce package of fine noodles in boiling salted water until tender. Brown 1 chopped onion and 3 sliced frankfurters in 2 tablespoons of bacon drippings. Add 1 can of tomato soup, ½ of a small can of chili peppers and ¼ pound of grated American cheese. Stir until the cheese melts. Season with 2 teaspoons of Worcestershire sauce, ½ teaspoon of salt, and ⅛ teaspoon of black pepper. Stir in the noodles and bake in a casserole in a moderate oven (350°) for 25 minutes. Serves 6.

VEGETABLE SALAD PLATTER

In the center of a salad platter place a whole boiled head of cauliflower. Arrange around it separate mounds of vegetables, alternating to have a diversion of color: cooked and diced carrots, beets, turnips, string beans, and potatoes. Peas, canned kidney beans, and canned asparagus tips may also be added. Season well and add French dressing. Sprinkle chopped parsley over the cauliflower. (Cook vegetables the day before and chill or use canned vegetables.)

BAKED APPLES WITH SOUR CREAM RUM SAUCE

Core 6 apples and peel halfway down. Make a syrup of 1 cup of sugar and 1 cup of water. Mix together 2 tablespoons of soft butter, 1 tablespoon of cinnamon, and 1 cup of finely chopped nuts, and place in the center of the apples. Pour the syrup around the apples in a baking dish, cover, and bake in a slow oven (275°) until soft. Serve with Sour Cream Rum Sauce.

Sour Cream Rum Sauce. — Mix sour cream with powdered sugar to taste. Flavor with rum.

Menu

BEEF STEW WITH RED WINE

BOILED NOODLES WITH FRIED BREAD CRUMBS

SALAD OF MIXED VEGETABLES WITH
MUSTARD DRESSING

FRENCH BREAD HEATED WITH GARLIC BUTTER

PEARS IN KIRSCH

BEEF STEW WITH RED WINE

Cut 4 slices of bacon in small pieces and brown in an earthenware casserole with 10 tiny onions. Add 2 pounds of beef cut in small pieces and cook until brown. Sprinkle 1 tablespoon of flour over the meat and cook together for a few minutes, stirring constantly. Add 1 tablespoon of chopped parsley and a pinch of mixed dried herbs, and season with salt and pepper. Add ½ cup each of red wine and water, and bring to a boil. Reduce the heat and simmer slowly with the lid on for 2½ hours. Add more of the wine and water mixture, if necessary. When the meat is cooked, thicken the gravy with a little cornstarch dissolved in cold water. (Prepare the day before.) Serves 4 to 6.

BOILED NOODLES WITH FRIED BREAD CRUMBS

Cook fine noodles in boiling salted water until tender but not too soft. Drain in a colander and rinse with hot water. Fry an onion and a clove of garlic in 4 tablespoons of butter. Remove onion and garlic, and add ½ cup of fine dried bread crumbs. Reheat noodles in the top of the double boiler. Serve hot, covered with the crumbs.

SALAD OF MIXED VEGETABLES

Mix 1 cup of celery, cut in short, match-like sticks, with 1 cup each of diced, boiled beets and shredded, cooked string beans. Add ½ cup of finely minced green pepper. Mix with Mustard Dressing. Serve with water cress. (Prepare vegetables in the morning and chill until ready.) Serves 6.

Mustard Dressing. — Mix ¼ cup of prepared mustard, ¾ cup of mayonnaise, and a little lemon juice.

PEARS IN KIRSCH

Heat 1 cup of brown sugar with 1 cup of water until the sugar dissolves. Peel 8 pears, leaving the stems on, and add to the syrup. Baste frequently and turn the pears so that all sides come in contact with the syrup. When the pears are tender, remove from the syrup and dip in ½ cup of kirsch. Place the pears in a serving dish and chill. Add the remainder of the kirsch to the syrup and boil 10 minutes. Pour over the pears and serve very cold. (Prepare the day before.) Serves 8.

Menu

CASSEROLE OF ARTICHOKES WITH CRAB

BAKED STUFFED EGGPLANT

SLICED ORANGES WITH CARAMEL SAUCE

CASSEROLE OF ARTICHOKES WITH CRAB

Make a white sauce with 2 tablespoons of butter, 2 tablespoons of flour, and 2 cups of milk. Season with salt, pepper, and Worcestershire sauce; mix in ½ cup of grated yellow cheese. Hard-boil 5 eggs and cut in slices. Use 1 No.-2 can of artichoke hearts and cut them lengthwise in halves. Pick over and remove bones from 1 large-sized can of crab meat (or the equivalent in fresh crab). In a small casserole place alternate layers of eggs, crab meat, and artichokes, with a little cream sauce between layers, and continue with the layers until the casserole is filled. Cover the last layer with cream sauce and Parmesan cheese, grated. (Prepare in the morning and store in the refrigerator.) Bake in a moderate oven (350°) about three quarters of an hour. Serves 6.

BAKED STUFFED EGGPLANT

Cut the eggplant in half lengthwise and bake in the oven until tender. Remove the pulp and mix it with a stuffing made of 1 cup of whole-wheat bread crumbs, 3 tablespoons of tomato catsup, ½ tablespoon of poultry seasoning, 2 tablespoons of melted butter, 1 grated onion, salt, and pepper. Fill the shells with this mixture and store in the refrigerator. When needed, place in the oven until heated through and browned. Serves 4.

SLICED ORANGES WITH CARAMEL SAUCE
(Viola's)

To make the caramel sauce, put 1 cup of granulated sugar and ½ cup of water in a deep aluminum pan, and cook without stirring until the syrup has turned a light brown. Remove from the stove and add 1 cup of cold water, but be careful, for it will bubble up. Cook over a slow fire until the caramel has melted; then continue cooking, without stirring, for about 7 minutes or until thick. Cool.

Peel 8 seedless oranges, removing all the yellow and white skin. Slice the oranges, but replace them in their original shape. Save any juice. Stand the oranges in a shallow serving dish, add any orange juice, and pour over ½ of the caramel sauce. (Prepare in the morning.) Chill until ready to serve; then pour over the rest of the sauce and sprinkle with 1 cup of chopped pecans.

Menu

BAKED ACORN SQUASHES FILLED WITH MEAT

CREAMED ONIONS WITH CARROTS

TOMATO AND AVOCADO SALAD

MAPLE FREEZETTE

TEA CAKES

BAKED ACORN SQUASHES FILLED WITH MEAT

Cut squashes in halves lengthwise and remove seeds. Fill with highly seasoned chopped meat, either beef, veal, pork, or a mixture of them. Cover pan and bake in a 400° oven for about 30 minutes or until the squashes are tender.

CREAMED ONIONS WITH CARROTS

Peel and boil 12 medium-sized onions. Drain. Scrape 5 carrots, cut into julienne strips, and boil until tender. Arrange the cooked onions in the bottom of a baking dish, and sprinkle the carrots over them. Add 1 tablespoon of chopped parsley to 2 cups of cream sauce and pour it over the onions and carrots. Cover with dried crumbs and dot well with butter. (Prepare in the morning.) Bake for ½ hour in a moderate oven (350°). Serves 8.

TOMATO AND AVOCADO SALAD

Peel 6 tomatoes, cut a lid from the top of each, and remove the pulp. Mash 2 avocados and 1 grated onion and add to the tomato pulp. Mix with well-seasoned French dressing and fill the tomatoes. Serve chilled on lettuce leaves. Serves 6.

MAPLE FREEZETTE

Mix 2 tall cans of evaporated milk and 2 cups of maple syrup or maple-flavored syrup. Add 1 cup of finely ground walnuts. Freeze until mushy, take out, place in a chilled bowl, and beat until creamy. Return to the refrigerator and freeze. (The strenuous beating is the secret of the lightness of this dessert.) Serves 6.

TEA CAKES
(Aunt Ella's)

Beat together 1 egg and ¾ cup of sugar until fluffy. Add 1 cup of sour cream and ½ teaspoon of vanilla. Sift together 1½ cups of flour, ½ teaspoon of soda, ⅛ teaspoon of salt, and ½ teaspoon of nutmeg. Add the dry ingredients to the sugar mixture and beat well. Pour into greased muffin tins and bake in a moderate oven (350°) for 35 minutes. These little cakes are delicious and will keep for a long time, if you hide them.

Menu

VEAL BAKED WITH WINE

RIPE TOMATOES STUFFED WITH
GREEN PEAS AND NUTS

LEMON CHIFFON PIE WITH CRUMB CRUST

VEAL BAKED WITH WINE

Cut 1½ pounds of veal in 1-inch cubes. Heat 2 tablespoons of bacon fat in an earthenware casserole. Add the meat, put on the lid, and cook over a very slow fire for 20 minutes. Remove the cover and sauté until brown. Add 1 tablespoon of flour and stir until mixed. Add 1 large can of evaporated milk and cook until smooth. Add 2 tablespoons of chopped green pepper and 2 tablespoons of onion. Season with salt and pepper. Bake in a moderate oven (350°) for 45 minutes. Add slowly 1½ cups of dry white wine and continue baking until veal is tender. When ready to serve, cover the top with canned chow-mein noodles or dried bread crumbs browned in butter. Serves 4.

RIPE TOMATOES STUFFED WITH GREEN PEAS AND NUTS

Peel firm, ripe tomatoes and scoop out the pulp. Turn upside down to drain and place in the refrigerator to chill until ready to serve. Mix cold cooked peas with chopped walnuts and add mayonnaise, well-flavored with lemon. Season to taste. (Prepare in the morning.) Fill the tomatoes and serve on lettuce leaves.

LEMON CHIFFON PIE WITH CRUMB CRUST

Into 1 cup of zwieback crumbs, crushed fine, stir ½ cup of sugar and ½ cup of melted butter. Mix thoroughly and press into a deep, 9-inch pie pan. Pat it firmly with the palm of the hand against the bottom and sides of the pan to form a pie shell. Bake in a moderate oven (375°) for 15 minutes.

Lemon Chiffon Filling. — Beat 4 egg yolks with ½ cup of sugar and the juice and grated rind of 1 lemon. Cook in a double boiler until thick. Beat the 4 egg whites stiff, adding gradually ½ cup of sugar. Remove enough of the beaten whites and sugar for a meringue to cover the pie; then fold the remainder into the cooked yolks and pour into the crust. Cover with the meringue and brown under the broiler. Serve cold.

Menu

BAKED AVOCADO STUFFED WITH HAM

MOLDED SPINACH WITH MUSHROOMS

BLANC MANGE

BAKED AVOCADO STUFFED WITH HAM

This recipe solves the problem of what to do with leftover ham or canned luncheon meat.

Cut 3 avocados in half lengthwise; remove seed. Fill the cavity and also cover the cut edges with vinegar and let stand for about half an hour. (Spiced vinegar may be used.)

Prepare 1 cup of thick cream sauce. Season with 2 teaspoons each of dry mustard and grated onion. Add 1 cup of ground ham or canned luncheon meat. Pour vinegar out of avocados and fill with creamed ham, heaping the amount high over the top. Cover with buttered crumbs and place on a greased pan. Set in a moderate oven (350°) for 20 minutes to heat through and brown the crumbs. Serves 6.

MOLDED SPINACH WITH MUSHROOMS

Drain thoroughly 4 cups of cooked spinach. Chop fine and season with pepper and salt. Press into a buttered ring mold, cover, and store in the refrigerator until later. Reheat in a moderate oven (350°). Unmold on a hot platter and fill the center with creamed mushrooms, made by adding 1 pound of sautéed mushrooms to 2 cans of mushroom soup. Serves 6.

BLANC MANGE
(Grandma Martin's)

Mix ¾ cup of milk with ¼ cup of cornstarch, 2 tablespoons of sugar, and ¼ teaspoon of salt. Add this mixture to 2¼ cups of scalded milk. Stir until blended; then cook in a double boiler until the mixture thickens and there is no taste of cornstarch. Beat 1 egg with 2 tablespoons of sugar and pour the hot mixture over it. Return to the fire until the egg thickens, stirring constantly. Flavor with vanilla and pour into a large mold or small individual molds. Chill. (Prepare the day before.) Serve with a pitcher of cream sweetened with powdered sugar and flavored with grated nutmeg. Serves 6.

ASPARAGUS AND SHRIMPS WITH CHEESE SAUCE

Dilute 1 can of mushroom soup with 1¼ cups of milk. Add ½ pound of Velveeta cheese and ⅛ pound of walnuts or almonds, chopped. Place all in the top of a double boiler and heat until well blended. Clean 1 pound of shrimps, either canned or fresh, and add to the mixture. (Prepare in the morning.) Reheat and pour over individual servings of asparagus — about 6 stalks on each slice of toast. This will serve 8.

GREEN SALAD WITH SPECIAL DRESSING

Chop radishes, hard-boiled eggs, and green pepper. Add to French dressing and pour it over a mixture of salad greens.

MINT SOUFFLÉ WITH STRAWBERRIES

Dissolve 1 package of lime gelatine in 1 cup of boiling water. Add ½ cup of cold water and flavor with a few drops of oil of peppermint. Chill until it begins to thicken. Beat the gelatine until it becomes light and fluffy. Fold in 1 cup of whipped cream. Pour into a ring mold rinsed in cold water. Chill until firm. (Prepare the day before.)

Unmold on a platter and fill the center with a bowl of powdered sugar and surround with unhulled strawberries. The guests help themselves to the powdered sugar and use it to sweeten the strawberries. Serves 6.

Menu

CURRIED SHRIMPS AND OYSTERS

BOILED NOODLES

ASSORTED VEGETABLE RELISHES

BANANAS IN SHERRY

CURRIED SHRIMPS AND OYSTERS

This dish is excellent for a "hurry-up" dinner before going to the theater.

Scald in a double boiler 1 cup of milk, 1 bay leaf, and a pinch of thyme. Sauté 1 clove of minced garlic and 4 young onions, chopped fine, in 2½ tablespoons of butter. When the onion is lightly browned, pour the flavored butter into the scalded milk. Mix 1 teaspoon of cornstarch, 1 tablespoon of curry powder, and 1 tablespoon of chutney with a little cold water. Stir the hot milk gradually into the mixture, return to the double boiler, and let cook for 20 minutes. Strain. Add 1 cup of cream or evaporated milk and let stand until ready to use. (Curry is better if made the day before.) Just before serving, add 1 large cup each of shrimps and oysters, and cook for 3 or 4 minutes. Serves 4.

Serve with boiled thin noodles and accompanied by chopped peanuts, grated fresh cocoanut, broiled chopped bacon, pickled onions, chopped dry ginger, chutney, and Bombay duck.

ASSORTED VEGETABLE RELISHES

Clean radishes, leaving a few green leaves, and heap in the center of a round platter. Cut celery and carrots into match-like sticks and arrange alternate bunches of the carrots and celery, interspersed with baby green onions. Decorate with parsley and scatter shaved ice over the vegetables.

BANANAS IN SHERRY

Place 6 peeled bananas in a shallow baking dish and dot with butter. In a separate pan put 1 cup of brown sugar, the juice and grated rind of 1 orange, and 3 tablespoons of sherry. Heat until the sugar is melted. Pour over the fruit. Sauté ¼ cup of chopped almonds in butter and sprinkle over the bananas. Bake in a 350° oven for about 20 minutes. Baste frequently. Just before removing from the oven, add a little more sherry.

Menu

VEAL AND MUSHROOMS EN CASSEROLE

SALAD DIABLE

PULLED BREAD

BAKED CHOCOLATE PUDDING WITH
COFFEE CUSTARD SAUCE

VEAL AND MUSHROOMS EN CASSEROLE

Heat 3 tablespoons of fat in an earthenware casserole and add 4 pounds of stewing veal cut in small pieces. Brown well; then add 1 finely chopped onion. Sprinkle lightly with flour and continue cooking over a moderate fire until the flour is brown, stirring constantly to prevent burning. Add 1 cup of white wine and stir until it boils; then add 2 minced cloves of garlic, 1 teaspoon of mixed dried herbs, and 1 teaspoon of chopped parsley. Peel and remove the seeds from 2 pounds of tomatoes, chop fine, and add to the meat. Simmer over a low fire for 1½ hours, or until the meat is tender.

Remove the meat, increase the heat, and let the sauce cook

until thickened. Strain. Replace the meat and the sauce in the casserole. Add ½ pound of sautéed fresh or canned mushrooms. Cover and let cook for 20 minutes. (Prepare in the morning.) Reheat. When ready to serve, stir in a few drops of lemon juice and sprinkle chopped parsley over the top. Serves 6 to 8.

SALAD DIABLE

In a salad bowl mash 1 clove of garlic and then discard it. Add 1 teaspoon of salt, 3 tablespoons of vinegar, a dash of Tabasco, ½ cup of olive oil, 1 teaspoon of dry mustard, and ½ teaspoon of pepper. Slice green onions fine, also 4 hard-boiled eggs. Mix well. Add 2 heads of lettuce, broken into 2-inch pieces. Toss lightly in the dressing and serve. Serves 4 to 6.

BAKED CHOCOLATE PUDDING

Cream 1 cup of sugar with ½ cup of butter. Beat in 2 egg yolks and 2 squares (or 2 ounces) of melted chocolate. Add ⅔ cup of sifted flour to the butter mixture. Flavor with 1 teaspoon of vanilla. Add ⅛ teaspoon of salt to 2 egg whites, whip until stiff and fold into the batter. Bake in a glass pie plate in a slow oven (275°) for 30 minutes. Serve hot with Coffee Custard Sauce. Serves 4 to 6.

Coffee Custard Sauce. — In the top of a double boiler, heat 1½ cups of cream, 3 tablespoons of sugar, and ½ cup of strong coffee. Add the well-beaten yolks of 3 eggs. Stir and cook until thick. Flavor with vanilla. (Prepare the day before.) Serves 6.

Menu

ESCALOPED HALIBUT

PEAS WITH GARLIC BUTTER

TOSSED GREEN SALAD

LEMON CRUMB PUDDING

ESCALOPED HALIBUT

Make a cream sauce with 2 tablespoons of butter, blended with 2 tablespoons of flour and 1 cup each of milk and cream. Season with salt, pepper, celery salt, and a pinch of mace. Add 1 tablespoon of chopped parsley, 1 tablespoon of onion juice, and a little lemon juice. Mix in 1 cup of boiled halibut, flaked, 1 small can of mushrooms, and 2 hard-boiled eggs, chopped fine. Pour into a buttered baking dish, cover with buttered bread crumbs, and bake for 15 minutes. (This may be prepared ahead of time and baked when needed.) Serves 4.

PEAS WITH GARLIC BUTTER

Sauté a crushed clove of garlic in butter. Remove the garlic and add drained cooked peas to the butter and sauté lightly. Remove to a serving dish and sprinkle with grated Parmesan cheese.

TOSSED GREEN SALAD

Rub a salad bowl with a clove of garlic. Break chilled crisp lettuce into 2-inch pieces and place a layer in the bottom of the bowl. Sprinkle with chopped hard-boiled egg and grated cheese. Add a few drops of lemon juice, a little olive oil, a sprinkle of salt, and some freshly ground pepper. Continue until the bowl is about three quarters full. Turn gently and mix lightly with your hands until all the lettuce is coated with the dressing.

LEMON CRUMB PUDDING

Soak 3 cups of soft bread crumbs in 2 cups of boiling water and let cool. Add the juice and grated rind of 1 lemon, ⅔ cup of sugar beaten with 3 egg yolks, ¼ cup of melted butter, and a pinch of salt. Mix well and bake in a moderate oven (350°) for 45 minutes. Beat the whites of 3 eggs until stiff, adding 6 tablespoons of sugar gradually while beating. Cover top of the pudding with the egg whites and brown in a slow oven (275°). Serves 6.

Menu

CASSEROLE OF LAMB WITH VEGETABLES

BEET SALAD RING

PEACHES AND FIGS WITH CREAM

CASSEROLE OF LAMB WITH VEGETABLES

Melt 2 tablespoons of bacon fat in an earthenware casserole. Add 4 pounds of lamb stew meat, cut from the shoulder, and brown on all sides. Remove the meat, add 2 tablespoons of flour to the fat, and brown. Add 2 cans of consommé and boil until thickened. Season with salt and pepper. Add ½ bay leaf, chopped parsley, and a pinch of thyme. Replace the meat and add 12 small onions and 6 carrots, diced. Cover the casserole and cook slowly in the oven for 2 hours or until the meat is tender. (May be prepared the day before.) Add 12 little peeled potatoes and cook for ½ hour more until the potatoes are tender. Remove the bay leaf and serve. Serves 6.

BEET SALAD RING

Dissolve 2 packages of lemon gelatine in 3 cups of boiling beet liquid and water. Add ⅓ cup of vinegar, 1 teaspoon of grated onion, and 2½ tablespoons of horse-radish. Chill, and when jelly is nearly set, add 1½ cups of cooked, diced beets and 1 cup of diced celery. Pour in a ring mold rinsed in cold water and place in the refrigerator until firm. (Prepare the day before.) Unmold on a platter and surround with chicory. Place a bowl of mayonnaise in the center. Serves 6.

PEACHES AND FIGS WITH CREAM

Place 6 halved, peeled peaches (fresh or canned) in a serving bowl. Pour over them 1 can of figs, mixed with ½ cup of brandy. Chill thoroughly. Pour sour cream over the top or a mixture of cream cheese, mashed and whipped with cream. Serves 6.

Menu

LAMB KIDNEYS AND MUSHROOMS
À LA HENRI

FRENCH BREAD

SPINACH RING AND CUCUMBERS

NEVER-FAIL HOLLANDAISE SAUCE

BROWN BETTY WITH FLUFFY HARD SAUCE

LAMB KIDNEYS AND MUSHROOMS À LA HENRI

Wash 12 lamb kidneys and remove the fat and membranes. Cut in thin slices but do not include any of the hard, white part. Slice 1 pound of mushrooms, excluding the stems.

Melt ¼ cup of butter in an earthenware casserole and add 12 green onions, shredded fine, including the tops; add the kidneys and mushrooms, and saute them all together. Cook gently until tender. Moisten with ½ cup of dry white wine, ¼ cup of dry red wine, and 2 tablespoons of brandy. Cover and simmer gently, stirring occasionally, for 1½ hours, adding more wine if necessary. Cream ½ tablespoon of butter with ½ tablespoon of flour and add to the gravy. Cook until thickened and season with salt and freshly ground black pepper. Flavor with 1 teaspoon of tarragon vinegar. Serve in the casserole. Serves 6.

SPINACH RING AND CUCUMBERS

Drain boiled spinach and chop fine. Pack a greased ring mold with the spinach and set the mold in a pan of hot water until heated through. Unmold on a hot platter and fill the center with chopped, boiled cucumber, completely masked in Never-Fail Hollandaise Sauce. (The spinach ring may be prepared the day before.)

NEVER–FAIL HOLLANDAISE SAUCE
(Mary's)

Place 1 cup of melted butter or margarine and 3 tablespoons of lemon juice where they will keep warm. Have a small pan of boiling water on the stove. Next to it place the bottom part of a double boiler, with about 1 inch of water boiling in it. Have a bowl which will fit in the opening of the boiler, but which will not touch the water. In the bowl place 6 egg yolks, and beat with a wire whisk as you add 1 tablespoon of boiling water from the little pan. Whip the yolks again, add another tablespoon of boiling water, and continue whipping until 8 tablespoons of boiling water have been used in all. Remove the bowl from the boiler and beat again and continue beating as you slowly add the lemon juice and melted butter. Add 1 tablespoon tarragon vinegar and 1 teaspoon dry mustard. Season with ¼ teaspoon of salt, a pinch of pepper and a dash of cayenne.

If you are using the sauce soon, place the bowl back over the boiler but do not let the water boil again. Cover the bowl to keep the sauce warm and beat again before serving. This sauce may be stored in the refrigerator in a glass jar and reheated over hot water, whipping it as it reheats. But remember, *over, never in hot water!*

BROWN BETTY

Mix 1 cup of brown sugar with ½ teaspoon of cinnamon, ¼ teaspoon of nutmeg, and ¼ teaspoon of salt. Cover the bottom of a covered baking dish with fresh bread crumbs and dot with butter. Arrange 1 cup of sliced, peeled apples on top of the crumbs. Sprinkle half of the sugar mixture over them. Add another layer of the bread crumbs and butter, another cup of apples, topped with the sugar mixture. Cover with fresh bread crumbs and plenty of butter. Cover and bake in a moderate oven (350°) for 40 minutes. Remove the lid and brown. Serve with Fluffy Hard Sauce. Serves 6.

Fluffy Hard Sauce. — Mix thoroughly 1 tablespoon of soft butter with 1 cup of sugar. Add 1 tablespoon of cream. Beat 3 egg whites with a pinch of salt and fold into the sugar mixture. Add 1 tablespoon of rum and mix well.

Menu

CASSEROLE OF VEAL AND CREAMED PEAS

BAKED TOMATOES STUFFED WITH CORN

RAW CAULIFLOWER SALAD

RASPBERRIES WITH SOUR CREAM

BROWN SUGAR COOKIES

CASSEROLE OF VEAL AND CREAMED PEAS

Cut 3 pounds of sliced veal into strips about 2 inches long and ½ inch wide. Roll in flour, then in beaten egg, and last in sifted bread crumbs. Sauté until crisp and brown. Arrange in a casserole with 1 pound of sliced mushrooms (either canned or fresh) and 1 chopped onion. Sprinkle with 1½ cups of uncooked peas and then add enough evaporated milk (or diluted mushroom soup) to cover. Season with salt, pepper, and a dash of mace. Cover and bake slowly for 2½ hours. (May be prepared in the morning.) About half an hour before serving, cover with grated Parmesan cheese and reheat. Serves 6.

BAKED TOMATOES STUFFED WITH CORN

Cut a lid from the required number of tomatoes and scoop out the pulp. Sprinkle the inside of the tomato with salt. Mix the tomato pulp with fresh or canned whole kernel corn and some green pepper, chopped fine. Season with grated onion, celery salt, and freshly ground black pepper. Fill the tomato shells, dot with butter, and replace the lids. (Prepare in the morning.) Bake in a moderate oven (350°) until the tomato is cooked through but is not too soft.

RAW CAULIFLOWER SALAD

Separate 1 medium-sized head of raw cauliflower into small florets and mix with 1 cup of diced celery. Moisten with French dressing or mayonnaise and add ¾ cup of chopped, stuffed green olives. Taste for seasoning and add onion salt, freshly ground pepper, and a little Worcestershire sauce. Serve on lettuce leaves. Serves 6.

RASPBERRIES WITH SOUR CREAM

Place fresh raspberries in a serving dish. Cover with a layer of sour cream. Sprinkle liberally with brown sugar. Chill and serve.

BROWN SUGAR COOKIES
(Helen's)

Cream together ½ cup of shortening and 1 cup of brown sugar. Beat in 1 egg and 1 teaspoon of vanilla and continue beating until well blended and smooth. Sift ½ teaspoon of baking powder with 1¾ cups of flour and ½ teaspoon of salt. Stir into the sugar mixture and beat until smooth. Roll out very thin on a floured board and sprinkle with brown sugar. Cut with a round cutter and bake in a moderate oven (350°) for 10 minutes.

Menu

CRAB EN CASSEROLE WITH NUTS

ARTICHOKES COOKED IN WHITE WINE

STUFFED TOMATO HALVES

FRESH PEACHES WITH CURACAO

CRAB EN CASSEROLE WITH NUTS
(Margaret's)

Make 1 cup of cream sauce and add 2 cans of crab meat (or the equivalent in fresh crab), flaked and all bones removed. Season with salt, paprika, and a dash of nutmeg. Add 1 tablespoon of lemon juice. Place in a casserole or individual shells. Cover with 1 cup of ground nuts and bake for 20 minutes in a moderate oven (375°). Sprinkle with chopped parsley. Serves 4 to 6.

ARTICHOKES COOKED IN WHITE WINE

Trim the tops off 6 small artichokes. Put 1 minced onion and 1 minced clove of garlic in a covered pottery casserole. Add 1 tablespoon of olive oil. Season with 2 teaspoons of salt. Place the artichokes upright in the casserole and pour over them 1 cup of white wine. Put on the lid and simmer slowly for 45 minutes, adding more wine and oil, if necessary, keeping the same proportions. Serve hot. Serves 6.

STUFFED TOMATO HALVES

Select tomatoes all the same size. Peel and cut in half crosswise. Scoop out the pulp and seeds. Invert to drain and chill until ready. Season with salt and pepper. Fill the hollowed halves with a mixture of chopped hard-boiled eggs, minced ripe

olives, and a little anchovy paste. Mix horse-radish with mayonnaise (1 tablespoon horse-radish to ½ cup mayonnaise) and pour
over the tomato halves.

FRESH PEACHES WITH CURAÇAO

Boil halved fresh peaches in a light sugar syrup to which
has been added vanilla flavoring. Let the peaches cool in the
liquid. Flavor with orange curaçao, and serve with thick cream
and a sauce of crushed fresh raspberries. (Vanilla and raspberry
ice cream may be used.)

The Husband Cooks

If your husband appreciates good food, he may for years have had a desire to try his hand at cooking. Most men, while disdaining the regular routine of the cook, thoroughly enjoy concocting some dish at which they excel, be it only scrambled eggs.

Some evening suggest that he mix the salad. Perhaps, at first, it may be that all he can manage is to shred and arrange the greens, tossing them with the salad dressing that you have already prepared. Later show him how to make French dressing. Have him practice in the privacy of the family until he is so well drilled that he can make the dressing and complete the salad with the confidence of a professional. Then, but not until then, is he ready to make his first public appearance as a chef.

As soon as he has mastered the salad-making technique, he can start on more advanced cookery. How about his trying one of the egg dishes for breakfast next Sunday morning? Select a recipe that may be used also as a supper dish so that after a little practice he may preen himself in front of guests while making a tasty "supper entree."

Men, as a rule, have a sweet tooth, but no desire for the concoctions that ladies "whip up" for their luncheon parties; none of the marshmallow and whipped cream froufrou for them! Men want something they can get their teeth into. Apple pie is one of their weaknesses, but pie crust always presents a real stumbling block. One man told me quite seriously that he had "spent hours" mixing the pie crust, and when the pie was baked it was so heavy he had difficulty in removing it from the oven. In this book he will find a recipe for apple pie with an easy cracker-crumb crust, and if he wishes to pass his time that way, he can "spend hours" mixing it with no disastrous results.

If your husband likes assorted cheeses, the problem of a sweet does not exist. Place fresh fruit in the center of the table and arrange on the cheese board the different cheeses. As your husband will undoubtedly wish to be in a position to hold forth to admiring guests on the relative merits of different cheeses, he should go to a shop or counter which specializes in them. The quickest way to learn about anything is to admit your ignorance; so if he questions the clerk about the different varieties, he will probably be enlightened as to the entire history of cheese making and the why and wherefore of their differing flavors.

By this time, your husband should be nicely started on his way toward becoming a distinguished chef. Next try him on corned beef hash or kidneys in red wine. After mastering these, he is ready to plan his own parties. Possibly you women may be asked to join the men guests, but these menus are really for the husband and his poker friends.

Your husband may already be a food enthusiast, a really good cook. In that case, let him glance over the recipes in this chapter. He will surely find some of interest and, it may be, an intriguing combination that he never heard of before. But whether he is a new convert to the thrills of cooking or an old one, let him give his own party. Let your husband entertain!

```
┌─────────────────────────────────────────┐
│                                           │
│              Menu                         │
│                                           │
│        OYSTERS  WITH  CHEESE              │
│                                           │
│           POTATO  SALAD                   │
│                                           │
│           CRISP  PICKLES                  │
│                                           │
│          HOT  GINGERBREAD                 │
│                                           │
└─────────────────────────────────────────┘
```

OYSTERS WITH CHEESE
(Margaret's)

Butter liberally a glass pie dish. Cover with a layer of large oysters and their liquor, and add about 3 tablespoons of cooking sherry. Sprinkle with finely chopped water cress, pepper, and paprika. Spread well with grated cheese and brown in a hot oven (400°) until the oysters wrinkle on edges.

POTATO SALAD
(Frances's)

Boil in their skins 6 medium-sized potatoes. Let cool (or cook the day before). Peel and dice. Place in a mixing bowl and pour highly-seasoned French dressing over them. Add 4 sliced hard-boiled eggs and 2 onions, chopped fine. Dice 6 stalks of celery and 1 large cucumber. Mix the salad well and season with salt, pepper, and a dash of cayenne. Let it stand in the refrigerator for several hours until well chilled. When ready to serve, mix with mayonnaise and arrange in a shallow bowl. Decorate the top of the salad with stars cut from canned pimiento and dot the spaces between with stuffed olives. Sprinkle capers over all. Serves 6 to 8.

CRISP PICKLES

Slice 3 dill pickles very thin and put in a jar. Heat a mixture of ½ cup of vinegar, 1 cup of brown sugar, and 1 teaspoon of celery salt. Pour over the pickles. Pour 2 tablespoons of olive oil over the top to keep the pickles crisp. Put on the lid and store in the refrigerator for 1 week before using.

Menu

CHEESE FONDUE WITH WHITE WINE

FRENCH BREAD HEATED

MIXED GREENS SALAD

FRUIT ARRANGEMENT

CHEESE FONDUE WITH WHITE WINE

Whenever I read this recipe, I see again a group of congenial people gathered around a crackling fire in a huge studio remodeled from an old barn. Our host brings in a chafing dish and, placing it in the center of our group, prepares this delicious concoction. We help ourselves to chunks of French bread, and as each dunks his small bits in the melted cheese our host stands watching us with smug satisfaction.

Grate 1 pound of Swiss cheese. Rub the chafing-dish pan with a clove of garlic. Put in the cheese and add gradually 2 cups of dry white wine. Use a wooden spoon and stir constantly, always in the same direction. Cook until the cheese melts; then add 1 tablespoon of cornstarch blended with a little cold wine and ½ teaspoon of pepper. Cook a few minutes longer and add a jigger of brandy. Serve at once with toast or with buttered French bread heated, which the men dunk in the cheese. Serve with dry white wine. Serves 4 to 6.

MIXED GREENS SALAD

In a glass salad bowl put the required amount of French dressing (already mixed). Add to it a little anchovy paste or chopped anchovies, some chopped celery, and 1 hard-boiled egg, chopped very fine. Have the greens washed and ready in a towel, so that all your husband has to do is dump them in the bowl and toss them lightly around in the dressing.

FRUIT ARRANGEMENT

In the center of the table from which your husband will serve his guests have an attractive arrangement of fruit. This will serve two purposes. It is a table decoration as well as a dessert. If your guests are anything like mine, the men will eat the fruit anyway; so you might as well make the most of it.

Menu

BEEF KIDNEYS IN RED WINE

HASHED BROWN POTATOES

ASSORTED VEGETABLE RELISHES

TOASTED ENGLISH MUFFINS

APPLE PANDOWDY

BEEF KIDNEYS IN RED WINE

Cut 2 beef kidneys in small pieces and remove the membrane. Put the pieces of kidney in a French pottery casserole and sauté in butter. Add 1 large can of solid-packed tomatoes. Mince 2 cloves of garlic and 4 onions, and add to the meat with a pinch of assorted dried herbs. Put the lid on the casserole and cook slowly for 2 hours. Then add 1 cup of red wine, season with salt and pepper, and cook without a lid until the gravy is thick enough to serve. Serves 4 to 6.

HASHED BROWN POTATOES

Chop fine 4 cold, boiled potatoes and mix with ½ cup of cream or evaporated milk. Add seasoning. Melt 2 tablespoons of butter in a pan but do not brown. When hot, put in the potatoes, press down into the pan, and cook for a moment over a quick fire. Lower the flame and cook for 10 minutes longer over a slow fire, being careful not to burn. Then fold over like an omelet and serve on a heated platter. Serves 4.

APPLE PANDOWDY

Peel and slice thin 6 apples and put in layers in a buttered baking pan. Dot each layer with bits of butter and sprinkle with sugar, nutmeg, cinnamon, and a little lemon juice.

Mix 2 cups of prepared biscuit flour with a little more milk than the recipe calls for. Drop by spoonfuls on top of the apples. Bake in a hot oven (400°) for half an hour. Serve hot with cream or cheese. Serves 6.

Menu

SPANISH EGGS

SPANISH RICE

FRENCH BREAD HEATED WITH GARLIC BUTTER

CELERY AND ROMAINE LETTUCE SALAD

SLICED ORANGE DESSERT

SPANISH EGGS

Slice 3 onions and 1 bell pepper very fine. Fry in olive oil until a delicate brown. Beat 6 eggs, adding salt, pepper, and chopped parsley. Pour over the onions and stir the mixture until the eggs are cooked like scrambled eggs. Serves 4.

SPANISH RICE

Heat 4 tablespoons of olive oil in an earthenware casserole; add 2 chopped onions, 2 cloves of garlic, minced fine, and 2 cups of rice. Cook for about 10 minutes, stirring gently to keep from browning. Add 1 chopped green pepper and 1 can of tomato paste diluted with boiling water (the canful). Season with salt and pepper. Cook for about 5 minutes, add 2 cups of boiling water, and cook slowly for 1 hour, or until the rice is tender. Add more boiling water as it is needed. (May be prepared ahead of time and reheated.) Serves 6.

CELERY AND ROMAINE LETTUCE SALAD

Cut in small slices 6 crisp stalks of celery. Save the leaves and place with 2 heads of romaine lettuce in a damp bag in the refrigerator. In a glass salad bowl mash 1 clove of garlic and 3 hard-boiled eggs and mix with ⅓ cup of French dressing. When ready to serve, break the romaine lettuce into 2-inch pieces and put into the salad bowl with the celery and leaves. Mix gently with a wooden fork and spoon. Serve at once. Serves 6.

SLICED ORANGE DESSERT

Make a sugar syrup by boiling together 1 cup of sugar with 1 cup of water and 2 tablespoons of grated orange rind. Boil for 10 minutes. Peel 8 oranges, removing all the white skin, and slice them. Arrange in a serving bowl, pour the hot syrup over the oranges, and baste from time to time. When well cooled, put in the refrigerator (may be prepared the day before). When ready to serve, sprinkle generously with shredded fresh cocoanut. Serves 6.

Menu

LAMB ROLL STUFFED WITH SAUSAGE

FRIED CAULIFLOWER

SALAD WITH CHIVES

PULLED BREAD

FIGS IN ORANGE JUICE

LAMB ROLL STUFFED WITH SAUSAGE

Have a lamb breast boned, spread with ¾ pound of pork sausage, and roll and tie into shape. (Perhaps your butcher will do this for you.) Place in a covered earthenware casserole. Brown on all sides in bacon fat. Season with salt and pepper and a few mixed herbs. Add 1 can of tomato soup diluted with water, 1 sliced onion, 1 minced clove of garlic, and 2 tablespoons of Worcestershire sauce. Cover closely and cook very slowly for about 2 hours or until tender. If necessary, add water flavored with bouillon cubes for additional moisture. Serves 4.

FRIED CAULIFLOWER

Break the cauliflower into separate florets and parboil until almost tender. Drain. (Do this early.) Roll the cauliflower in 4 tablespoons of melted butter. Cover and cook gently for 10 or 15 minutes, turning occasionally. Let it get delicately brown, but not cooked sufficiently to darken or dry out.

SALAD WITH CHIVES
(Joan and Jean's)

Wash and chill 3 heads of lettuce. Thin mayonnaise with French dressing, and add 1½ tablespoons each of chopped chives and fresh tarragon leaves. Break the lettuce leaves into a salad bowl and gently fold in the dressing. Serves 6.

FIGS IN ORANGE JUICE

Peel purple figs and place in a serving dish. Cover with orange juice and sprinkle with a dash of nutmeg. Chill. (These should be prepared ahead of time.)

Menu

FLANK STEAK WITH DRESSING

BAKED POTATOES SUPRÊME

MIXED VEGETABLES WITH
THOUSAND ISLAND DRESSING

STRAWBERRIES WITH BROWN SUGAR

FLANK STEAK WITH DRESSING

Sprinkle a seasoning of salt, pepper, paprika, and a little ginger over a flank steak. Sauté a medium-sized chopped onion and 3 tablespoons of chopped celery in 1 tablespoon of drippings. Mix and stir in 1 cup of bread crumbs. Add a little poultry seasoning and season to taste. Stir in a well-beaten egg and spread the dressing over the flank steak. Roll and tie with string.

In an earthenware casserole heat 3 tablespoons of bacon drippings and sear the flank steak on all sides. Dilute 1 can of tomato soup with a little water and pour over the meat. Cover and bake in a moderate oven from 1½ to 2 hours. Thicken the gravy, if necessary. Serves 4.

BAKED POTATOES SUPRÊME

Select potatoes of uniform size and scrub with a very stiff brush to remove any rough skin. Rub with soft butter, or for a better flavor, rub with bacon drippings. Place in a greased pan and bake in a hot oven until done. This is an excellent recipe for those who enjoy eating the skin of the potato.

MIXED VEGETABLES WITH
THOUSAND ISLAND DRESSING

Cook Lima beans, string beans, and peas. Drain and mix with raw, chopped zucchini. Place a bowl of Thousand Island Dressing in the center of a platter and surround with a ring of the assorted vegetables. Around the edge of the platter arrange halved, peeled tomatoes covered with chopped chives. Decorate with water cress.

Thousand Island Dressing. — To 1 cup of mayonnaise add ½ cup of chili sauce. Season with salt, pepper, and Tabasco sauce. Add chopped green pepper and chopped chives. Mix thoroughly. Serve ice cold. (Canned tomato paste may be used instead of chili sauce.)

STRAWBERRIES WITH BROWN SUGAR

Wash and hull strawberries ahead of time. Cover with brown sugar and serve with unsweetened thick cream, or with cream cheese beaten smooth with cream and served cold. (A little brandy may be poured over the strawberries.)

Menu

CRAB STEW

A MAN'S GREEN SALAD

FRENCH BREAD HEATED

FRUIT ARRANGEMENT

ASSORTED CHEESE AND CRACKERS

CRAB STEW

Melt 2 tablespoons of butter and add 1 small can of chopped or sliced mushrooms, drained. Cook for a few minutes; then add 2 teaspoons of grated onion and 2 tomatoes, peeled and chopped. Cook for about 5 minutes; then add 1 pound of fresh crab meat or the same amount of canned crab meat, cleaned and picked over for bones. (Leave in as large pieces as possible.) Heat through, add 1¼ cups of cream (or evaporated milk), and stir gently until well heated. At the last moment, stir in 1 teaspoon each of chopped chives and parsley. This is rather liquid, so it is best to serve it in soup dishes or in the pottery soup bowls which may be bought with lids. Serve with heated French bread and let the guests break off their own pieces. They may want to dunk their bread in the stew. This recipe will serve 4 for bridge, but double it if the men are playing poker.

A MAN'S GREEN SALAD

In a wooden or glass salad bowl mix 2 mashed potatoes and 2 hard-boiled eggs put through a coarse sieve. Add a little anchovy paste and a little grated cheese. In a glass jar make some good French dressing of olive oil and lemon, salt, pepper, and mustard. (Never any sugar in a French dressing.) Have the dressing ready, as well as an assortment of greens, washed, wrapped in a damp napkin, and placed in the refrigerator. Show your husband how to break the greens into pieces before placing in the bowl. Tell him to shake the dressing well, pour over the salad, and dip down into the potato-egg mixture as he gently folds the salad together to blend everything. Any greens may be used — all the different kinds of lettuce and even young spinach leaves.

ASSORTED CHEESE AND CRACKERS

On a large, round, glass platter arrange an assortment of cheeses in the center. Innumerable kinds are already packaged in the shops, and you might add a few which come in bulk. Around the edge of the platter arrange at least 2 different types of crackers: a hard cracker, as well as any small, salted cracker you may particularly like.

Menu

SUPERLATIVE CORNED BEEF HASH WITH
MAYONNAISE AND HORSE-RADISH SAUCE

CELERY, CHIVES, AND LETTUCE SALAD

FRENCH BREAD HEATED WITH
GARLIC BUTTER

PEARS WITH ORANGE JUICE

SUPERLATIVE CORNED BEEF HASH

Wash 4 large potatoes and boil with the skins on until not quite done. Chill, peel, and cut into ½-inch cubes. Cut in similar-sized pieces the contents of 1 can of corned beef and add to the potatoes. Add 1 grated onion with its juice. Using a fork, blend in ¾ cup of evaporated milk. Melt 2 tablespoons of bacon drippings in an iron frying pan, spread the hash evenly, and brown slowly. Any extra milk which drains to the outside edges should be dipped back into the center again. As parts of the hash brown, lift them lightly with a spatula and fold over onto the top, so that the brown parts will be distributed throughout the hash. When partially browned, fold over like an omelet and pour over more of the evaporated milk. Brown under the broiler. Sprinkle coarsely-ground black pepper over the top. Place in the center of a serving platter and surround with 6 poached eggs on round slices of buttered toast. Serve with Mayonnaise and Horse-radish Sauce. Serves 6.

Mayonnaise and Horse-radish Sauce. — Mix 1½ cups of mayonnaise with freshly grated horse-radish to taste. Season with a little salt and white pepper. Serve in a bowl to accompany the corned beef hash.

CELERY, CHIVES, AND LETTUCE SALAD

In a wooden salad bowl mix 3 heads of crisp lettuce broken into 2-inch pieces, the hearts of 2 bunches of celery cut into slices, including the tops, and 2 tablespoons of finely chopped chives. Place in the refrigerator until ready to use. Mash the yolk of 1 hard-boiled egg and add to French dressing. Pour over the salad and mix gently until well blended. Serves 6.

PEARS WITH ORANGE JUICE

Drain 1 can of pears. Place in a serving dish and pour over them orange juice flavored with curaçao or kirsch. Baste frequently while chilling. (Prepare ahead of time.) Serves 6.

Menu

BOILED BRISKET OF BEEF WITH
HORSE-RADISH GRAVY

BOILED POTATOES

CHOPPED SPINACH IN CREAM

CAMEMBERT CHEESE IN ASPIC

BUTTERY MELBA TOAST

BOILED BRISKET OF BEEF WITH HORSE–RADISH GRAVY

Place 3 pounds of brisket of beef in a stewing kettle. Add ½ cup each of chopped celery, carrots, and onions; also 1 garlic bean, minced fine. Add boiling water to cover, and flavor with bouillon cubes. Cover and simmer gently for about 4 hours, or until the meat is tender.

Slice the meat and serve with new potatoes boiled in their jackets. Arrange on a platter surrounding a bowl of gravy flavored with horse-radish, made by adding ⅓ to ½ cup of horse-radish to 2 cups of the strained meat liquor. Thicken with 2 tablespoons of flour and add 1 onion, chopped fine. Taste for seasoning and add a little sugar, if necessary. Serves 6.

CHOPPED SPINACH IN CREAM

Cook 2 pounds of well-washed spinach for 2 minutes in 1 cup of boiling salted water with 1 teaspoon of sugar. Drain and plunge into cold water. Squeeze out moisture and chop fine. Sauté 1 cut clove of garlic in 2 teaspoons of butter for 2 minutes. Remove the garlic and put in the chopped greens; then add ½ cup of evaporated milk, salt to taste, and a dash of nutmeg. Let the mixture cook gently for 5 minutes. (May be prepared ahead of time.) Serves 6.

CAMEMBERT CHEESE IN ASPIC

(Serve in place of dessert.)

Dissolve 1 package of salad gelatine in 1½ cups of boiling water. Flavor with 1 teaspoon each of tarragon vinegar and Worcestershire sauce. Use a mold a little larger than a whole Camembert cheese and cover the bottom with about 1 inch of the aspic. Chill until firm. Scrape off the outside of a Camembert cheese and place the whole cheese on the aspic. Pour the rest of the aspic into the mold, completely surrounding and covering the cheese. Place in the refrigerator until firm. (Prepare the day before.) Unmold and serve with a plate of assorted crackers.

```
┌─────────────────────────────────────────┐
│                                          │
│                 Menu                     │
│                                          │
│             EGGS RANCHO                   │
│                                          │
│           LETTUCE SALAD WITH             │
│        ROQUEFORT CHEESE DRESSING          │
│                                          │
│         TEXAS CRISP CORN CAKES           │
│                                          │
│            FRUIT ARRANGEMENT             │
│                                          │
└─────────────────────────────────────────┘
```

EGGS RANCHO

Chop and fry 4 strips of bacon. Cut 1 bunch of onions very fine, including the tops. Heat 1 large can of tomatoes and add the bacon and onions. Let simmer for 10 minutes. Mash the tomatoes with a fork, add seasoning to taste, and pour into an earthenware casserole or baking dish until the sauce is about 1 inch deep. Dot 8 raw eggs over the top and sprinkle with chopped nuts. Bake in a moderate oven (350°) until the eggs are set. Serves 4 to 6.

LETTUCE SALAD WITH
ROQUEFORT CHEESE DRESSING

Wash and thoroughly chill lettuce leaves. Break into a salad bowl and gently mix with Roquefort Cheese Dressing.

Roquefort Cheese Dressing. — Crumble ¼ pound of domestic Roquefort cheese into 1 pint of French dressing (made without sugar).

TEXAS CRISP CORN CAKES

To 2 cups of yellow corn meal and 1 teaspoon of salt add enough boiling water to make a stiff batter. Cool. Dip your hands in cold water and shape the mixture into the thinnest cakes possible, about the size of the palm of your hand. Have a baking pan very hot, melt 1 tablespoon of bacon drippings, and place the corn cakes in the pan. Flatten still thinner with a pancake turner and brown in a hot oven. Serve hot. Serves 4 to 6.

Help your husband make these cakes ahead of time. If he prefers, he can brown them on the top of the stove in an iron skillet.

Menu

POT ROAST IN SOUR CREAM

NEW YORK SALAD

TOASTED FRENCH BREAD

LEMON BANANA GELATINE

POT ROAST IN SOUR CREAM

I learned to prepare this delicious dish while visiting a Norwegian family on a farm outside Oslo. They generally used veal, but I find that beef is equally delicious.

Rub an earthenware casserole with garlic and add ¼ cup of bacon fat. Rub a 6-pound pot roast with salt, pepper, and ground ginger. Dredge with flour and brown in the bacon fat. Add 1 cup of thick sour cream and turn the meat until thoroughly covered and the cream is brown. Add 2 bay leaves, 2 onions chopped fine, 1 diced peeled tomato or 1 cup of canned tomato, and 1 pint of water. Cover tightly and bake in a moderate oven (350°) for about 3 hours. Remove the meat to a serving platter. Strain the juice, thicken for gravy, and season to taste. Serves 6 to 8.

NEW YORK SALAD

Peel ripe tomatoes and cut crosswise. Press gently to eliminate seeds and then cut into thin strips. Cut tender pieces of celery into strips and cold boiled potatoes into thin slices. Season with French dressing and arrange in a bowl with chopped hard-boiled eggs and minced green onions on the top.

TOASTED FRENCH BREAD

Split French bread lengthwise and toast under the broiler. For a garlic-flavored bread, rub with a clove of garlic and then spread with butter. For anchovy flavor, mix anchovy paste with the butter and spread on the bread. Heat in a slow oven (275°) until the butter has melted.

LEMON BANANA GELATINE

Mash 4 medium-sized bananas to a pulp; add ¼ cup of orange juice, ¼ cup of lemon juice, and ¼ cup of canned pineapple or other canned juice, and ¼ cup of rum. Dissolve a package of lemon-flavored gelatine in ¾ cup of boiling water. Cool and add the fruit mixture. Sweeten with powdered sugar, if necessary. Stir frequently until almost congealed; then turn into a mold. Place in refrigerator until firm. (Prepare the day before.) Serve with chilled custard sauce made from packaged custard pudding, thinned with cream and flavored with rum. Serves 6.

Menu

BACHELOR'S BOUILLABAISSE

BUTTERY MELBA TOAST

MIXED GREEN SALAD

ORANGES WITH ALMONDS

TOASTED ANGEL FOOD CAKE

BACHELOR'S BOUILLABAISSE

Simmer in a large kettle 1 pound of fillet of sole and 1 pound of scallops in enough boiling salted water to cover well. Add 4 whole cloves, 1 small chopped onion, and 4 tablespoons of sherry. Cook 15 minutes. Set aside.

In an iron skillet heat 2 tablespoons of olive oil and 1 tablespoon of butter. Add 2 large onions, chopped fine, and 2 finely minced cloves of garlic. Brown lightly; then add 1 can of tomato soup, 1 canful of hot water, 3 whole cloves, and 2 bay leaves. Dissolve 2 teaspoons of curry powder in ¼ cup of sherry and pour into the mixture. Add 1 cup of diced cheese and let all simmer slowly for about 20 minutes.

Clean 1 pound of canned or fresh shrimp; slice mushrooms (1 large can) and add to the cheese mixture. Add all to the fillet of sole and scallops and bring to a boil. Remove the cloves and bay leaf. Then add 1 pound of canned or fresh lobster meat, cut in pieces, and cook slowly until heated through.

Serve in a soup tureen, with Buttery Melba Toast. Serves 8.

ORANGES WITH ALMONDS

Peel 6 oranges and separate into sections. Place in a glass serving bowl and pour over the oranges ½ cup of honey. Chill. Sprinkle liberally with shredded almonds.

TOASTED ANGEL FOOD CAKE

Place slices of angel food cake on a pan and toast under the broiler. Then turn them over and toast on the other side. Or you can place the slices of cake on a cookie sheet and toast them in the oven. Serve cold.

Menu

BRAISED SHORT RIBS OF BEEF WITH
VEGETABLES

TOASTED ROLLS WITH CHEESE

SALAD BOWL

APPLESAUCE PIE

BRAISED SHORT RIBS OF BEEF WITH VEGETABLES

In a roasting pan melt 3 tablespoons of bacon fat. Cut 4 pounds of short ribs into serving pieces and sear in fat until well browned on all sides. Add ½ cup of sliced onions, a pinch of mixed dried herbs, 1 minced clove of garlic, ½ teaspoon of salt, and a dash of pepper. Dissolve 1 bouillon cube in 1 cup of warm water and pour over the seasonings.

Put the lid on the pan and roast in a slow oven for about 2 hours, or until the meat is tender. Baste the meat often. The last hour of cooking, add 6 peeled potatoes and 6 carrots. Remove the meat to a heated platter and surround with the vegetables. Add more bouillon to the pan if necessary to make the right amount, and thicken with flour for gravy. A crumbled ginger snap and a dash of Kitchen Bouquet will darken the gravy and give an added flavor. Serves 4.

TOASTED ROLLS WITH CHEESE

Split French rolls, spread with butter, and sprinkle with grated American cheese. Place them under the broiler until toasted and the cheese is browned. Dust with paprika.

APPLESAUCE PIE
(Graham Cracker Crust)

Mix 1½ cups of finely ground graham cracker crumbs with ½ cup of butter, ½ cup of sugar, and 1 teaspoon of cinnamon. Reserve half of this mixture. Press the remainder evenly over the bottom and sides of a 9-inch pie pan. Bake 15 minutes in a 375° oven.

Applesauce Filling. — Peel and core 6 apples and cook into applesauce (or use canned applesauce). Put through a purée sieve and sweeten to taste. Let cool and put into the crumb shell. Cover with the remainder of the crumbs, mixed with ½ cup of chopped walnuts. Brown slightly under the broiler. (Prepare ahead of time.) Serve cold with or without whipped cream, or with sour cream sweetened with powdered sugar and flavored with rum or brandy. Serves 6.

Menu

BAKED WHOLE FISH

**NEW POTATOES WITH
LEMON BUTTER AND CHIVES**

BAKED EGGPLANT WITH TOMATOES

**PINEAPPLE AND CHERRIES WITH
STRAWBERRY SAUCE**

BAKED WHOLE FISH

Slice onions into a baking pan and cook until brown in bacon fat. Sprinkle ginger and salt inside any fish suitable for baking, and place on the onions. Surround with sliced tomatoes, sprigs of parsley, and a few chopped fresh or pickled tarragon leaves. Mix canned consommé and white wine and pour over the fish. Bake until tender. Baste frequently. Cover with buttered bread crumbs and brown. Serve on a platter surrounded with the sauce from the pan.

NEW POTATOES WITH
LEMON BUTTER AND CHIVES

Scrape and boil 3 pounds of new potatoes. Melt ¼ cup of butter, stir in a pinch of flour and nutmeg, and add salt and pepper and the grated rind of 1 lemon. Cook for about 1 minute. Pour over the potatoes and let them heat in the mixture but do not boil. Add 1 teaspoon of chopped chives and the juice of 1 lemon. Serve hot. Serves 6.

BAKED EGGPLANT WITH TOMATOES

Peel 2 eggplants and slice crosswise in ¼-inch slices; sauté in butter 10 to 15 minutes with 12 chopped green onions, tops and all, and 2 cloves of garlic, sliced thin. Peel and slice 6 tomatoes and sauté. Cover the bottom of a buttered baking dish with the slices of eggplant mixture and then add the tomato. Season with salt, pepper, and cayenne, and pour over the juice from the frying pan, including the onions. Cover with grated cheese. If there is too much eggplant and tomato for 1 layer, continue until the baking dish is filled. Bake in a slow oven (275°) for 1 hour. Serves 6.

PINEAPPLE AND CHERRIES WITH STRAWBERRY SAUCE

Chill and drain 1 can each of pitted Bing cherries and pine-apple cubes. Mix in a serving bowl and pour Strawberry Sauce over them. (Fresh fruit, sweetened, may be used instead of canned fruit.) Serves 6.

Strawberry Sauce. — Wash and hull 1 quart of strawberries and cut into pieces. Add ½ cup of sugar and cook for 5 minutes. Press through a wire sieve and reheat. Blend 1 tablespoon of corn-starch with 2 tablespoons of cold water and add to the straw-berries. Cook 3 minutes and then chill. Add 3 tablespoons of kirsch or brandy and pour the sauce over the mixed fruit. Serves 6.

Menu

LAMB KIDNEYS IN RICE RING

MIXED GREEN SALAD

FRENCH BREAD HEATED WITH
GARLIC BUTTER

GINGER FIGS

LAMB KIDNEYS IN RICE RING

Split 30 lamb kidneys in half and remove the membrane. Heat 4 tablespoons of bacon fat in an iron skillet and add 1 onion, chopped fine. Flour the kidneys and add to the bacon fat. Toss lightly with a fork, allowing them to brown and cook through, about 10 or 15 minutes. Season with salt and pepper. Remove from the pan and place in the center of a rice ring. Add 1 can of mushrooms to the pan, brown and add a little water. Let come to a boil and pour over the kidneys. Serve surrounded with fried bacon. Serves 8.

Rice Ring. — Boil 2 cups of rice. Drain and mix in gently with a fork ⅓ cup of butter. Pack lightly in a well-greased ring mold. (Do this part ahead of time.) Cover with brown paper and re-heat in oven. Turn out on a platter.

GINGER FIGS

Remove stems from 1 pound of. dried figs. Cover with cold water. Add 1 large ginger root and the juice and grated rind of ½ lemon. Stew until the figs are soft and puffed. Remove figs to a serving dish. Measure the juice and add an equal amount of sugar. Simmer until thick. Strain over the figs and serve with sour cream sweetened with powdered sugar.

Menu

FILLET OF SOLE À LA STUART

BAKED STUFFED POTATOES WITH
CHEESE SAUCE

WATER CRESS AND NUT SALAD

MINT ICE WITH RIPE PEARS

FILLET OF SOLE À LA STUART

Dice 1 onion and 2 tomatoes fine and season to taste. Place in an earthenware casserole and on top of them place 4 fillets of sole. Melt ¼ cup of butter and pour over the fish; then sprinkle with dried mixed herbs. Bake in a hot oven for 15 minutes. Add 1 cup of dry white wine, reduce the heat to medium, and bake 15 minutes longer. Serves 4.

BAKED STUFFED POTATOES WITH CHEESE SAUCE

Prepare baked stuffed potatoes ahead of time. Reheat in a medium oven for 15 minutes. Prepare cheese sauce by adding ½ cup of grated cheese and 1 teaspoon of dry mustard to 1 cup of cream sauce. Serve the baked potatoes on a platter, accompanied by a bowl of cheese sauce and a bowl of chopped green onions. The cheese sauce is poured over the potato and the onions sprinkled over the top.

WATER CRESS AND NUT SALAD

Wash and pick over water cress. Add chopped walnuts and toss lightly with tart French dressing.

MINT ICE WITH RIPE PEARS

Either buy or make lemon ice. Add 3 or 4 tablespoons of crème de menthe and serve over ripe pears, peeled and cut into sections lengthwise.

You may make quite a ceremony of serving this dessert. Bring in one bowl with the pears previously prepared (Lemon juice diluted with water and poured over them will keep them from discoloring.) and a second bowl with the lemon ice. Before the attentive eyes of your guests, whip the crème de menthe into the lemon ice and pour it over the pears.

Menu

SPAGHETTI KATHERINE

FRENCH BREAD HEATED WITH
GARLIC BUTTER

SALAD OF CANNED ARTICHOKES AND
CELERY WITH MUSTARD DRESSING

SUGARED STRAWBERRIES WITH
PORT WINE

SPAGHETTI KATHERINE

Heat 2 tablespoons of olive oil and in it brown 1 onion and 1 clove of garlic, both minced. Add 3 slices of Italian sausage, chopped fine, ¼ cup of minced ham, ½ dozen finely cut dried or fresh mushrooms, 1 can of consommé, 1 can of tomato soup, salt, and pepper. Cover pan and cook slowly until well blended. Transfer the sauce to a bowl. Cover and leave in the refrigerator until the next day. Heat and mix with 1 pound of spaghetti cooked for 20 minutes. Serve with grated Parmesan cheese. Serves 4.

SALAD OF CANNED ARTICHOKES AND CELERY

Serve chilled canned artichoke hearts with finely minced celery. Mix with Mustard Dressing (p. 75).

SUGARED STRAWBERRIES WITH PORT WINE

Hull firm, ripe strawberries, sprinkle with port wine, and cover with sugar. Serve from a bowl and with this pass heavy cream or cream cheese whipped with a little top milk. Sour cream may also be used.

Emergencies Must Be Met

Emergencies may suddenly arise to confront any hostess. Your husband, like mine, may hospitably invite six extra guests for the very formal dinner you have planned for twelve. And to make matters worse, he doesn't even tell you that he has asked them! Imagine any hostess's thoughts as the table is hastily enlarged and reset, the hors d'oeuvres stretched by additions from the emergency shelf, and the soup eked out by adding other varieties out of a can.

But don't be disturbed. Remember it is flattering to have a husband who likes your parties well enough to include everyone he meets and who has enough faith in your ability as a hostess to feel it is safe for him to do unpredictable things. A well-stocked emergency shelf is the hostess's salvation in such a case.

Your reserve supply of food may fill a storeroom, a cupboard, or one shelf, but no matter how small your space may be, you really should have some food put away for that emergency. You may not wish to buy everything at one time, but if you watch the sales and buy at reasonable prices, you will be amazed to see how soon your storeroom, cupboard, or shelf will be filled.

Canned soups are always good, not only when served with croutons or hot crackers, but they are wonderful food stretchers, especially vegetable, mushroom, and tomato soups. If you find yourself confronted suddenly with guests who have lingered after the cocktail hour, utilize that bit of meat left over from last night's dinner. Simply cut it in strips, add mushroom soup, put it in a casserole, top with buttered bread crumbs, and bake until brown; you will have at least the main part of your dinner. Or, if you prefer something heartier, you might add vegetable soup to the meat in place of mushroom, season well with onion juice and herbs, place in a casserole, and when covered with biscuit crust you have an old-fashioned meat pie.

Canned clam chowder, mixed with evaporated milk and thinned with fresh milk, is almost a meal in itself. And as a first course for a luncheon or dinner, nothing could be better than madrilène or chicken soup. Leftover lamb, ground and moistened with gravy, then sandwiched between layers of boiled rice, makes a wonderful emergency dish, if served with canned tomato soup as a sauce.

A can of grated cheese is essential for your emergency shelf. Add some of it to the bread crumbs on top of any dish and see how it improves the flavor; or try mixing some through your green salad before adding the dressing.

Your supplies should include cheese spreads for sandwiches or *canapés;* spread them on bread, cover with chopped bacon and toast under the broiler. A wonderful Welsh rarebit may be made by adding cheese spread to a cream sauce or mushroom soup; season strongly with mustard, cayenne, and a dash of sherry; pour over hot buttered toast.

Canned fish — salmon, tuna, sardines, lobster, crab, and shrimp — should be in everyone's emergency cupboard. The salmon can be served cold with Green Mayonnaise (p. 40), or hot with hollandaise sauce. Lobster and crab can be extended with a cream sauce, made from evaporated milk, or with mushroom soup, flavored with sherry, and baked in individual shells or served on toast. Sardines placed on a strip of toast, broiled with a slice of cheese on top, and served with a sauce made of canned tomato soup, make an excellent snack.

Canned artichokes may be used hot as a vegetable with a lemon-butter sauce or with hollandaise. (By all means, always keep a jar of Never-Fail Hollandaise (p. 89) in your refrigerator.) If the artichokes are bottled in olive oil they may form the basis of a salad platter, interspersed with stuffed eggs and sliced canned meat. Both asparagus and whole string beans are useful in an emergency, for they may be served hot or cold the same as the artichokes. Try layers of asparagus and salmon **mixed** with cream sauce or cream of mushroom soup and baked with a covering of mashed potatoes.

Another helpful vegetable is canned spinach. It may be chopped, mixed with a cream sauce flavored with cheese, dotted with raw eggs over the top, and then baked in the oven. You may mix shredded canned tongue with cooked macaroni and mushroom soup. Pour this over canned spinach and bake in the oven.

For dessert, there is nothing that can be relied upon more than the old stand-by, canned fruit, whether you or someone else canned it. Add a bit of leftover wine to the fruit, bake it in the oven, and serve very hot. Pears soaked in brandy and served with hot apricot jam make a quick and easy last course. Peaches covered with melted raspberry jelly, flavored with sherry, and dotted with whipped cream cheese, make an excellent dessert, emergency or otherwise.

A "must have" are an assortment of herbs, seasonings — including onion, garlic, and celery salts — also spiced or wine vinegar and an extra jar of mayonnaise. If you have no mint in your garden, or no garden, keep a can of dried mint as well as dried parsley and dried onion chips. A sauce of a combination of horse-radish and mustard comes in bottles and adds just the right flavor to salad dressing and to gravies.

Don't forget the anchovies and anchovy paste. You won't be able to make Green Goddess Salad (p. 124) without them. In fact, they improve any green salad. Try inserting them in slits in a leg of lamb or adding the paste to your scrambled eggs when you want something different.

Also don't forget the "ready-mixed" cake, gingerbread, pie crust, and biscuit mixtures now on the market. They will help you out of many difficulties.

You may, if you wish, include expensive delicacies — caviar, smoked turkey, smoked oysters, *pâté de foie gras,* and fruits in brandy. These will add interest to any emergency meal but they really aren't necessary. The important thing is to have the right supplies to meet that emergency, to be able to prepare a meal quickly and with very little effort.

Menu

SALMON TIMBALES WITH
HOLLANDAISE OR EGG SAUCE

FRENCH FRIED ASPARAGUS

CANNED ARTICHOKE SALAD ON LETTUCE

BAKED CHOCOLATE CRUMB PUDDING
or
LEMON CRUMB PUDDING

SALMON TIMBALES

Bone and flake a 1-pound can of salmon. Beat 4 eggs and add 1 tablespoon of onion juice, 2 teaspoons of lemon juice, 1 cup of milk, and 2 tablespoons of butter. Mix with the salmon. Put in buttered timbale molds, place them in hot water, and bake in a moderate oven (350°) for 30 minutes. Makes 8 timbales. Serve with Never-Fail Hollandaise Sauce (p. 89) or Creamed Egg Sauce. Serves 6.

Creamed Egg Sauce. — While your salmon is baking, hardboil 2 eggs. Make a cream sauce and add the eggs, chopped. Sprinkle chopped parsley over the top and serve.

FRENCH FRIED ASPARAGUS

For 24 stalks of canned asparagus use 2 eggs and 1 cup of fine, dried bread crumbs. (Always keep a jar of dried bread crumbs handy.) Beat eggs and season with salt and pepper. Roll each stalk in egg, and then in bread crumbs. Brown in deep fat. Serves 4.

CANNED ARTICHOKE SALAD ON LETTUCE

Drain canned artichokes and marinate in French dressing. Chill thoroughly. Serve on shredded lettuce leaves.

BAKED CHOCOLATE CRUMB PUDDING

Scald 2 cups of milk. Add 2 cups of fresh bread crumbs and let cool. Mix ⅓ cup of cocoa, ½ cup of sugar, ½ cup of finely chopped nuts, and ½ teaspoon of salt. Add to the crumb mixture. Lastly add 1 well-beaten egg, 1 teaspoon of vanilla, and ¼ cup of melted butter. Pour into individual molds or a large baking dish and bake in a moderately slow oven (325°) for about 1 hour. Serve with or without whipped cream. Serves 6.

Menu

CHICKEN AND VEGETABLE SOUP

CANNED RED KIDNEY BEANS EN CASSEROLE

GREEN GODDESS SALAD

QUICK PRUNE DESSERT

CHICKEN AND VEGETABLE SOUP

Mix 1 can of chicken gumbo with 1 can of vegetable soup. Thin with water and heat. Garnish each serving with 1 teaspoon of finely chopped, raw Bermuda onion and a generous sprinkling of grated Parmesan cheese. Serves 4 to 6.

CANNED RED KIDNEY BEANS EN CASSEROLE

In an earthenware casserole heat canned red kidney beans with cream, but do not make too thin. (Evaporated milk may be used.) Fry bacon, drain on brown paper, place on top of beans in casserole, and serve hot.

GREEN GODDESS SALAD

Mash 5 fillets of anchovies. Chop fine 1 green onion or 1 small dried onion, a little parsley, and a few bottled tarragon leaves. Thin 1½ cups of mayonnaise with a little tarragon vinegar and add the anchovies and chopped greens. Mix in finely chopped chives. Chill. Rub a salad bowl with garlic and fill with the broken leaves of chilled romaine, escarole, chicory, or lettuce, or a mixture of all. Fold in the dressing and serve. Serves 6.

QUICK PRUNE DESSERT

Add ½ cup of sugar to the juice from 1 can of prunes and cook until a thick syrup is formed. Chill and pour over the prunes. Serve with whipped cream flavored with sugar and brandy or a custard sauce made from packaged custard pudding thinned with additional milk. Serves 4 to 6.

Menu

BRIDE'S TUNA AND CORN EN CASSEROLE

CANNED ASPARAGUS WITH
MUSTARD DRESSING

BAKED CANNED PITTED BING CHERRIES

BRIDE'S TUNA AND CORN EN CASSEROLE

This is a good recipe for a bride to try. It looks intricate and is sure to impress her friends. It is not necessary for her to confess it all came out of cans!

Beat 2 eggs and add the contents of 1 large can of evaporated milk. Add 1 No.-2 can of cream-style corn, 1 7-ounce can of flaked tuna, 1 grated onion, and 1 chopped green pepper. Mix all the ingredients and put in a buttered casserole. Bake in a 325° oven until the custard is firm — about 1 hour. Serves 6.

CANNED ASPARAGUS WITH
MUSTARD DRESSING

Serve chilled canned asparagus with Mustard Dressing (p. 75).

BAKED CANNED PITTED BING CHERRIES

In an earthenware casserole heat 1 can of pitted Bing cherries and 2 tablespoons of canned cocoanut. Thicken the juice with 2 teaspoons of cornstarch, blended with 2 tablespoons of sherry. Stir until thick. Serve hot with chopped walnuts and additional cocoanut sprinkled over the top. Serves 6.

Menu

TOASTED CRAB SANDWICH

BAKED PURÉED PEAS

MIXED GREEN SALAD

PEACHES EVALINE

TOASTED CRAB SANDWICH

Mix 1 can of flaked crab meat with mayonnaise highly seasoned with Worcestershire sauce, horse-radish, a dash of Tabasco, and coarsely ground black pepper. Toast 4 slices of bread on one side, turn and spread crab mixture on the other side. Cover with grated cheese or a square slice of cheese and toast under the broiler. Serves 4.

BAKED PURÉED PEAS

Mix 2 cans of green pea soup with 3 tablespoons of butter, ½ teaspoon of sugar, ½ cup of sweet cream, and salt and pepper to taste. Stir until well blended; then pour into a glass baking dish. On the top of the purée spread 2 tablespoons of crisp bacon, finely chopped. Over this put the stiffly beaten white of 1 egg, to which ⅛ teaspoon of salt has been added. Place in the oven to bake until the mixture is well heated and the egg white is slightly brown. Serves 4.

PEACHES EVALINE

Place canned peach halves in a baking dish and sprinkle brown sugar in the hollows. Dot with butter. Cook under the broiler very slowly until the sugar crusts. Pour brandy over them and send to the table lighted. Serve with ice-cold custard. (The custard may be made from prepared custard pudding mixture thinned with additional milk.)

Menu

BAKED CANNED BEANS

ONIONS STUFFED WITH MEAT

CORN BREAD STICKS

CANNED APRICOTS IN PORT

BAKED CANNED BEANS

Chop fine 2 onions and mix with 1 teaspoon of dry mustard and 1 tablespoon of molasses. Place in the bottom of a casserole and pour in 3 cans of baked small beans. Cover with strips of bacon and bake covered for ½ hour in a slow oven; then remove the cover and brown the bacon. Serves 6.

ONIONS STUFFED WITH MEAT

Peel and parboil whole onions. Remove the center and fill the opening with well-seasoned ground canned meat or well-seasoned bread crumbs. Coat the top and bottom openings with beaten egg and sauté the onions in melted butter until well browned.

CORN BREAD STICKS

Mix 1 tablespoon of bacon fat with 2 cups of corn meal and stir in enough boiling water to make the mixture hold its shape. Beat in 1 egg and a pinch of salt. Fill well-greased bread-stick molds and bake in a hot oven until golden brown. Serves 6.

CANNED APRICOTS IN PORT

Soak canned apricot halves (1 large can) in ½ cup of port wine mixed with 1 tablespoon of brandy. Place in the refrigerator to chill. Serves 6.

Menu

CURRIED TUNA AND RICE

PEAS EN CASSEROLE

CANNED ASPARAGUS SALAD

CANNED FIGS BAKED IN BRANDY

CURRIED TUNA AND RICE

Boil ½ cup of brown rice or use 1 cup of cooked rice. Add 1 small can of flaked tuna, 3 chopped hard-boiled eggs, 1 chopped onion, and 1 tablespoon of chopped parsley. Mix lightly. Dissolve 1 teaspoon of curry powder in 2 cups of cream sauce. Add to the tuna mixture. Pour in a baking dish and cook in a slow oven for 1 hour. Serve chutney and chopped green onions with this. Serves 4.

PEAS EN CASSEROLE

Fill a casserole with alternate layers of cooked peas (fresh or canned), sliced canned mushrooms, and diced celery. Add diluted canned mushroom soup between the layers. Add 1 grated onion to 1 can of tomato soup and pour over all. Cover with bread crumbs, dot with butter, and bake in a hot oven for 15 minutes.

CANNED ASPARAGUS SALAD

Drain canned asparagus and marinate in a dressing made by adding chopped pickle to French dressing. Mix a little grated cheese with a finely chopped hard-boiled egg and sprinkle over the top of the asparagus before serving.

CANNED FIGS BAKED IN BRANDY

Pour 1 large can of figs into an ovenproof serving dish and sprinkle over them ½ cup of canned moist cocoanut (reserving the rest until later). Add ½ cup of chopped walnuts and ¼ cup of brandy. Cover the dish and bake in the oven until heated through. Serve hot, sprinkled with the remaining cocoanut. Whipped cream may be added. Serves 6.

Menu

BREADED CANNED TONGUE WITH
TOMATO SAUCE

CANNED KIDNEY-BEAN-AND-PEA SALAD

FLUFFY LEMON PIE

BREADED CANNED TONGUE WITH TOMATO SAUCE

Season slices of canned tongue with salt and pepper. Dip in a beaten egg and roll in dried bread crumbs. Sauté in hot butter or fat. Serve with a tomato sauce made by adding a bouillon cube and ½ can of water to 1 can of tomato soup.

CANNED KIDNEY–BEAN–AND–PEA SALAD

Drain 1 can each of peas and kidney beans. Add ½ cup of chopped celery, 1 hard-boiled egg diced, and 1 canned pimiento cut in shreds. Season with salt and paprika and moisten with French dressing. Arrange on a bed of lettuce leaves with mayonnaise on top. Serves 6.

FLUFFY LEMON PIE

Prepare a crumb crust of zwieback (p. 80). Fill with lemon filling.

Fluffy Lemon Filling. — Beat the yolks of 3 eggs until lemon colored. Add the grated rind of 1 lemon and the juice from 1½ lemons. Mix with 1 cup of powdered sugar, 3 tablespoons of boiling water, and ⅛ teaspoon of salt. Cook in a double boiler until thick. Cool and fold in the stiffly beaten egg whites. Fill the baked zwieback shell and place in a 400° oven for 3 minutes to brown. Serves 6.

Menu

BALTIMORE STEW

SALAD OF CELERY AND CANNED ARTICHOKES

CORN MEAL MUFFINS

BUTTERSCOTCH TARTS

BALTIMORE STEW

A group of us were attempting to revive our youth by an evening of ice skating. The evening grew very cold, our muscles soon were stiff, and we were starved; so we returned to a friend's apartment for a snack. By the time our hands and feet were thawed, she had prepared a casserole of this appetizing stew, which surprised me, as I knew she was not particularly interested in cooking. Later she admitted that she simply combined the contents of the four cans left on her emergency shelf.

1 can mushroom soup	½ grated onion
Little cream	1 tablespoon Worcestershire sauce
1 jar chicken and egg noodles	Salt and pepper
1 can whole kernel corn	Bread crumbs
1 can green peas	¼ cup grated cheese

Butter

Pour the soup into an earthenware casserole and thin with a little cream. Add the chicken and egg noodles, corn, peas, grated onion, and Worcestershire sauce. Season to taste. Heat thoroughly. Cover with bread crumbs and grated cheese, dot with butter, and bake in a moderate oven (350°) until the crumbs are browned. Serves 6.

SALAD OF CELERY AND CANNED ARTICHOKES

Mix a dressing of 1 teaspoon each of lemon juice and tomato catsup with ½ cup of mayonnaise. Add 2 tablespoons of cream and season with salt, celery salt, pepper, and a dash of Tabasco. Slice fine 2 stalks of celery, leaves and all, and mix with 1 can of drained artichoke hearts. Fold in the dressing and serve on a bed of lettuce leaves. Serves 4 to 6.

BUTTERSCOTCH TARTS

Make a pie crust from the prepared pastry flour, using the recipe on the package. Roll thin. Cut into circles and fit them into muffin tins or tart pans. Bake. Make ready-packaged butterscotch pudding according to the recipe on the package. Add chopped nuts. Fill the shells when cool. Top with whipped cream.

Menu

EASY SHRIMP CURRY WITH BOILED RICE

CHUTNEY

CASSEROLE OF TOMATOES AND CORN

QUICK PRUNE WHIP

EASY SHRIMP CURRY

Dissolve 1 teaspoon of curry powder in 1 cup of milk and add to 1 can of mushroom soup. Clean 1 can of shrimps and add to the curry. Cook for 20 minutes in the top of a double boiler. Serve with boiled rice. Serves 4.

CASSEROLE OF TOMATOES AND CORN

1 cup bread crumbs	1 large can solid pack tomatoes
½ cup melted butter	1 can whole kernel corn

Sugar, salt, pepper, and celery seed

Mix the crumbs with the melted butter. Fill a casserole with layers of tomato, crumbs, corn, and seasonings. Cover the top with crumbs and bake slowly until brown and bubbling. Serves 6.

QUICK PRUNE WHIP

Put enough canned prunes through a purée sieve to make 1 cup. Place in the refrigerator to chill and just before serving add ½ cup of powdered sugar and 1 teaspoon of lemon juice. Gently fold in 2 stiffly beaten egg whites and serve.

Make a boiled custard, using the egg yolks, and serve well chilled with the prune whip. Serves 4.

Menu

SPINACH AND NOODLE CASSEROLE WITH
SLICED TONGUE

HARVARD BEETS

CHOCOLATE CORNSTARCH PUDDING

SPINACH AND NOODLE CASSEROLE WITH SLICED TONGUE

Cook 1 package of fine noodles in boiling salted water until tender. Place in the bottom of a baking dish. Cover with 1 can of spinach, drained thoroughly, chopped, and seasoned well with butter, salt, pepper, and grated onion. Over this arrange slices of canned tongue, cut in strips, and cover with 2 cups of medium white sauce. Sprinkle buttered bread crumbs and grated cheese thickly over the top. Bake in a moderate oven (350°) until heated through and well browned. Serves 6.

HARVARD BEETS

Slice 3 cups of freshly boiled beets or canned beets. Mix ½ cup of sugar with ½ tablespoon of cornstarch and ½ teaspoon of salt. Add ½ cup of mild vinegar and stir until smooth. Cook in the top of a double boiler until clear. Add the beets and keep warm for about 30 minutes to allow the seasoning to penetrate. Just before serving add 3 tablespoons of butter. Serves 6.

CHOCOLATE CORNSTARCH PUDDING
(Grandma Martin)

Place in a double boiler 2 squares of chocolate with 2 cups of milk and heat until the chocolate melts. Mix ¼ cup of cold milk with ½ cup of sugar, 3 tablespoons of cornstarch, and ¼ teaspoon of salt. Add to the chocolate mixture and stir constantly until it thickens, for about 10 minutes. Add ½ teaspoon of vanilla and turn into a serving dish. Serve with thin cream. Serves 4 to 6.

Menu

MINCED CLAMS EN CASSEROLE

POTATO PUFFS

LOUISIANA STEWED TOMATOES

FRUIT CUP

CHOCOLATE CUP CAKES

MINCED CLAMS EN CASSEROLE

Soak 1 dozen square salted crackers in 1 cup of milk until soft. Add 1 can of minced clams, 2 well-beaten eggs, 4 tablespoons of melted butter, pinch of salt and pepper. Mix well. Put in a casserole and bake in a moderate oven (325°) for ½ hour or longer, until the custard is set and brown. Serves 4.

POTATO PUFFS

Boil and mash enough potatoes to make 1 cupful. Add 2 egg yolks beaten until lemon colored. Sift 1 cup of flour with 1 teaspoon of baking powder and add to the potato mixture alternately with 1 cup of milk. Fold in the 2 egg whites, beaten stiff with a pinch of salt. Drop small portions from a teaspoon into deep fat. Cook until puffed and brown. Drain on brown paper. Serves 4 to 6.

LOUISIANA STEWED TOMATOES

Mince fine 1 large onion, 1 clove of garlic, and 1 sprig of parsley. Sauté in 1 tablespoon of bacon drippings for about 15 minutes but do not brown. Add 2 large cans of tomatoes, 1 teaspoon of sugar, and 1 tablespoon of butter. Place in an earthenware casserole and cook slowly on top of the stove for 1½ to 2 hours, stirring occasionally to prevent burning. Serves 4 to 6.

FRUIT CUP

Peel 1 grapefruit and 2 oranges, and separate the fruit into sections. Add 1 14-ounce can of pineapple cubes with juice and 1 small can of drained seedless grapes. Mix in 1 teaspoon of preserved ginger cut in small pieces. Chill in the refrigerator. Serves 4.

CHOCOLATE CUP CAKES

Use the ready-mixed chocolate cake mixture and bake into cup cakes. Serve warm. They may be baked in the oven at the same time as the Clam Casserole.

Menu

TUNA OR SALMON RING WITH
SHRIMP SAUCE

BAKED ASPARAGUS AND ONIONS WITH
CHEESE

BEET SALAD

BRANDIED PEARS WITH FRUIT SAUCE

TUNA OR SALMON RING

Flake as fine as possible 1 13-ounce can of tuna or salmon. Make a cream sauce with 2 tablespoons of butter, 1 tablespoon of flour, and 1 small can of evaporated milk, diluted with ½ cup of water. Season with ½ teaspoon of salt and ¼ teaspoon of pepper. Add ½ cup of fresh bread crumbs. Add the finely flaked fish, the beaten yolks of 3 eggs, and 2 tablespoons of chopped parsley. Add 1 teaspoon of crushed dill seed. (If you are making this ahead of time, suspend preparations at this point.) Remove from the refrigerator about 1 hour before it is to be served and fold in 3 stiffly beaten egg whites. Grease a small ring mold and pour in the fish. Bake in a moderate oven (350°) for about 30 minutes, until the custard is set. Unmold on a platter and serve with Shrimp or Cream Sauce. Serves 6.

Shrimp Sauce. — Make a cream sauce of 2 cups of milk, 2 tablespoons of butter, and 2 tablespoons of flour. Clean shrimps from a 5½-ounce can (or the equivalent in fresh shrimps), and chop into small pieces. Add to the sauce and season to taste.

BAKED ASPARAGUS AND ONIONS WITH CHEESE

Place a layer of canned asparagus tips in the bottom of a baking dish. Cover with fried onions and sprinkle with grated cheese. Continue the layers until the casserole is full. Sprinkle with bread crumbs, dot with butter, and bake in a slow oven (275°).

BEET SALAD

Place a bowl of mayonnaise, well seasoned with horse-radish, in the center of a platter. Surround with sliced beets arranged on bed of lettuce and sprinkled with chopped parsley.

BRANDIED PEARS WITH FRUIT SAUCE

Pour ¼ cup of brandy over canned pears. Chill. Cover with whipped cream or cream cheese mashed and thinned with cream. Serve with a hot sauce made with equal parts of orange marmalade and apricot jam, flavored with brandy.

Menu

CREAMED TOMATO AND PEA SOUP

CREAMED CHIPPED BEEF

BROWNED CARROTS

CANNED PEAR AND CHERRY SALAD

PECAN BISCUITS WITH BUTTERSCOTCH

CREAMED TOMATO AND PEA SOUP

Mix 1 can each of tomato and pea soup and stir in the same amount of milk and cream mixed. Heat in the top of a double boiler. Season to taste with salt, pepper, and Worcestershire sauce. When ready to serve, flavor with ⅓ cup of sherry. Serves 6.

CREAMED CHIPPED BEEF
(Lillyon's)

Soak ¼ pound of dried beef for a few moments in warm water. Put 2 tablespoons of butter in a frying pan and brown well but do not burn. Drain the beef and add to the butter. When well saturated with butter, sprinkle with 2 tablespoons of flour. Pour in 2 cups of hot, light cream and continue stirring as the cream thickens. Serve very hot on thin slices of freshly toasted bread. Evaporated milk, diluted with an equal amount of fresh milk, may be used in place of the cream. Browning the butter gives this dish its piquant flavor. Serves 4.

BROWNED CARROTS

Cook small, tender carrots in boiling salted water. Drain. Roll in melted butter or bacon fat and then in crushed corn flakes. Place in a pan and broil under medium heat until brown, adding more butter or fat, if necessary.

CANNED PEAR AND CHERRY SALAD
(Serve with Pecan Biscuits in place of dessert)

Place halves of canned pears on lettuce leaves and fill with pitted, canned white cherries stuffed with nut meats. Serve with Orange and Lemon Mayonnaise (p. 64).

PECAN BISCUITS WITH BUTTERSCOTCH
(Hazel's)

Prepare biscuit dough from a ready-mixed preparation. Roll the dough to ¼-inch thickness. Spread with melted butter and sprinkle thickly with brown sugar. Cover with pecan halves (or other nuts) and roll like a jelly roll. Cut in 1-inch slices and place close together in a buttered pan. Bake in a quick oven (450°).

The Versatile Hamburger

No matter what kind of beef you grind or how fine you grind it, it is still hamburger! Some like it made from sirloin; others insist it must be top round and will be satisfied with nothing else. But many persons buy hamburger just as they find it and manage very well. With clever seasoning, it can be made delicious. After all, what we do with our material is what counts, whether it is wool for a dress, straw for a hat, or meat for dinner.

Really, no other article of food will allow you to "save face" like a pound of hamburger. When you have lingered too long over the afternoon game of bridge and are faced with the problem of preparing dinner quickly hamburger can be relied upon. Or perhaps you have succumbed to the lure of a much too-extravagant hat so that the end of the month finds you and your budget in a befuddled condition. Again hamburger will come to your rescue!

So because of its usefulness, please treat the hamburger with a little consideration. Don't bang it between your hands with such vigor that it emerges from the frying pan looking like a badly laid slab of cement. Instead, season it highly, *mix it lightly,* and *mold it gently!*

The hamburger can be the basis of an endless array of dishes. For a hearty meal try combining it with spaghetti, noodles, or rice. This needs only the addition of tomato and cheese with a suggestion of garlic to become a deliciously flavored casserole dish. Or it may be broiled and served with any one of several sauces, such as mushroom sauce made by adding broiled mushrooms to the well-seasoned meat gravy. Tomatoes and onions make another sauce that may be enriched with the addition of red wine.

With a little ingenuity, you can originate all kinds of combinations as well as create new sauces. But no matter what recipe you use or how many other ingredients you decide to add, don't forget to use the onion! Hamburger and onion are inseparable.

If you are an advocate of the use of ground round or sirloin, then pat your meat gently into a glass pie dish, dot it generously with butter, and place it under the broiler to brown. Through the transparent sides of the glass dish, you can watch the cooking until the meat is just the right shade of pinkness to satisfy you. Cut the meat into wedges like a pie, and serve it to your family from the dish in which it was cooked. Its flavor will be as fine as, if not finer than, that of the most expensive cut of steak, and you will be surprised at the rich, delicious gravy that appears as though by magic.

Hamburger may be combined with several other kinds of meat and baked in the oven as a meat loaf. This may be turned into an entire meal by surrounding the meat loaf with potatoes and vegetables and serving it in its earthenware casserole. Chopped parsley, sprinkled over the top at the last moment, will give that welcome festive touch, or, if you feel affluent, use freshly cooked green peas.

To add a new interest to your next cocktail party, try offering your guests tiny meat balls, sautéed crisp and brown, and subtly flavored with herbs and onion. Spear them with toothpicks and heap them in the center of a platter, or they may surround a bowl of mustard sauce. When made in a larger size, these same meat balls may be served at a buffet dinner accompanied by tomato, steak, or mushroom sauce. Or perhaps you may like to experiment with your own sauce, using a combination of the different kinds of pepper with the addition of salt, dry mustard, garlic, and other seasonings. Canned soups may be used in an emergency to make a quick sauce; for example, tomato, celery, asparagus, and mushroom. The mushroom soup may be flavored with sherry.

If you want a quick shepherd's pie, add a can of vegetable soup to the hamburger and bake it in a casserole with mashed potatoes on top, or you may use leftover mashed potatoes by adding warm milk and beating them again.

A Spanish touch may be acquired by covering well-seasoned hamburger with mashed canned tamales. Cover the top with a thick sprinkling of cheese and bake in the oven. With a tossed green salad, some toasted French bread, and a bowl of fresh fruit, you have a delicious and satisfying supper.

But no matter whether you broil your hamburger or bake it, it still won't be right unless you handle it with a light touch. This light touch is far more important than the seasoning or the cut of meat which you use. So remember, lift it tenderly, toss it lightly, pat it gently!

HAMBURGER ROLL

Soak 1 slice of bread in a little water. Squeeze out the excess water and mix with 1 pound of ground round steak or hamburger, 2 well-beaten eggs, and a few canned mushrooms. Season with salt and pepper.

Sprinkle dried bread crumbs on a mixing board, place the meat mixture on the crumbs, and flatten it lightly. In a frying pan cook 1 chopped onion in a little butter. Mix in ½ cup of cooked rice and season. Spread this over the meat and roll carefully. Place in a baking pan in a 400° oven and bake for 15 minutes. Reduce the heat to 325° and roast for 45 minutes. Just before removing from the oven, pour sour cream or canned mushroom soup over the meat. Serves 4.

QUICK HAMBURGER STEAK SANDWICH

Toast the desired number of slices of bread on one side. On the other side spread a mixture of butter and prepared mustard.

Mix ground round steak or hamburger with chopped onion and milk (1 pound of meat to ½ cup of milk and 2 tablespoons of onion). Season with salt and pepper. Spread the meat mixture on the buttered side of the bread, covering to the very edge. Put a dab of butter on each slice and broil for about 5 minutes.

HAMBURGER WITH RED WINE

Have the butcher run 2 pounds of round steak through the chopper 3 times. (Hamburger may be used.) Place in a bowl and mix lightly with a fork, adding a seasoning of salt, freshly ground pepper, a little chopped parsley, and ¼ teaspoon of mixed herbs. (These can be bought packaged from any herb store.) Pour over this 2 cups of red wine. Do this in the morning and let it stand in a cool place until you are ready to cook it in the evening. Shape the meat into a loaf and bake in the oven or make it into patties. Serves 6.

HAMBURGER WITH MUSHROOM SAUCE

Mix 1½ pounds of ground round steak or hamburger with 3 tablespoons of grated onion, 1 teaspoon of salt, a pinch of coarsely ground black pepper, a dash of Worcestershire sauce, and 1 cup of evaporated milk. Make into patties. Place in a casserole and sauté in bacon fat until brown. Add 1 can of mushroom soup thinned with evaporated milk. Simmer for about 20 minutes, basting with the sauce occasionally. Sprinkle chopped parsley over the top. (The patties may be shaped in the morning, covered with waxed paper, and kept in the refrigerator until ready to cook.) Serves 6.

HAMBURGER WITH NOODLES

Brown 1 medium-sized onion, chopped fine, in about 2 tablespoons of bacon drippings. Mix in 1 pound of hamburger and continue cooking until the meat is brown. Stir in 1 can of tomato soup and 1 cup of water. Mix in 2 cups of uncooked noodles and continue cooking until the noodles are tender. (Add more water if necessary.) Season to taste. Add 1 can of corn and 1 can of pitted ripe olives. Pour into a buttered casserole and cover with 1 cup of grated cheese. Cook in a 350° oven for about 45 minutes. Serves 6.

DELICIOUS PATTIES

Shape ground round steak into a loaf, handling as lightly as possible. Cut in slices and place in a glass pie dish. Make an indentation in the top of each slice and fill with a piece of butter. Broil. Do not turn.

MEAT CAKES À LA MARIE

Grind together ⅓ pound each of round steak, veal, and fresh pork, 1 green pepper, and 1 onion. Mix in ½ cup of cracker crumbs. Season with 2 teaspoons of anchovy paste and a dash of pepper. Mix in 4 beaten eggs, ¼ cup of milk, and ¼ cup of capers. Shape into patties about 1½ inches thick. Heat olive oil or bacon drippings in a hot skillet and brown the patties on both sides. Remove to a glass pie dish, cover, and bake in a moderate oven for 15 minutes. Serves 4 to 6.

GROUND MEAT BALLS WITH HERBS

Season 1½ pounds of ground round steak or hamburger with 1 teaspoon of salt, ½ teaspoon of pepper, and a dash of paprika. Add 1 teaspoon each of chopped chives and chopped parsley and a pinch of thyme and marjoram. Fry 1 slice of bacon, mince very fine, and add to the meat. Make small cakes of the mixture, roll in flour, and brown in bacon drippings. Pour 1 can of mushroom soup into the pan for gravy. Serves 4 to 6.

BEEF PATTIES IN HORSE–RADISH SAUCE

Peel 4 bananas and place in a baking dish with 2 tablespoons of butter. Bake 30 minutes in a moderate oven (350°). To 1½ pounds of ground round steak add 1 teaspoon of salt and ¼ teaspoon of white pepper. Form into cakes. Broil until well cooked. Make a white sauce of 4 tablespoons of butter, 2 tablespoons of flour, and 1 cup of evaporated milk. Season with salt, a little onion juice, and 3 tablespoons of horse-radish. Pour sauce on a hot platter, lay the meat cakes in it with the bananas, cut in halves, on top. Serves 3 to 4.

BAKED HAMBURGER AND VEGETABLES

Boil ½ pound of macaroni and chop fine. Brown 2 medium-sized onions, chopped fine, in bacon fat with 1 pound of ground round steak or hamburger, stirring well with a fork. Add 1 small can of tomatoes or tomato soup, 1 small can of peas, and 1 small can of mushrooms (pieces and stems). Stir in macaroni and place in a casserole. Cover with bread crumbs mixed with grated cheese and dot with butter. Bake in a moderate oven (350°) for 1 hour. (This is one of those dishes which may be prepared in the morning and kept in the refrigerator until ready to bake.) Serves 4 to 6.

CHEESEBURGER

Mix very lightly 1 pound of ground round steak or hamburger with 1 cup of milk. Add salt, pepper, and a little Worcestershire sauce. Pat lightly into a glass pie dish and place under a hot broiler for about 10 minutes. Sprinkle ½ cup of grated cheese over the top and broil for about 3 minutes more. Serve hot mushroom soup or tomato soup with this as a sauce. Serves 3.

BARBECUED PATTIES
(Jane's)

½ cup soft bread crumbs	2 tablespoons Worcestershire sauce
¼ cup milk	1 tablespoon vinegar
1 pound hamburger	2 tablespoons sugar
Salt and pepper	½ cup catsup
2 tablespoons bacon drippings	1 onion, chopped

Moisten the bread crumbs with milk. Add meat, salt and pepper. Form into 4 large patties. Brown on both sides in bacon drippings in a frying pan. Add remaining ingredients. Cover and cook 10 minutes. Serves 4.

BROILED HAMBURGERS WITH ROQUEFORT

Season hamburger, mold into patties, and broil. Cream butter with Roquefort cheese and spread over the broiled meat. Return to the broiler until the cheese is melted.

HAMBURGER WITH SAUCE

Season hamburger, mold into patties, and sauté in a skillet. About 3 minutes before they are done, add cream and Worcestershire sauce to the pan in which they are sautéed. (For 2 patties use ¼ cup of cream and 2 tablespoons of Worcestershire sauce.)

PATTIES IN SHERRY SAUCE

1 pound ground round steak	3 tablespoons butter
Salt and pepper to taste	1 can condensed mushroom soup
¼ cup sherry	

Mix beef with salt and pepper; shape into patties. Melt butter in a skillet; brown patties on both sides. Remove to a baking dish. Combine mushroom soup and sherry; heat in a skillet. Pour soup over patties and bake in a moderately hot oven (375°) about 15 minutes. Serves 4.

CRISP MEAT CAKES

Soak 5 slices of rye bread in 1 cup of milk. Squeeze out part of the milk, leaving the bread still moist. Place in a mixing bowl and add 1 pound of ground round steak or hamburger, 1 grated onion, 1 beaten egg, 1 teaspoon of salt, and ½ teaspoon of pepper. Mix all together lightly, using a fork. Shape into patties and roll in dried bread crumbs. Melt bacon fat in an iron skillet and brown the meat quickly. Let cook 10 minutes. Remove meat cakes to a serving platter and keep warm. Add either evaporated milk, sour cream, or canned mushroom soup to the gravy in the pan and heat. Serve the gravy in a bowl in the center of the platter, surrounded with the meat cakes. Do not pour the gravy over the cakes as that will destroy their crispness. Decorate with parsley. Serves 4.

MEAT STUFFED WITH CABBAGE

Brown lightly in 2 tablespoons of bacon fat, 1 large chopped onion and ½ cabbage, shredded. Mix with 2 cups of boiled rice. Moisten with a little water flavored with a bouillon cube.

Roll out 1½ pounds of seasoned ground beef on a piece of waxed paper and shape into a square. Fill half with the cabbage mixture and fold the other half of the meat over it. Remove from the waxed paper and place in a buttered baking dish. Dot with bacon drippings and pour 1 can of evaporated milk around the meat. Bake 1 hour in a moderate oven. Baste often. (One can of mushroom soup may be used instead of the milk.) Serves 6.

BROILED HAMBURGERS WITH NUTS

1½ pounds hamburger steak	6 tablespoons chopped walnuts
2 teaspoons salt	6 tablespoons chopped parsley
Pepper	3 tablespoons minced onion

3 strips bacon

Season hamburger with salt and a dash of pepper. Divide into 6 portions. Form each portion into 2 cakes and flatten gently. Combine nuts, parsley, and onion, and spread on top of 6 cakes. Cut the bacon in half lengthwise and place around the hamburgers. Place remaining cakes on top and pinch cakes together. Place on a heatproof dish and broil under a hot flame for 8 minutes. Turn and brown on the other side.

STEAK DIABLE

Grind 2 pounds of round steak and 12 anchovies three times. Season highly with 2 tablespoons of onion juice, 1 tablespoon of lemon juice, 1 tablespoon of Worcestershire sauce, a dash of Tabasco, salt, and pepper. Mix with 2 uncooked egg yolks. Place mounds of the meat mixture on pieces of toast and garnish each with rolled anchovies and minced onions. This is served raw! Serves 6.

THIN HAMBURGERS WITH CHEESE

1 pound hamburger	1 onion, chopped fine
Salt and pepper	¼ pound cheese, sliced thin

Make patties of the meat, place between sheets of waxed paper and roll thin. Sprinkle with salt, pepper, and chopped onion. Place on each patty a slice of cheese, then cover with another patty. Broil. Serves 3.

HAMBURGERS WITH PAN GRAVY

Have your butcher grind 1 pound of round steak, 1 pound of veal, and a piece of suet the size of a walnut, putting them through the grinder three times. Mince 1 large onion and sauté in bacon drippings until brown. Put the meat in a bowl and add 4 well-drained canned tomatoes, chopped. Add the onion and ½ teaspoon each of ginger and mace. Season with salt and pepper. Beat with a fork for at least 10 minutes. Shape into round patties, handling as lightly as possible. Dot butter on the top of each cake. Put in a heatproof serving dish. Brown under the broiler until cooked to taste. Serve in the baking dish, surrounded with pan gravy. Serves 6.

HAMBURGER GOULASH

Brown 1 pound of ground round steak or hamburger in 2 tablespoons of bacon fat, stirring as the meat cooks. Add ¼ cup each of chopped onion and celery, 1 can of Lima beans, and 1 No.-2½ can of tomatoes. Season with salt and pepper and add a pinch of herbs. Cover and cook for 1 hour over a slow fire. Serves 4.

BROILED GROUND STEAK WITH PIQUANT SAUCE

Lightly form 3½ pounds of ground round steak or hamburger into a cake about 1½ inches thick. Dot with butter and broil.

In the meantime, mix the sauce on a heatproof platter. Melt 3 tablespoons of butter and add 1 clove of garlic, minced. Sprinkle the melted butter generously with salt, pepper, and paprika. Then add 1 teaspoon of dry mustard, a little lemon juice, 1 onion grated, and 1 teaspoon of Worcestershire sauce. Place the platter in the oven, and when the steak is cooked, remove to the platter and move the meat gently back and forth until the sauce has been absorbed. If you place the meat in a pan when you broil it, the juices of the meat will be saved and can be added to the sauce. Serves 8.

PART II

RELAX AND ENTERTAIN

The Cocktail Party

If you feel like giving a party and are minus a maid, the cock-tail party is an easy solution. The party may be the result of a hasty invitation to "drop by for cocktail" or of a more elaborate plan that may include serving a buffet supper for those who linger after the cocktail hour.

Or you may plan to give one large party during the year, which you will find far less expensive than several small ones. In that case, why not give the type of party that could become a tradition — such as a Christmas cocktail party? If so, plan to have it the day after Christmas — to most people the dullest day of the year. No one seems to have anything to do on that day, so your friends will all be thrilled to receive your invitation. And another suggestion, you might make this a family party, allowing each member of the family, married or single, to invite a certain number of his friends. The assortment of varied ages and personalities will add to the interest, making the party amusing as well as unique. Don't be afraid to try something different.

To give a successful cocktail party is not difficult, if you make your plans ahead of time and do not attempt more than can be handled with ease.

If you are not planning to have a professional mix the drinks, you had better ask some friend to assist you by acting as bartender. But remember this requires a tactful approach. Don't forget to have everything ready to work with and in sufficient quantities. If you need extra ice, be sure to get the kind frozen in cubes or else someone will have to chip ice all evening. If you haven't a portable bar, a card table or two, if firm, will do nicely.

Remember that it is far better to serve one excellent cocktail than to offer several varieties badly mixed. If you are serving Martinis, try mixing them ahead of time. I keep mine in an antique glass decanter; in fact, I always have some on hand so that if anyone drops in for a drink, I can serve a Martini quickly and with no effort. I think this particular cocktail becomes more mellow if the ingredients are allowed to mix and become acquainted before they are expected to push someone's spirits up where they should be.

If you are serving Old-Fashioneds at your party, you may have some of the glasses filled with the right amount of sugar, bitters, and a little water; then all that has to be done at the last minute is to put in the bourbon, a couple of pieces of ice, and give it a stir. If no one happens to want an Old-Fashioned, you haven't wasted your liquor. You may have a few highball glasses filled with the right amount of Scotch, which, if not used, may be poured back in the bottle.

And don't forget the guests who might want a non-alcoholic drink. Have chilled ginger ale, Coca-Cola, fruit juices, tomato or clam juice ready, so that those who prefer them are not made conspicuous by having to ask for them.

Don't, I beg of you, have any canapés that will "die on the vine." Don't serve any food which will look even faintly wilted before the party is over. It isn't necessary, for there are plenty of good things that will not grow stale. Don't try to serve anything that has to be looked after at the last moment unless you have someone to do it. In case you are having hot canapés, prepare them in advance up to the stage where they go under the broiler. Place them in pie tins, and cover with waxed paper until ready to broil. Cook only a small number at a time. Remember, your guests won't all arrive at once.

Personally, I favor serving food on the buffet or on the table in the dining room, instead of passing it. When it is passed to the guests, it never seems to reach all of them as they move about. Also, if you have a servantless home, you will find it helpful to arrange the food in the dining room ahead of time.

If you do serve food on the buffet or table, have a platter filled with an assortment of cold meats, patterned off with strips of dill pickle which are good to eat as well as decorative. A pot of mustard, or, better still, Mustard Sauce, should be at hand. Nearby place a platter of thinly sliced white and rye bread, already buttered and the crusts removed. You can prepare the bread early in the morning, provided you cover it with waxed paper and then with a damp napkin. Keep it in the refrigerator until it is time to serve it.

Another platter may hold the ever-popular stuffed eggs, but do something special with them this time. They should be small or pullet eggs, but if you have been unable to get them, cut hard-boiled large ones lengthwise in three wedges. The filling may be flavored with anchovies or shrimps and may include capers, chives, or a little chopped fried bacon.

Then consider the cheese spreads. I am, of course, referring to the blended cheeses for which I have given recipes, not to the commercial mixtures. Prepare two or more different kinds and serve in bowls surrounded with crackers, potato chips, or thin slices of pumpernickel bread.

Ground meat makes an excellent spread, and you may be surprised to learn that one of the best is boiled soup meat left after you have made your weekly supply of soup stock. Have some ready the day before your party so that it will be well chilled. Grind it fine and mix with chopped green onions, prepared mustard, Worcestershire sauce, and mayonnaise. Place in a bowl, sprinkle with chopped parsley, and serve with buttered rye bread or crackers.

If you have a chafing dish or can borrow one, it is a good idea to serve one hot dish. Try Welsh rarebit made with a cream sauce and a goodly amount of grated fresh cheese. But remember, this involves using plates! Another suggestion is shrimp in hot curry sauce, or tiny fish balls in a lobster sauce. One of my own specialties is bits of hot wieners speared with toothpicks and dunked in a sour cream sauce.

Sometimes I serve French Onion Soup (p. 165), quantities of

it, because it is always popular. The soup is not expensive and is best if made the day before the party to give it time to ripen. It may be served on a side table from one of those peasant pottery soup kettles and kept hot on an electric plate or an alcohol burner. Nothing tastes better on a cold night than a cup of hot onion soup with a dash of grated Parmesan cheese on the top, especially after you have had your share of ice-cold Martinis and are too full of cold canapés to think of dinner.

It may be that you are giving one of those "balance the budget" parties — the "she had me, so I'll have her" type of party — which is your privilege. In that case, you probably invited your guests "from five to seven." But on the other hand, if you are giving a party just for the joy of seeing your old friends and of having them together in your home, you will probably invite them to drop in for cocktails from six o'clock on. But don't include the "on" unless you mean it, because if they have as good a time as I hope they will, they will stay for the "on" side of the invitation. Be prepared! Have the chafing dish ready.

So the first time the spirit moves you, sit right down with a pad and pencil and (I hope) this book of tricks and plan for yourself a perfectly superb cocktail party, and, as they said in the gay nineties, "Don't spare the horses!"

CANAPÉS SERVED HOT

FRIED ARTICHOKE CHIPS

Peel and cut Jerusalem artichokes in very thin slices. Place in ice water for 1 hour. Drain and dry between towels. Drop a few at a time into hot fat, drain on absorbent paper, and sprinkle with salt.

CORNED BEEF BALLS

Grind fine the contents of 1 can of corned beef. Mix with 1 raw egg. Shape into balls with a small pickled onion in the center of each. Roll in dried crumbs and fry in deep fat. Serve on toothpicks.

CHEESE AND BACON CANAPÉS

Beat the yolk of 1 egg, add ½ cup of grated cheese and 1 tablespoon of cream, and season with salt and pepper. Toast rounds of bread on one side and spread the cheese mixture on the untoasted side. Cut bacon in 1-inch pieces and place on top. Toast in the oven until the bacon is crisp.

PIMIENTO CHEESE PUFFS

Blend 1 8-ounce package of pimiento cheese with 1 well-beaten egg. Season to taste. Toast rounds of bread on one side. Spread the untoasted side with butter and the pimiento cheese. Broil until brown and puffed. (A slice of dill pickle or tomato may be placed on the bread and topped with the cheese before broiling.)

BACON SLICES STUFFED WITH SARDINES

Mash sardines and season with Worcestershire sauce, dry mustard, and pepper. Spread pieces of bacon with this mixture, roll, and fasten with toothpicks. Sauté until the bacon is crisp. Serve on toothpicks.

FRENCH FRIED SHRIMPS

Clean shrimps and, if too large, cut in half. Dip in beaten egg to which a little milk has been added. Roll in fine bread crumbs and fry in deep fat. Spear with a toothpick. Serve on a large plate, in the center of which is a bowl of mayonnaise seasoned with mustard.

ROLLED CHEESE CANAPÉS

Mix softened cream cheese, pimiento cheese, and butter. Spread on slices of white bread. Roll and fasten with a toothpick. Toast under the broiler and serve hot.

BRAZIL NUTS IN BACON

Shell and peel some Brazil nuts, sprinkle them with salt and paprika, and then roll each one in a half slice of bacon, secured with a toothpick. Place under the broiler until the bacon is crisp. Drain on brown paper and serve hot.

CANAPÉS OF SCALLOPS

Fry scallops in deep fat. Serve on toothpicks. Place on a platter around a bowl of tartare sauce.

LIVER SAUSAGE CANAPÉS

Mash liver sausage, add chopped salted nuts, Worcestershire sauce, and lemon juice. Form this paste into small balls, dip in beaten egg, roll in bread crumbs, and fry in deep fat until brown.

HAM AND CHUTNEY SANDWICHES

Toast small rounds of bread on one side. Mix chutney sauce with deviled ham. Put a mound of this on untoasted side of bread. Cover with the following mixture: Mash ¼ pound of American cheese with 2 tablespoons of butter. Add ¼ teaspoon of mustard and season with salt and paprika. Beat in 1 egg. Spread on the toast and bake in a quick oven. Sprinkle with paprika and serve hot.

DEVILED CHEESE

Put 1 tablespoon of butter into a pan. Add 2 teaspoons of dry mustard, 2 tablespoons of vinegar, 2 teaspoons of anchovy paste, pepper, cayenne, and ¼ pound of cheese cut into pieces. Stir well until melted; then spread on toasted bread and serve hot.

ROLLED CHEESE AND OLIVE FINGERS

Work cream cheese to a smooth paste with a little cream. Add finely chopped olives and chill. Spread slices of bread with the mixture, roll, and toast under the broiler. Serve very hot.

CHEESE AND ANCHOVY SPREAD

Mash equal parts of yellow packaged cheese and cream cheese. Add anchovy paste to taste. Spread on crackers, and toast under the broiler.

AVOCADO AND BACON STRIPS TOASTED

Make a spread of 1 avocado, mashed and seasoned with ¼ teaspoon of salt, ⅛ teaspoon of paprika, and 1 teaspoon of lemon juice. Spread on strips of toast and cover with chopped bacon. Broil until crisp.

DEVILED HAM ROLLS

Mix ¾ cup of sifted flour with ⅛ teaspoon of salt. Add ¼ cup of shortening, blending well with tips of fingers. Mix in 2 tablespoons of cold water to make a stiff paste. Roll very thin in an oblong shape. Spread with deviled ham and roll the short way like a jelly roll. Chill thoroughly, slice thin, and bake in a hot oven for 15 minutes. These may be served hot or cold.

ONION AND CHEESE CANAPÉS

Slice an onion paper-thin, place on rounds of buttered bread and sprinkle with grated cheese. Heat slowly under the broiler.

BROILED SAUSAGE WITH PECAN

Slit an opening in a small sausage, insert a pecan nut meat, and broil. Serve hot.

ROLLED SANDWICHES FILLED WITH FRIED ONION

Sauté chopped onions in butter until soft but not brown. Season with salt and pepper. Spread on thinly sliced bread, roll, fasten with a toothpick, and cover with a damp cloth until ready to toast. Place a few of them at a time in a pan and toast under the flame of the broiler.

FILLED BISCUIT CANAPÉS

Bake small baking powder biscuits made from rich dough. Split open and fill with liverwurst, mashed and mixed with mayonnaise and chopped fried bacon.

TOMATO AND CHEESE CRACKERS

Spread small round crackers with tomato catsup. Cover with freshly grated American cheese and place in the oven until the cheese melts. Serve hot.

HAM AND CHEESE CANAPÉS

Melt 2 tablespoons of butter in a pan and add 2 tablespoons of flour. Blend and pour in 1 cup of hot milk. Stir until thickened and add ¼ pound of freshly grated cheese. Cool. Beat 2 egg yolks into the mixture. Season with salt and pepper. Cover squares of dry bread with pieces of lean, boiled ham. Spread the cheese mixture over the ham and place in a pan under the broiler to brown. Sprinkle with paprika and serve.

ANCHOVY PUFFS

Mash 2 6-oz. packages of cream cheese and add 2 egg yolks. Mix well and add 1 small grated white onion. Stir in 2 teaspoons of anchovy paste and a pinch of cayenne. Spread thickly on small rounds of toast, heaping toward the center. Arrange on a baking sheet and place under a hot broiler. Watch carefully! They will puff slightly and come out a light golden brown.

MEAT PASTRIES

These are delicious for a cocktail party or to be served with a hearty soup as a whole meal. (They may be reheated.)

Mix 2 egg yolks, ½ cup of butter, 2 tablespoons of cream, 2 cups of flour, and a pinch of salt. Roll very thin and cut into circles with a cooky cutter. Fill with the following meat mixture and fold over, pressing the edges together. Bake in a moderate oven (350°).

Meat Mixture. — Grind cooked meat and add a small amount of grated onion. Season with salt and pepper and add leftover gravy to moisten.

OYSTER AND BACON ROLLS

Wrap medium-sized oysters in ¼ strips of bacon and fasten with a toothpick. Grill under the broiler until the bacon is golden brown.

CHEESE BALLS A LA ALLEN

Mix 1½ cups of freshly grated cheese, a little salt, a pinch of cayenne pepper, and the beaten whites of 2 eggs. Roll in small balls, dip in beaten eggs and bread crumbs, and fry in deep fat.

PARMESAN STRIPS
(Kay's)

Mix 6 tablespoons of grated Parmesan cheese, 3 tablespoons of butter, and 3 tablespoons of minced parsley. Season to taste. Spread 12 narrow toast strips with the mixture, sprinkle 3 tablespoons of chopped peanuts over the top, and place in a hot oven (400°) for 10 minutes.

CLUB CANAPÉS

Mix 3 tablespoons of cream cheese with 1 tablespoon each of chopped onion and chopped green pepper. Mix thoroughly and spread on small round crackers, sprinkle with paprika, and place in a hot oven until brown.

LIVERWURST ROLLS

Roll liverwurst sausage in biscuit dough, slice, and bake.

CANAPÉS SERVED COLD

PINWHEELS

Slice bread very thin. Spread with butter seasoned with mustard, Worcestershire sauce, and chopped parsley. Place a small Vienna sausage (the kind that comes in glass jars) at one end of the slice and roll the bread. Wrap in a damp towel and put in the refrigerator. Slice the rolls into 1-inch sections and put a toothpick in each one.

CHEESE COOKIES

(Mary's)

Mix 1 package of Shefford's cheese, ¼ pound of butter, 1 cup of flour, and a dash of cayenne. Form into a roll and wrap in waxed paper. Place in the refrigerator until chilled and firm. Slice and bake in a moderate oven until firm and slightly brown. This is one of my very best recipes.

EGGS STUFFED WITH LIVER SAUSAGE

Hard-boil eggs; cut in half lengthwise. Remove yolks and mash; add liverwurst and mash again. Season with salt, cayenne, dry mustard, Worcestershire sauce, lemon juice, and mayonnaise. Stuff the whites with this mixture.

SMOKED SALMON ROLLS

Mix cream cheese with horse-radish to taste. Spread on thin slices of smoked salmon, roll, and secure with a toothpick.

STUFFED CUCUMBER SANDWICHES

Peel a cucumber and remove the center and seeds with an apple corer. Mix 1 package of cream cheese, 2 tablespoons of chopped chives, 2 teaspoons of chopped parsley, and ¼ teaspoon of mustard with enough mayonnaise to soften. Stuff the cavity in the cucumber with this mixture, wrap in waxed paper, and place in the refrigerator. Serve cut in thin slices on rounds of toasted rye bread, which has been well buttered.

FRIED ALMOND ROUNDS

Brown lightly ¼ cup of chopped almonds in ¼ cup of butter. Mix with 2 tablespoons of chutney, 2 tablespoons of chopped sweet pickle, 1 tablespoon of Worcestershire sauce, and a pinch of salt. Spread on toasted squares of bread.

RED CAVIAR AND SOUR CREAM
(Kay's)

Mix 1½ pounds of cream cheese with ½ cup of sour cream and add 2 tablespoons of onion juice. Put in a closed container with 1 clove of garlic and let stand in the refrigerator. Just before serving, remove the clove of garlic and gently fold in 1 pound of red caviar. Place in the center of a flat glass dish and surround with slices of pumpernickel bread.

CHEESE MIXTURE FOR STUFFING CELERY

Mix ½ pound of Roquefort cheese, ½ cup of sherry, and 1 teaspoon of Worcestershire sauce. Add enough cream cheese to make a stiff paste. Season with salt, pepper, and paprika. Fill celery stalks.

This mixture is especially delicious spread between 2 pecan halves.

TINY TOMATOES STUFFED WITH SMOKED OYSTERS

Cut off the tops of tiny red tomatoes and hollow out. Mix canned, smoked oysters, minced, with a few chopped capers, a little horse-radish, and some mayonnaise. Fill tomatoes and use to decorate an hors d'oeuvres platter.

HUACAMOLE

Mash avocados, flavor with grated onion and lemon juice, and season with salt and pepper. Thin with mayonnaise. Serve in a bowl, surrounded with potato chips.

EGGS STUFFED WITH BACON

Cut in half lengthwise 12 hard-boiled eggs. Fry 6 slices of bacon and chop fine. Add to the mashed yolks of the eggs and mix in 3 tablespoons of chopped chives, 2 tablespoons of soft butter, 1½ tablespoons of vinegar, and salt and pepper to taste. Fill the whites with this mixture.

ANCHOVY NUT TIDBITS

Season cream cheese with a small amount of anchovy paste, and spread between halves of walnuts or pecans.

STUFFED EGGS
(Jane's)

Hard-boil 12 eggs. Cut in half lengthwise and mix the yolks with the following seasoning: 2 teaspoons of prepared mustard, 1 teaspoon each of minced tarragon leaves, celery salt, grated onion, and curry powder. Add 2 tablespoons of mayonnaise, a dash of lemon juice, and salt and pepper to taste. Blend thoroughly and put back in the whites.

LIPTAUER CHEESE

This is one of the recipes that all my friends will look for! For the past few years we have served it at all our cocktail parties. It was given me by Mrs. Victor Jacomini and she has most generously consented to allow me to include it in my book, so that everyone may enjoy it.

5 packages cream cheese	2 teaspoons dry mustard
3 tablespoons capers	2 teaspoons paprika
2 tablespoons onions, finely chopped	4 tablespoons chopped chives
1 tube of anchovy paste	1 tablespoon caraway seed

Mix all together until well blended. Soften with beer to make the right consistency for spreading, being careful not to make it too thin. Serve with potato chips or crackers.

OPEN PUMPERNICKEL SANDWICHES

Mix a little anchovy paste with butter and mayonnaise. Add chopped hard-boiled eggs, spread on pumpernickel fingers, and sprinkle with chopped green olives on top.

ONION AND GREEN PEPPER SPREAD

(Men enjoy these sandwiches with beer.)

Grind together 2 large green peppers and 1 large onion; then add ½ cup of cider vinegar and 1 tablespoon of sugar. Let stand overnight. When ready to use, drain and press dry. Mix with a little mayonnaise and season with salt and pepper. Spread on thinly sliced, buttered rye bread.

HAM AND ROQUEFORT CHEESE ROLLS

Slice square boiled ham the same thickness as for sandwiches. Spread with a mixture of 1 tablespoon each of Roquefort and cream cheese. Roll tight like a jelly roll and then cut into ½-inch slices. Serve on toothpicks.

STUFFED CUCUMBER SLICES

Peel and slice cucumbers in 1-inch slices. Scoop out a small place in the center and fill with deviled ham. Chill.

EGGS STUFFED WITH MUSHROOMS AND HAM

Hard-boil 6 eggs and slice lengthwise. Remove yolks and mash with 3 anchovies, ¼ cup of chopped, cooked mushrooms, 2 tablespoons of minced ham, 2 teaspoons of olive oil, and a little vinegar. Mix together well. Refill the whites and serve.

CHEESE APPLES

Mash 1 8-ounce package of American cheese until soft. Chop fine 12 small pickled onions and mix with the cheese. Add ½ cup of chopped nuts. Form into small balls, roll in paprika, and stick a clove in one side. (These are attractive when used to decorate a platter of assorted sandwiches.)

STUFFED CELERY WITH LIVERWURST

Mash liverwurst. Add chopped stuffed green olives and lemon juice to taste. Thin with mayonnaise. Use mixture to stuff small, inner stalks of celery.

BRANDIED STUFFED DATES

Use bottled brandied dates or soak fresh dates overnight in brandy. Next day remove pits and fill with peanut butter mixed to taste with horse-radish.

COLESLAW AND COOKED HAM SPREAD

Cut a head of cabbage in half and shred paper thin, discarding the heart. Place shredded cabbage on a bread board and chop with a long knife until reduced to a fine mince. Put ham scraps or sliced boiled ham through a chopper and add to the cabbage with mayonnaise strongly flavored with lemon juice. Add celery seed and a little mustard seed and mix all together. Season with salt and pepper.

COCKTAIL FRANKFURTERS

Parboil frankfurters 5 minutes, peel, and cut in ½-inch pieces. Marinate in tart French dressing 1 hour. Serve with toothpicks.

CHEESE–STUFFED ROLLS

Mix 3 packages of Philadelphia cream cheese with 2 tablespoons of butter and 3 tablespoons of chopped chives. Season with Worcestershire sauce, paprika, and salt. Hollow out the centers of square French rolls and fill with the mixture. Wrap in waxed paper, place in the refrigerator, and let stand for 4 hours. Slice and serve.

ROQUEFORT CHEESE SPREAD

Mix ¼ pound each of butter and Roquefort cheese; add 2 cakes of cream cheese and mash together. Add 1 teaspoon of minced parsley, 1 teaspoon of anchovy paste, ½ teaspoon of lemon juice, and a dash of paprika. (Leave in refrigerator overnight.) When ready to use, thin to right consistency with cream. Serve in the center of a plate surrounded with crackers.

CHEESE AND SARDINE MOLD

Mix well the contents of 1 bottle of capers and 2 cans of sardines with 6 cakes of cream cheese. Add ½ cup of chopped parsley and the grated rind and juice of 1 lemon. Season well with salt, paprika, and a dash of Worcestershire sauce. Press into a round mold, cover, and chill in the refrigerator. Unmold on a platter and surround with Melba toast or pumpernickel fingers.

SPICED SARDINE PASTE

Mix mustard and mayonnaise with minced sardines and chopped water cress. Spread on thin slices of pumpernickel bread and sprinkle with paprika.

GREEN AND WHITE CHEESE

Blend thoroughly 4 tablespoons of butter with 2 packages of cream cheese. When smooth add 1 teaspoon of salt, 1 teaspoon of capers, ¼ teaspoon of paprika, 3 finely chopped green onions (using both green and white parts), and 2 finely chopped anchovies. Spread on small pieces of crisp toast.

PECAN AND CHEESE ROLL

Mix 3 packages of cream cheese and 1 section of Roquefort cheese with the juice of 1 small onion and a little cream. Form into a roll about 5 inches long. Roll in 2 tablespoons of ground pecans and then in chopped parsley. Chill in the refrigerator. Slice and serve on crackers or surrounded with squares of crisp toast.

MOCK PÂTÉ DE FOIE GRAS

Mix 3 tablespoons of mayonnaise and 1 cup of mashed liverwurst. Add ¼ cup of cooked mushrooms, finely chopped. Season to taste with salt and pepper. Add a little onion juice and combine all the ingredients. Serve with rounds of toast.

CHEESE STRAWS

Mix 1 cup of flour, ½ teaspoon of salt, 1 cup of freshly grated cheese, and 2 tablespoons of butter the size of an egg. Mix well, roll out, cut in long strips, and bake in a moderate oven.

MEAT AND CHEESE BALLS

Mash 1 6-ounce package of soft yellow cheese. Add 3 tablespoons of canned tongue and 3 tablespoons of any strongly flavored ready-cooked sausage, put through the meat chopper. Season with 1 teaspoon of Worcestershire sauce, a dash of cayenne, 1 tablespoon of sour pickle, chopped, and ¼ teaspoon of Colman's mustard. Mash the ingredients all together and shape into balls the size of a marble. Pile in a mound in the center of a glass plate decorated with parsley and surrounded with small round crackers.

CORNED BEEF SPREAD

Grind the contents of 1 can of corned beef, using the fine blade. Add 1 finely chopped onion and flavor with horse-radish and prepared mustard. Mix in enough mayonnaise to make the proper consistency for spreading. Serve with buttered rye bread and sliced dill pickles.

SHRIMPS WITH SAUCE

Serve shrimps, each one speared on a toothpick, around a bowl of mayonnaise seasoned with dry mustard, lemon, and chopped chives.

BLENDED CHEESE
(Stored in Jars)

These blended cheeses are excellent spreads to keep in your refrigerator as well as savory additions to your cocktail party menu. (Save large cold cream jars, paint the tops in different gay colors and use them for storing the cheese.)

Mash 1 package of Old English cheese and add port or sherry to taste. Put in a closed container and store in the refrigerator.

or

Mash ¼ pound of Roquefort or Stilton cheese and add 2 packages of cream cheese. Flavor with 2 teaspoons of horse-radish and 1 teaspoon of onion juice. Mix well and put in a covered container in the refrigerator.

FRENCH ONION SOUP
(Bee's)

This is the soup that we often serve at our cocktail parties:

Slice 3 onions fine and brown in a saucepan with 2 table-spoons of butter. Cook 15 minutes. Add 1 tablespoon of flour and mix thoroughly. Heat 3 cans of consommé in an earthenware casserole and add the onions. Simmer for 25 minutes. Season with salt and pepper. Mix 2 ounces each of grated Swiss and Parmesan cheese. Slice sour-dough French bread or rolls very thin and toast. Place the slices of bread on top of the soup and sprinkle with the cheese. Put under the broiler and brown for about 15 minutes.

CHAFING DISH SUGGESTIONS

WIENERS IN SOUR CREAM SAUCE

Heat 1 pint of sour cream in a chafing dish. Add prepared mustard to taste, then tomato chili sauce. Season with salt and pepper. (Be sure to prepare in this order, for the mustard taste must predominate.)

Cook skinless wieners in boiling water for about 10 minutes. Cut into inch-long pieces, spear with toothpicks and serve in the sauce.

CURRIED SHRIMPS

Prepare a thick cream sauce, and add onion juice and curry powder to taste. Dot thickly with shrimps speared with tooth-picks and serve in the chafing dish.

WELSH RAREBIT

Prepare 2 cups of cream sauce, using 2 tablespoons of butter, 2 tablespoons of flour to 2 cups of whole milk. Add 3 cups of freshly grated cheese, ¼ teaspoon of cayenne, and 4 teaspoons dry mustard. Stir until cheese is thoroughly blended. Flavor with 4 tablespoons of sherry. Serve in a chafing dish with an accompanying plate of Buttery Melba Toast.

FISH BALLS

Cut 1½ cups of codfish in small pieces and soak in lukewarm water for 1 hour. Peel and dice 4 medium-sized potatoes. Drain the codfish and cook with the potatoes until soft. Drain again; then add 1 well-beaten egg and ⅓ cup of milk. Beat until light and fluffy. Roll by small spoonfuls in finely crushed corn flakes. Fry in deep fat and drain on brown paper.

Prepare a rich cream sauce and pour into a chafing dish. Spear the fish balls with toothpicks and arrange in the cream sauce. Sprinkle with chopped parsley. (Finely chopped lobster and a little sherry may be added to the sauce.)

LOBSTER AND MUSHROOMS

To 1 cup of cream sauce add 1 finely grated onion. Add a wineglass each of cognac and sherry. Pour into a chafing dish. Sauté 1 pound of mushrooms and spear with toothpicks. Cut 2 pounds of lobster meat into cubes and also spear with toothpicks. Place both in the sauce in the chafing dish.

SHRIMPS IN SAUCE

Mix 4 tablespoons of tomato catsup, 1 tablespoon of anchovy paste, and 1 tablespoon of butter, and put in a chafing dish. Flavor with 1 tablespoon of brandy, 1 tablespoon of Worcestershire sauce, and a dash of Tabasco. Add 2 tablespoons of cream. Serve hot in a chafing dish with shrimps, speared with toothpicks.

This same sauce may be poured over sardines which have been broiled and placed on pieces of toast. This is also a suggestion for Sunday night supper.

~~~~~~~~~~~~~~~~~~~~~~~~~~~~~~~~~~~~~~~

The Buffet Dinner

~~~~~~~~~~~~~~~~~~~~~~~~~~~~~~~~~~~~~~~

Early in my career as a wife, I was faced with a situation that resembled a nightmare from which one awakes with cold sweat upon the brow. One Thanksgiving we were expecting three important guests for dinner; they were all males, and not only important in the public eye, but to our future as well. A number of strays had been added to the list, mostly friends who had no families to go to on this day. The party finally numbered twenty.

When I awoke on Thanksgiving morning, I knew that something was wrong. It wasn't the lack of "bustle" in my household, nor yet the unusual silence, but some sixth sense that made me aware of the awful truth — I had no maid! She had left without a word of warning.

Fortunately, even in those days, I had formed the habit of preparing everything ahead of time.

My turkey was already roasted and wrapped securely in its coat of Patapar paper, needing only to be reheated. My pies — apple and mince — I had baked the day before. The cranberry sauce had been cooked and stored in the refrigerator. The creamed onions would be easy to prepare, and the potatoes needed only to be boiled, mashed, and kept warm in the huge double boiler, with the yellow turnips heating beside them. Because of this early preparation, I was able to complete my dinner for twenty by myself.

Yes, I could do that, but who would help me serve the dinner? The turkey, true to the tradition of Thanksgiving, would be carved at the table, the vegetables served from the buffet, but how could I be in the kitchen attending to last minute details and at the same time in the drawing room looking after my guests of honor?

At last, in my hour of desperation, an idea came to me. As my eminent guests arrived, I asked, "Are you from the Globe Catering Company? So nice of you to help us out!" and as I rattled on, I bundled each of them into a large white apron and led them to the kitchen. Perhaps you can guess the rest. It was one of the best parties we ever gave. The other guests when seated at the table, offered numerous suggestions as the "butlers," amid hilarious coaching from the sidelines, served the dinner efficiently and with great dignity. So, remember, if such an emergency should arise when you are giving a dinner, don't worry too much and don't let it flurry you. Just relax, everything will turn out all right — that is, if you have planned your work ahead of time.

Never give a party unless that is what you definitely want to do. Inviting a group of guests to your home solely to repay social obligations is not likely to please either your friends or yourself. You are unlikely to become a popular hostess, if you have no feeling but relief when you have paid what you consider a compulsory debt. Invite your friends when you really want to see them and if you serve food that is unusual as well as delicious, your party is sure to be a success.

Be definite about the hour of your dinner. A careless hostess will invite you, tell you the day, but give no further information, leaving you to cross-examine her to find out if you are to wear a long dress and if your husband is to "wear a black tie." Next, you are forced to inquire, "What time is dinner?" only to receive the vague answer, "Oh, I don't know! About seven-thirty or quarter to eight, or perhaps eight would be better."

Certainly, if the hostess doesn't know when dinner is to be served, the guests will not be definite about it. They will straggle in for hours, and the food, when it finally arrives, will have suffered from the delay just as much as the guests.

Popular parties open with a punch. So be sure to dust off that charm and have the warmth of hospitality ready for each group of guests as they arrive. And equally important — have a drink

ready for them — immediately! Don't let your guests feel they are
kept waiting for the curtain to go up. Remember it is important
that your party get off to a good start.

You may wish to seat your guests at one long table in the
dining room. If your table is too small, cover it with a false top;
you will be surprised at the number of additional guests this
will allow you to seat. Some hostesses prefer to arrange the dinner
on the dining-room table and seat their guests at small tables
placed throughout the house. But whether you use large or
small tables, do have place cards. Unless you plan your seating
ahead of time, you are sure to discover a group of "widows" all
alone at one table and a few timid souls huddled together at another. Place cards will eliminate all this confusion and everyone
will have a much better time.

Now that we have considered the guests, let us think about the
food. I hope you have courage enough to serve something new,
something different from the old stand-bys found at nearly every
supper. For example, have you ever tried braised oxtail? I
served this very delicious dish at a dinner party not long ago and
the reaction of my guests was: "I don't know why we never have
food like this in our home."

If you should decide to serve oxtail, arrange it attractively with
accompanying vegetables. The carrots should be little ones, fresh
from the garden; the onions should be wee bits of white; and
the potatoes tiny new ones or little balls cut from larger ones.
And don't forget the sherry in the sauce. It helps to make any
dish festive. If you have a large earthenware casserole, cook
the oxtail in it, and bring it right into the dining room with your
beautiful china, crystal, and silver. You'll be surprised to see
how well the casserole will look in its formal surroundings.

Start cooking your meat in the morning and let it bubble
peacefully over a slow fire while you fix the vegetables. Then
wash all the greens which you are going to put in the salad,
wrap them in a damp cloth, and pop them into the refrigerator.
See that your salad dressing is ready and set the table. You are
through until it is almost time to serve dinner, because undoubtedly you made your dessert the day before.

Perhaps your friends might like little hamburgers flavored with wine and floating in a sea of canned mushroom soup or sour cream; or they might prefer small codfish balls with a sauce of creamed lobster. Both are a change from the baked ham and roast turkey that you meet at so many buffet parties.

Many extra steps will be saved if the dessert plate is placed in front of the guest as the soiled dinner plate is removed. The dessert may be served from a large platter or arranged individually on each plate, or you may prefer to let your guests help themselves from the buffet.

The buffet dinner offers innumerable opportunities to add a touch of originality to your party. One friend of mine hung a large sign on her front door, "The Kit Kat Club." When her guests arrived, they were peeked at through the grating in the door — reminiscent of the days of the speak-easy—and were asked appropriate and amusing questions before they were allowed to enter. Another friend who serves marvelous Italian food calls her dining room "Little Joe's Restaurant — Open Thursday Night Only." The entire dinner is carried out in this atmosphere; red and white tablecloths, candles stuck in old wine bottles, bowls of fruit on the tables, and all food served in pottery casseroles. Innumerable other ideas can be originated for the informal buffet dinner, such as a Spanish motif or a beach or yacht party with appropriate decorations.

But remember that delicious food, attractively arranged, conveys the wish of the poised, relaxed hostess: "Accept this hospitality that comes from my heart, and share with me the best I have to offer."

Menu

CURRIED CHICKEN SERVED IN
PINEAPPLE SHELLS

CONDIMENTS

CHUTNEY

BOILED RICE

BOILED CELERY ROOT

PINEAPPLE CUBES IN RUM

PETITS SABLÉS PARISIENS

CURRIED CHICKEN SERVED IN PINEAPPLE SHELLS

Cook a 5-pound hen in boiling salted water until tender. Remove the skin and bones and cut the meat into small pieces. Put 4 onions and 1 clove of garlic through the food chopper. Simmer in 5 tablespoons of butter but do not brown. Add 5 tablespoons of flour and stir until blended. Then add 1 quart of hot chicken broth, 2 tablespoons of curry powder (dissolved in a little stock), juice of ½ lemon, and 1 teaspoon of grated lemon rind. Let simmer for 15 minutes. Add 1½ cups of cream or evaporated milk and taste for seasoning. Add the chicken. It may now be put in the refrigerator until about ½ hour before serving. Reheat in the top of a double boiler.

Cut a pineapple in half lengthwise and carefully remove as much of the fruit as possible. If you cut the fruit in slices across (being careful not to cut into the shell), you can work your knife between the fruit and shell and the fruit will come out in large pieces. Save all the fruit and juice to use for dessert. Cover shells with waxed paper until ready for use. About ½ hour before dinner, heat shells in the oven. Remove, and fill with the chicken, which has been heating in a double boiler. Serves 6 to 8.

CONDIMENTS

Condiments to be served with curry: homemade chutney, chopped peanuts, chopped white of hard-boiled egg, chopped yolks, chopped green onion, chopped fried bacon, and fresh or dried cocoanut. These are very attractive when served in little Chinese bowls with Chinese spoons and arranged on a lacquered tray.

CHUTNEY

2 whole lemons (seeds removed and lemons chopped fine)
1 box seeded raisins
2 pounds brown sugar
2 cloves of garlic, chopped fine
1 medium-sized jar preserved ginger, cut fine
2 pounds rhubarb, cut fine
Cayenne pepper and salt to taste

Mix all ingredients and cook very slowly until thick and syrupy. Fill sterilized jars and seal.

BOILED RICE

Wash and drain 1½ cups of rice. Boil 3 quarts of water and add 1½ teaspoons of salt. Drop rice slowly into water so as not to retard the boiling. Cook it without stirring until it is tender, about 25 minutes. Place rice in a strainer and let cold water run over it. To reheat, place the strainer of rice uncovered over boiling water, or cover and put it in a warm oven.

BOILED CELERY ROOT

Boil celery root in salted water. Peel and cut in small strips. Add grated onion and toss lightly with melted butter and chopped parsley. (Prepare in the morning and reheat.)

PINEAPPLE CUBES IN RUM

Cut pineapple in uniform pieces. Add juice and put into a glass bowl. Pour over 1 cup of rum and sprinkle with powdered sugar. Place in the refrigerator until thoroughly chilled. (Prepare in the morning.) Serve with sprigs of mint leaves over the top.

PETITS SABLÉS PARISIENS

Cream together ½ cup of sweet butter and ¾ cup of granulated sugar. Add 3 yolks and 1 white of egg beaten well together. Mix well; then add 1 teaspoon of vanilla and, if procurable, 1 teaspoon of orange flower water. Add 2 cups of sifted flour and mix until smooth. Toss onto a lightly floured board and roll out to about ¼-inch thickness. Cut with a large, fluted, round cutter, and then cut in fours. Put the cookies on buttered tins and bake in a moderate oven (350°) until a light brown.

Menu

SPICED BOILED TONGUE

CHOPPED SPINACH RING FILLED WITH
CREAMED RADISHES

BAKED STUFFED POTATOES

CUCUMBER SALAD WITH TOMATO
ANDRÉ DRESSING

ICEBOX CAKE OF PEACH AND PINEAPPLE

SPICED BOILED TONGUE

1 fresh beef tongue	2 chopped onions
1 tablespoon salt	1 cup vinegar
¼ cup mixed pickling spices	1 clove garlic

Place the tongue in a large kettle and cover with boiling water. Add the other ingredients and simmer for 3 hours, or until very tender. Remove tongue from liquor and peel. Serve hot with spinach ring or cold as a sliced meat.

CHOPPED SPINACH RING FILLED WITH CREAMED RADISHES

Boil 1 bunch, or ½ pound, of spinach for each person. Drain and chop fine. Press out the juice and put the spinach into a greased ring mold, pressing it down firmly. (Prepare in the morning.) Place mold in a pan of hot water, cover, and heat in a moderate oven. Unmold on a large serving platter and fill the center with Creamed Radishes.

Creamed Radishes. — Make a rich cream sauce. Peel and boil radishes until tender. Add to the cream sauce. (Prepare in the morning.) Reheat in a double boiler before serving.

CUCUMBER SALAD WITH TOMATO

Soak 1 tablespoon of gelatine in 1 tablespoon of cold water. Dissolve over hot water. Whip ½ pint of cream stiff and fold in the gelatine. Add 1 tablespoon of tarragon vinegar and season with salt, pepper, and cayenne. Fold in 1 cup of finely chopped cucumber. Fill individual molds and chill until firm. (Prepare the day before.) Place a thick slice of peeled tomato in a lettuce leaf on each plate. Season with salt and pepper. Place a cucumber jelly mold on top of each tomato slice and pour André Dressing over all.

André Dressing. — Mix ½ cup of French dressing with 4 tablespoons of mayonnaise. Season with salt, pepper, and paprika. Add 1 teaspoon of Worcestershire sauce and 2 tablespoons each of chopped parsley and chopped chives.

ICEBOX CAKE OF PEACH AND PINEAPPLE

Cook together in top of double boiler 1 cup of puréed peaches (from canned peaches), ½ cup of crushed pineapple, ½ cup of granulated sugar, and 2 well-beaten eggs. Stir constantly until thick. Cool. Cream ½ cup of butter with 1 cup of powdered sugar and add to the first mixture. Fold in 1 cup of cream which has been whipped. In the bottom of a mold arrange a layer of split ladyfingers and cover with some of the fruit and cream mixture; then more ladyfingers and fruit, and ladyfingers for the top layer. Put in the refrigerator for 24 hours. Unmold and serve with whipped cream. Serves 6.

Menu

BEEF WITH TOMATOES AND SOUR CREAM
EN CASSEROLE

ZUCCHINI AND CORN PUDDING

RICE BROWNED IN OLIVE OIL

CELERY ROOT SALAD

APRICOTS WITH RUM SAUCE

BEEF WITH TOMATOES AND SOUR CREAM EN CASSEROLE

Cut 1½ pounds of round steak in strips 1½ inches long and ¼ inch wide. Cut the meat across the grain; otherwise it will be stringy and tough. Melt 2 tablespoons of butter or bacon fat in a skillet, and when hot add the meat strips and brown quickly. In a French earthenware casserole melt 2 tablespoons of bacon fat and add 1 grated onion. Cook until slightly brown and then stir in 2 tablespoons of flour. Blend. Add 1 can of tomato soup, 1 teaspoon of prepared mustard, 1 cup of sour cream, 1 teaspoon of salt, and a dash of pepper. Let boil up and then add the meat. Add 4 tablespoons of water to the pan in which the meat was browned, boil, and add to the casserole. Mix thoroughly. (Prepare in the morning.) Bake in a moderate oven (350°) for 40 minutes. Serves 6.

ZUCCHINI AND CORN PUDDING

Cook 6 large zucchini in boiling salted water until tender. Chop and drain. Chop fine 2 onions, 2 cloves of garlic, and 1 bell pepper. Sauté in butter. Cool and mix with the zucchini. (Prepare in the morning.) Add ½ cup of grated cheese, 5 well-beaten eggs, and 1 can of small kernel corn. Stir in ¼ cup of butter and pour into a baking dish. Place in a pan of hot water and bake in a slow oven for half an hour. Serves 6.

CELERY ROOT SALAD

Cut raw celery root in julienne strips, keeping it white by covering it with water to which lemon juice has been added. (Prepare in the morning.) Drain, when ready to serve, and toss lightly with French dressing. Serve on lettuce leaves, accompanied by a bowl of Mustard Dressing (p. 75).

APRICOTS WITH RUM SAUCE

Place 1 can of halved, peeled apricots in a baking dish with the cut-side up. Fill the cavity with coarsely chopped almonds dotted with a little butter. Brown under the broiler and serve with Rum Sauce.

Rum Sauce. —

2 eggs	3 tablespoons rum
4 scant tablespoons sugar	¼ cup whipping cream

Beat eggs thoroughly and slowly add sugar, then rum. At the last, fold in the whipped cream. Serves 6.

Menu

CHICKEN COOKED IN PORT WINE

STUFFED BAKED SWEET POTATOES

EGGPLANT FRITTERS

ITALIAN STRING BEANS

PULLED BREAD

TOSSED GREEN SALAD

ALMOND RING

CHICKEN COOKED IN PORT WINE

Cut 2 frying chickens, weighing about 2 pounds each, into serving pieces (discarding necks, backs, and tips of wings). Melt, but do not brown, ½ cup of butter in an earthenware casserole and, when hot, add the chicken pieces and cover immediately. Turn the fire very low and simmer for half an hour. Season with salt and pepper and add 1 cup of white port wine. Cook for another half hour and add ¼ pound of whole canned mushrooms. Continue cooking for 15 minutes. Stir in 1 cup of cream sauce, mixed with 1½ cups of cream. Cover and simmer slowly for about 15 minutes, until the chicken is tender. (Prepare in the morning.) When ready to serve, add ½ cup of sherry, and reheat in a slow oven. Sprinkle a thick covering of chopped, browned almonds over the top and serve in the casserole. Serves 4 to 6.

STUFFED BAKED SWEET POTATOES

Bake 6 sweet potatoes, cut in half lengthwise, and scoop out the pulp. Mash with butter, the juice and grated rind of 1 orange, and a pinch of salt. Pile mashed potato roughly in the skins, brush over with melted butter and sprinkle lightly with sugar. Prepare potatoes in the morning, cover with waxed paper, and keep in the refrigerator until later. Bake slowly in a covered pan for 30 minutes before serving. Brown under the broiler.

EGGPLANT FRITTERS

Peel and cook an eggplant until tender. Drain, mash, and season with salt and pepper. Add 1 egg, 2 teaspoons of baking powder, and enough flour to hold together. Form into round cakes, dredge with flour, and fry in deep fat. Serves 6.

ITALIAN STRING BEANS

String and shred 2 pounds of string beans and cook in boiling salted water until tender. Drain. Sauté 2 mashed cloves of garlic in 4 tablespoons of butter. Remove the garlic, pour the butter over the beans, and mix gently. (Prepare in the morning.) Reheat and sprinkle a little grated Parmesan cheese over the beans before serving. Serves 6.

ALMOND RING
(Peggy's)

Whip 3 whole eggs and 3 yolks with 1 cup of granulated sugar until very light. Crush fine 4 large soda crackers and add to the eggs. Grind ½ pound of almonds, including the brown skin, and add to the mixture. Stir in a pinch of salt, ½ teaspoon of nutmeg, and the grated rind of 1 lemon. Fold in 3 egg whites, beaten stiff, and pour the mixture into a buttered ring mold. Bake 40 minutes in a slow oven (275°). Invert the mold and let cool. Loosen the pudding (with a knife), remove to a platter, and dust with powdered sugar. When ready to serve, fill the center with 2 cups of sweetened whipped cream, flavored with vanilla, and mixed with 1½ cups of crushed raspberries. (Prepare ahead of time.)

Menu

POT ROAST WITH OLIVES

GRATED POTATO CAKES WITH BACON

CURRIED CELERY ROOT

CORN PUDDING RING FILLED WITH BUTTERED CARROTS

GREEN SALAD WITH SPECIAL DRESSING

NUT CRUST FILLED WITH BANANA CREAM

POT ROAST WITH OLIVES

Make gashes in a 4-pound pot roast and insert small stuffed olives and bits of bacon. Brown meat thoroughly in bacon fat. Add 1 onion chopped, 1 clove of garlic minced, 1 teaspoon of mustard, 1 teaspoon of ginger, 1 can of tomato paste, and 1 tablespoon of Worcestershire sauce. Cover and simmer slowly for 3 hours, adding hot water as needed. Serves 6.

GRATED POTATO CAKES WITH BACON

Grate 1 potato per person and mix with finely chopped raw bacon. Press down in an iron skillet to make a large cake or mold into small cakes. Brown first on one side and then on the other, cooking until the potatoes and bacon are done.

CURRIED CELERY ROOT

Boil celery root; peel and cut in narrow strips. Mix in finely minced onion and add cream sauce seasoned with curry, salt, and pepper. (Prepare in the morning and reheat in a double boiler.)

CORN PUDDING RING FILLED WITH BUTTERED CARROTS

Drain a No.-2 can of cream style corn and reserve the liquid. Melt 2 tablespoons of butter and stir in 2 tablespoons of flour until well blended. Add slowly 1 cup of cream and the corn liquid, stirring all the time. Cook until thick. Add the drained corn and heat again. Beat 2 egg yolks and pour part of the hot corn mixture over them. Beat well and return to the rest of the corn. Cook slowly until thick. Add ¾ teaspoon of salt and cool. (Prepare in the morning.) Add ⅛ teaspoon of salt to the 2 egg whites and beat until stiff. Fold them lightly into the corn and pour the mixture into a well-greased ring mold. Bake in a 350° oven for about 20 minutes, until firm. Unmold and fill with hot, chopped, buttered carrots. Serves 6.

NUT CRUST FILLED WITH BANANA CREAM
(Jane's)

Nut Crust. — Grind enough Brazil nuts to make 1½ cups of the powdered nuts. Add 3 tablespoons of sugar and press in the bottom and on the sides of a glass pie dish to make a crust. Fill with Banana Cream Filling.

Banana Cream Filling. — Beat 3 egg yolks and add gradually, while still beating, 2½ tablespoons of cornstarch, ⅔ cup of sugar, and ¼ teaspoon of salt. Melt 1 tablespoon of butter in 2 cups of scalded milk and pour over the egg mixture. Cook in a double boiler until thick. Cool. Flavor with 1 teaspoon of vanilla.

Pour half of this mixture into the nut crust and cover with peeled, sliced bananas. Cover the bananas with the rest of the custard and chill for several hours in the refrigerator. Grind glacéed Brazil nuts in the meat grinder and sprinkle them thickly over the top just before serving.

> ## Menu
>
> BAKED HAM SUPRÊME
>
> MUSTARD SAUCE
>
> BRANDIED SWEET POTATOES
>
> CABBAGE SOUFFLÉ WITH
> ASSORTED VEGETABLES
>
> TOMATO ASPIC WITH JELLIED MAYONNAISE
>
> FRUIT PLATTER
>
> THIN VANILLA WAFERS

BAKED HAM SUPRÊME

Our guests always comment on the fine flavor of our baked hams. I believe it is the seasonings added to the water when the hams are boiled that gives them this unusual touch. The coating of white pepper also adds a new note. But don't overlook Margaret's Mustard Sauce. It may be made ahead of time and keeps well in the refrigerator.

Wash and weigh the ham. Place in a large roasting pan with a lid. Add 2 cups of granulated sugar, 1 cup of apple cider vinegar, 1 stick of cinnamon, 1 dozen whole cloves, and 6 allspice berries. Fill the pan with water, place the lid on tight, put into a 350° oven, and cook 20 minutes per pound, turning the ham often. (Count the time after the water begins to boil. A tenderized ham will require only 15 minutes per pound for cooking.) When cooked, let cool in the liquid. (May be boiled the day before.)

When cooled, gently remove the top skin, being careful not to take the fat off with it. Place the ham in another pan and stud at intervals with cloves. Sprinkle liberally with white pepper; then spread a layer of brown sugar over all. Pour 1 cup of sherry into the pan and place the pan, without the lid, in a very slow oven, about 250°, for 1 hour. The slow heat allows the spicy flavor of the pepper to penetrate the meat. After ½ hour, gently baste the ham every 10 minutes with the gravy. Remove the pan from the oven, cover, and keep hot on top of the stove with a very low heat. Use asbestos mats under the pan.

The oven is now free to take care of the rest of the dinner. Serve the ham with Mustard Sauce, which may be made the day before and reheated in a double boiler. This sauce will keep indefinitely in the refrigerator.

MUSTARD SAUCE
(Margaret's)

Combine 2 teaspoons of dry mustard, ¼ teaspoon of salt, 1 teaspoon of granulated sugar, and 2 tablespoons of flour. Place in the top of a double boiler. Add ¾ cup of water and 2 tablespoons of heated vinegar, stirring as it cooks until it becomes a smooth, creamy sauce. Then add 2 egg yolks, slightly beaten, and 2 tablespoons of melted butter. When thickened, lift the pan from the hot water immediately to prevent the curdling of the egg yolks. Prepare the day before your party, but when reheating do not allow the water to boil underneath the sauce.

BRANDIED SWEET POTATOES

Boil 6 medium-sized sweet potatoes. Peel and arrange in a baking dish. (Prepare in the morning.) Mix ½ cup of water with 1½ cups of brown sugar. Bring to a boil and pour over the potatoes. Bake in a moderate oven (350°) for 20 minutes. Open the oven door (keeping potatoes warm), and pour ⅓ cup of brandy over the potatoes. Add 4 tablespoons of melted butter and baste with sauce continually for 10 minutes. Place under the broiler to brown, and serve. Serves 6.

CABBAGE SOUFFLÉ WITH ASSORTED VEGETABLES

Remove center and slice a large head of cabbage. Cook for from 5 to 10 minutes in boiling, salted water. (This should be done in the morning to eliminate the odor of cooking.) Drain and chop very fine. Use 4 cupfuls, season with salt and pepper, and add 1 tablespoon of butter and 3 tablespoons of cream. Beat the whites of 6 eggs very stiff and fold into the cabbage. Fill a buttered ring mold and place in a pan of hot water in a moderate oven. Bake for 25 to 30 minutes. Unmold on a platter and surround with mounds of well-seasoned, cooked string beans sliced lengthwise; fill the center of the mold with diced, buttered carrots. Serves 6 to 8.

TOMATO ASPIC WITH JELLIED MAYONNAISE

Jellied Mayonnaise. — For the jellied mayonnaise, soak 1 tablespoon of gelatine in ¼ cup of cold water. Dissolve in 1¼ cups of boiling water. Chill, and when it starts to thicken, add ½ cup of mayonnaise seasoned with a little onion juice and dry mustard. Pour into a fancy mold and place in the refrigerator until firm. Add the tomato aspic to make a second layer.

Tomato Aspic. — Cook tomatoes (1 large can) with 1 teaspoon of salt, ½ teaspoon of paprika, 3 tablespoons of chopped onion, 2 tablespoons of lemon juice, 1½ teaspoons of sugar, 4 stalks of celery, and 1 bay leaf. Let simmer for ½ hour. Strain. Add enough hot water to make 3 cups. Soak 2 tablespoons of gelatine in ½ cup of cold water and dissolve in the hot tomato juice. Season with Worcestershire sauce and a little horse-radish. Cool. Pour the gelatine on top of the jellied mayonnaise, which must be firm. (Prepare the day before your party.) Unmold on a platter and surround with water cress. Serves 6 to 8.

FRUIT PLATTER
(Harriet's)

Drain 1 can of peaches and 1 can of figs. Place in a bowl and pour over them 1 can of whole apricots, juice and all. Pour California brandy over the fruit, cover, and let stand overnight. Chill and drain canned grapes and canned pitted Bing cherries.

In the center of a large platter place a small bunch of mint leaves. Around the mint form the grapes in bunches, interspersed with groups of 2 or 3 cherries with green leaves. Beyond them should come the peaches, with the apricots and figs arranged alternately as to color, with more green leaves. Pour the brandied juice over all. Serves 6 to 8.

THIN VANILLA WAFERS

Mix thoroughly ½ cup of sugar and ½ cup of shortening. Add 1 well-beaten egg and beat all together. Sift together ¾ cup of flour and ½ teaspoon of salt. Stir into the egg mixture and beat vigorously. Add ½ teaspoon of vanilla. Drop like marbles from a teaspoon onto a well-greased cooky sheet, spacing them far apart. Place an English walnut meat in the center of each cooky. Bake in a 400° oven for 10 to 15 minutes.

Menu

BEEF À LA MODE

TINY CROOKED-NECK SQUASHES

BAKED TOMATO AND CHEESE À LA STUART

POTATO CROQUETTES WITH PEANUTS

WATER CRESS SALAD

PEPPERMINT BAVARIAN CREAM
WITH HOT CHOCOLATE SAUCE

BEEF À LA MODE

Lard a 4- or 5-pound pot roast with strips of salt pork, cutting the incisions to run with the grain of the meat. Place in a deep casserole or in a Dutch oven. Brown in bacon fat. Add ½ cup of chopped celery, 12 tiny onions or 2 large ones, sliced, ½ cup of diced carrots, 1 teaspoon of minced parsley, 1 bay leaf, salt, and pepper. Add 1 can of consommé and 2 cups of white wine. Cover and cook slowly on top of the stove for about 4 hours. Slice and serve hot with thickened gravy. Serves 6.

TINY CROOKED–NECK SQUASHES

Use the very tiny yellow squashes and cook whole in boiling salted water until they are nearly tender. (May be prepared in the morning.) Heat a mixture of oil and butter in an iron skillet to the depth of ¼ inch and reheat the squashes in the hot fat. Sauté gently until brown on all sides. Sprinkle with salt and pepper. Arrange around the roast as a garnish.

BAKED TOMATO AND CHEESE À LA STUART

Dice 1 onion and 1 green pepper into small pieces. Cook in butter, but do not brown. Mix in 1 tablespoon of flour, ½ teaspoon of salt, and ½ teaspoon of mixed herbs or thyme. Put 3 cups of canned tomatoes in a casserole, add the onion mixture, and stir until they are well mixed. (Prepare in the morning.) Later sprinkle grated Parmesan cheese over the top, dot with butter, and bake for 30 minutes in a moderate oven until nicely browned. Serves 4 to 6.

POTATO CROQUETTES WITH PEANUTS

Shape into small croquettes 4 cups of hot mashed potatoes. Cool. Dip in 1 egg, beaten with 2 tablespoons of water. Roll in peanuts, ground and crushed until fine. (Prepare in the morning.) Later fry in deep fat. Drain on brown paper, and serve at once. Serves 6.

WATER CRESS SALAD

Wash and pick over water cress. Place in a salad bowl and chill in the refrigerator. Sprinkle chopped green onions or chives over the water cress, and gently mix with French dressing when ready to serve.

PEPPERMINT BAVARIAN CREAM

Soak 1½ tablespoons of gelatine in ¼ cup of milk. Add ½ teaspoon of salt to 1¾ cups of milk and scald in the top of a double boiler with ½ pound of peppermint candy, which has been crushed. When the candy is melted, add the gelatine and stir until it is thoroughly mixed and dissolved. Cool quickly. When it begins to thicken, beat until light and fold in ½ pint of cream, whipped. Pour into a decorative mold. (Prepare the day before.) Serve with Hot Chocolate Sauce (p. 43) sprinkled with chopped nuts.

Menu

PORK LEG STUFFED WITH MUSHROOMS

BAKED ORANGES

HOMINY GRITS

PURPLE CABBAGE WITH GRAPE JUICE SAUCE

SPINACH CROQUETTES

STRAWBERRY MERINGUE

PORK LEG STUFFED WITH MUSHROOMS

Have the butcher bone a leg of pork. Fill with Mushroom Stuffing; tie the meat together or fasten with metal skewers. Place in a roaster, the fat side of the meat on the top. Roast in a hot oven (450°) for 30 minutes. Reduce temperature to 325° and cook according to the weight, allowing 40 minutes per pound.

Mushroom Stuffing. —

⅓ cup chopped onions	4 cups soft bread crumbs
¼ cup butter	½ teaspoon sage
1 teaspoon salt	Pepper
1 pound mushrooms, sautéed in butter	

Sauté onions in the butter, but do not brown. Add the bread crumbs, salt, sage, and pepper. Mix all lightly, then add the mushrooms, and place stuffing in the roast.

BAKED ORANGES

Cut large oranges in half, remove the pulp, and crimp the edges of the orange peel cups. Add finely diced canned pineapple to the orange pulp and mix with orange marmalade. Place back in the orange skins. (Prepare ahead of time.) Later bake for ½ hour in a moderate oven (350°). Ten minutes before removing from the oven, cover the fruit mixture with finely ground walnuts. Serve hot.

HOMINY GRITS

Cook in a double boiler 2 cups of hominy grits with 1½ quarts of water for about 2 hours. Add salt to taste and a large piece of butter. Serves 8.

PURPLE CABBAGE WITH GRAPE JUICE SAUCE

Chop fine 1 onion and cook in 4 tablespoons of fat for 3 minutes. Add 4 cups of shredded purple cabbage and 1 cup of grape juice. Slice 2 sour apples and add to the cabbage with 2 teaspoons of salt. Cook for 25 minutes, until the cabbage is tender. Add 4 tablespoons of vinegar and 2 tablespoons of sugar. Cook 5 minutes. Serves 6. (Prepare ahead of time and reheat.)

SPINACH CROQUETTES

Boil 3 pounds of spinach with as little water as possible for 20 minutes. Drain and chop fine. Chop 1 onion fine and cook in butter until soft, but do not brown. Mix well with the spinach and add 1 slice of fried bacon, chopped fine. Stir in 1 cup of cream sauce and heat slowly. Add the beaten yolks of 2 eggs and stir over the fire for 2 minutes. Spread on a buttered pan and let cool. Form into croquettes. Roll in sifted bread crumbs, then in a slightly beaten egg, and in the crumbs again. (Prepare in the morning.) Later fry in deep fat until brown. Serves 6 to 8.

STRAWBERRY MERINGUE

Grease a ring mold. Beat 6 egg whites very stiff and while beating add slowly 1 cup of sugar and 1 teaspoon of cream of tartar. Add 1½ teaspoons of vinegar and 1 teaspoon of vanilla. Put this mixture in the ring mold, set in a pan of water, and bake in a slow oven (325°) for 1 hour. When cool, take out of the mold and place on a glass serving platter. (Prepare in the morning.) Fill the center with strawberries mixed with whipped cream and arrange extra berries around the outside.

Serve with a custard sauce made from the egg yolks. Serves 6.

Menu

HUNGARIAN BEEF STEW

BAKED ONIONS STUFFED WITH
MASHED POTATOES

CORN BAKED WITH GREEN PEPPER

STRING BEAN SALAD

BLACKBERRY ICE CREAM

SPICED ANGEL FOOD CAKE

HUNGARIAN BEEF STEW

Cut 2 pounds of round steak in long strips, cutting across the grain. Brown in butter or bacon fat. Add 5 onions, chopped fine. Put in a covered casserole and add ½ teaspoon of salt, ¼ teaspoon of pepper, 1 clove of garlic cut fine, ⅛ teaspoon of marjoram, and ¾ cup of white wine. Stew until the meat is tender; then add ½ pound of fried, chopped bacon and 2 cups of sour cream. Put the lid on the casserole and leave in the oven about ½ hour, but do not let the cream bubble. Serve in the casserole. (May be prepared the day before and reheated.) Serves 6.

BAKED ONIONS STUFFED WITH MASHED POTATOES

Remove skins from 8 Bermuda onions and parboil 10 minutes in boiling salted water. Drain; then remove the center. Pour 1 cup of canned consommé over the onions and bake in the oven until tender, basting frequently. Peel and boil 6 potatoes; mash. Add hot milk. Season with salt, pepper, and butter. Beat until fluffy. Fill the centers of the onions with mashed potatoes, and sprinkle buttered crumbs over the top. (May be prepared in the morning.) Later bake in a slow oven to reheat and brown.

CORN BAKED WITH GREEN PEPPER

Mix 4 cups of freshly grated corn or cream style canned corn, 1 finely chopped green pepper, 4 beaten egg yolks, and ½ cup of butter, melted. Stir until well blended, pour into a casserole, and bake in a moderate oven until browned.

STRING BEAN SALAD

Remove the strings from 3 pounds of string beans, but leave whole. Tie in bunches and cook in boiling salted water until tender. Drain. When cool, marinate in French dressing. (Prepare the day before and leave in the refrigerator.) Remove ties and serve on a round platter; the bunches of string beans alternating with romaine lettuce leaves. Place a bowl of French dressing in the center.

BLACKBERRY ICE CREAM

Soak 1 tablespoon of gelatine in ¼ cup of cold water. Empty 1 large jar of blackberry jam into the top of a double boiler. Heat and strain. Add the gelatine to the strained jam and reheat in the top of a double boiler until the gelatine is dissolved. Cool. Add ¾ cup of cassis liqueur and 2 cups of cream, whipped. Pour into the freezing tray of the refrigerator and freeze. Serves 6.

SPICED ANGEL FOOD CAKE

Sift 1 cup of cake flour and mix with ½ teaspoon of salt, 1 teaspoon of cinnamon, ½ teaspoon of nutmeg, ¼ teaspoon of cloves, and ½ cup of sugar. Sift this mixture 4 times. Place 10 egg whites on a platter and whip with a wire whisk until fluffy; then add 1 teaspoon of cream of tartar and continue whipping until the whites are stiff. Sift 1 cup of sugar and whip gradually into the whites; later add 1 teaspoon of vanilla. Fold the flour mixture in gradually. Pour the batter into an ungreased 9-inch tube pan and bake for 1 hour, starting with the oven at 250° and increasing gradually to 325°.

Menu

LAMB SHANKS

SCALLOPED POTATOES WITH BACON ON TOP

STUFFED ARTICHOKES WITH
NEVER-FAIL HOLLANDAISE SAUCE

COLESLAW WITH CHOPPED PEANUTS

PINEAPPLE COTTAGE CHEESE CAKE

LAMB SHANKS

Have you the courage to serve these lamb shanks to your guests? If so, don't be surprised if they think they are turkey legs.

Allow 1 shank per person. (Do not allow the butcher to crack the bone.) Salt and pepper each one and roll in flour. Melt some fat in a roasting pan, add the shanks, and brown in a hot oven. Add some sliced onions and a tiny bit of garlic. Season with celery salt, sage, poultry seasoning, and coarse black pepper. Sprinkle a little water over the lamb. Put on the lid and bake in a medium oven (350°) for 1 to 1½ hours. These may be prepared the day before and reheated.

Remove shanks to a serving platter, add some Kitchen Bouquet to the gravy, if necessary, to darken it, taste for seasoning, and strain into a bowl. Place the bowl of gravy in the center of the platter, surround with the lamb shanks, and decorate with parsley.

SCALLOPED POTATOES WITH BACON ON TOP

Peel and slice thin the required number of potatoes. Put a layer of potatoes in a baking dish, sprinkle with salt and pepper, and dot with butter. Cover with other layers of potatoes, seasoning, and butter, until all the potatoes have been used. Cover with milk to the depth of the potatoes. Place strips of bacon on the top and bake in a moderate oven (350°) until the potatoes are soft and well browned.

STUFFED ARTICHOKES

Boil artichokes until tender. Remove the leaves and the choke (the prickly center) and fill the cavity with chopped, boiled onions. Cover with a layer of bread crumbs mixed with butter and grated Gruyère cheese. (Prepare in the morning.) Reheat in a casserole in a hot oven until the crumbs are brown. Serve with Never-Fail Hollandaise Sauce (p. 89).

COLESLAW WITH CHOPPED PEANUTS

Cut a head of cabbage in half and shred the leaves paper-thin, discarding the heart. Place shredded cabbage on a breadboard and chop with a long knife until reduced to a fine mince. Chop peanuts in a wooden chopping bowl, or put them through the grinder, using the coarse blade, and add to the cabbage. Mix with mayonnaise flavored with lemon. Season with salt and pepper.

PINEAPPLE COTTAGE CHEESE CAKE

Mix 2 cups of finely rolled corn flakes, ½ cup of melted butter, 4 tablespoons of sugar, and 1 teaspoon of cinnamon. Pack three quarters of this mixture in the bottom and on the sides of a spring mold. Pour in the pineapple filling and sprinkle with the remaining crumbs. Chill in the refrigerator until firm.

Pineapple Filling. — Beat 3 egg yolks with ½ cup of sugar, a pinch of salt, and 1 cup of milk. Place in the top of a double boiler and cook until thick. Soak 2 tablespoons of gelatine with 2 tablespoons of cold water and dissolve in the hot custard mixture. Press 1 pound of cottage cheese through a wire sieve. Add the juice and grated rind of 1 lemon, 1 teaspoon of vanilla, and ½ cup of crushed pineapple. Mix thoroughly and fold in the stiffly beaten egg whites and ½ cup of cream, whipped. Pour into the crust. Serves 6. (Prepare the day before.)

Menu

PORK CHOPS BAKED WITH
MUSHROOMS AND NUTS

CINNAMON APPLES

SWEET POTATO PUDDING

PEAS WITH CREAM AND BACON

HORSE-RADISH MOLD

SHREDDED CARROT AND CELERY SALAD

BRANDIED FRUIT RING

PORK CHOPS BAKED WITH MUSHROOMS AND NUTS

Brown 6 pork chops in a French casserole. Add 1 small can of evaporated milk. Cover and bake in a slow oven for 1 hour. Add 1 can of mushroom soup, 1 small can of mushrooms, and 1 teaspoon of salt. Bake for half an hour. Sprinkle with 1 cup of chopped walnuts or almonds, browned in butter. Serve in casserole. Serves 6.

CINNAMON APPLES

Peel and core 4 baking apples. Boil ½ cup of sugar, 1 cup of water, and ¼ cup of cinnamon drops. Let the cinnamon drops dissolve and then add the apples. Put the lid on the pan and cook gently until the apples are tender. Baste the apples with the syrup as they are cooking. (Prepare the day before.) Serves 4.

SWEET POTATO PUDDING

Boil 5 sweet potatoes until tender. Peel and mash while hot. Let cool. Cream ⅓ cup of butter with 1 cup of brown sugar and add 4 beaten egg yolks. Mix well. Combine the sugar mixture with the mashed potatoes and add ½ cup of sherry and 1 tea-spoon of nutmeg. Fold in 2 stiffly beaten egg whites and pour into a well-buttered casserole. Bake in oven at 350° for about 40 minutes. Serves 6.

PEAS WITH CREAM AND BACON

Cut 6 slices of bacon in small pieces and fry in an earthenware casserole. Add 2 cups of cooked peas (boil peas in the morning), 1 cup of cream or evaporated milk, and season with salt and pepper. Cover with ½ cup of bread crumbs, dot with butter, and brown under the broiler. Serves 4 to 6.

HORSE–RADISH MOLD

Make 1 recipe of Aspic Gelatine (p. 237), leaving out ½ cup of water. Let chill; then add ½ cup of mayonnaise and 3 table-spoons of horse-radish. In the bottom of a ring mold make a design of sliced stuffed olives and add the gelatine. (Prepare the day before.) Unmold and fill with Carrot and Celery Salad. Serves 6.

SHREDDED CARROT AND CELERY SALAD

Slice 5 stalks of celery wafer-thin. Shred 5 carrots fine and mix with the celery. Add salt, pepper, celery salt, and the juice of 1 lemon. Add mayonnaise according to taste. Serves 6.

BRANDIED FRUIT RING

Drain the juice from 1 can of pitted Bing cherries and 1 No.-2 can of pineapple cubes. Pour 1 cup of brandy over the fruit, cover, and let it stand for 1 hour. Stir occasionally. Add the juice of 1 lemon to the drained fruit juice and heat. Soak 2 tablespoons of gelatine in ¼ cup of cold water; then dissolve in the heated fruit juice. Cool. Drain off the brandy and place the fruit in a rinsed ring mold. Add the brandy to the gelatine mixture. When it begins to stiffen, pour it over the fruit. Place in the refrigerator for several hours until firm. (Prepare the day before.) Unmold and place a bowl of sweetened whipped cream in the center. Serves 6.

Menu

BEEF STROGANOFF

RICE BROWNED IN OLIVE OIL

ZUCCHINI STEWED WITH TOMATOES

BAKED CARROTS

GREEN SALAD MOLD WITH AVOCADO

PECAN GELATINE MOLDS

PEACHES WITH BRANDY AND
MARSHMALLOWS

BEEF STROGANOFF

Cut 1½ pounds of round steak in strips 1½ inches long and ¼ inch wide. Cut the meat across the grain, otherwise it will be stringy and tough. Melt 2 tablespoons of butter or bacon fat in a skillet; when hot add the beef strips, cover, and cook for 15 minutes. Stir occasionally. Cut in small pieces ½ pound of fresh mushrooms or use 1 small can of chopped mushrooms. Add to meat and cook for 10 minutes, adding more butter if necessary. Put meat and mushrooms into the top of a double boiler. In the skillet melt 1 tablespoon of butter, add 1 tablespoon of flour, and stir until blended. Continue stirring while adding 1 cup of sour cream. Bring to a boil. Pour this over the meat and mush-rooms in the double boiler and cook over boiling water for 15 minutes, stirring occasionally. Season with salt and pepper. Serve with rice, browned in olive oil. (This is better if prepared the day before and reheated.) Serves 4 to 6.

ZUCCHINI STEWED WITH TOMATOES

Wash and slice 2 pounds of zucchini. Slice 2 stalks of celery and mince 1 onion. Sauté onion in olive oil until golden in color;

then add zucchini and celery. Turn slowly in oil until well coated and then pour in 1 can of Italian tomatoes. Season with basil, a tiny piece of bay leaf, parsley, and a minced clove of garlic. Add salt and pepper. Let simmer over a slow fire for 1 hour. If too moist, pour off some of the liquid. Add a dash of Worcestershire sauce. Serves 6.

BAKED CARROTS

Put 3 cups of grated carrots in an earthenware casserole. Add 3 tablespoons of butter, salt and pepper to taste, and a slight sprinkling of ginger. Cover and bake in a moderate oven for half an hour. Serves 6.

GREEN SALAD MOLD WITH AVOCADO

Dissolve 1 package of lime gelatine in 1 cup of boiling water. Mix in 1 package of cream cheese, mashed, and add 1 can of pineapple cubes, drained, and 1 avocado, diced. Pour the mixture into a ring mold and place in the refrigerator until firm. Unmold and surround with Pecan Gelatine Molds. Serve with Orange and Lemon Mayonnaise (p. 64). Serves 6.

Pecan Gelatine Molds. — Dissolve 1 package of lemon gelatine in 1½ cups of boiling water. Add 2 tablespoons of vinegar and a pinch of salt. Chill and when it begins to thicken, add ½ cup of pecan meats, ½ cup of diced, peeled apples, and 1 cup of diced celery. Pour into individual molds and chill until firm. Serves 6.

PEACHES WITH BRANDY AND MARSHMALLOWS

Peel and slice peaches. Put in water with a little lemon juice added to prevent discoloration. An hour before dinner, drain the peaches and place in a casserole or open baking dish. Pour a little brandy or sherry, or a combination of both, over the peaches and sprinkle with brown sugar. Cover the entire surface with marshmallows. Put in a slow oven to heat, allowing the marshmallows to melt. Place under the broiler just before serving, if additional browning is necessary. Canned peaches may be used.

Menu

BRAISED OXTAIL WITH WINE AND CHESTNUTS

BAKED STRING BEANS WITH LIMA BEANS

ASPARAGUS PARMESAN

POTATO AND CELERY SALAD

FILLED ANGEL FOOD CAKE

BRAISED OXTAIL WITH WINE AND CHESTNUTS

Cut 2 oxtails into serving pieces. Soak for 1 hour in salted water, drain, and dry on a towel. Brown quickly and place in a French earthenware casserole. Cover with 2 cans of consommé, adding 1 onion which has been sliced and browned, 1 diced green pepper, 1 small-sized can of tomatoes, 3 carrots sliced, 2 teaspoons of salt, 6 whole black peppers, and a pinch each of basil, marjoram, and thyme. Add 1 cup of claret and 1 teaspoon of Worcestershire sauce. Cover and cook in the oven for 4 hours at 325°. Remove the meat and strain the broth. Taste for seasoning. Replace the meat in the casserole and pour over it the strained broth. Arrange previously cooked baby carrots and onions around the meat, dipping the gravy over them. Add potato balls and peeled, boiled chestnuts. Cook covered in the oven until the potato balls are tender. Sprinkle chopped parsley over the top just before it is served. (The meat may be prepared the day before, adding the vegetables when it is reheated.) Serves 6.

BAKED STRING BEANS WITH LIMA BEANS

String and shred diagonally 3 pounds of string beans and boil until tender. Drain. Add 2 cans of Lima beans (or equivalent of freshly cooked), drained. Season with salt and pepper, and add some butter. Make 2 cups of rich cream sauce, using cream or evaporated milk diluted with fresh milk. Season the sauce with a little grated onion and 4 tablespoons of grated Parmesan cheese. Mix half of the sauce with the vegetables and put in a French earthenware casserole. (Prepare in the morning.) Reheat over a low fire. Pour the rest of the sauce over and place under a very slow broiler until brown. Serves 8 to 10.

ASPARAGUS PARMESAN

Arrange freshly cooked or canned asparagus tips on a flat baking dish. Paint with melted butter, using a pastry brush or the tip of your finger. Sprinkle with grated Parmesan cheese and brown quickly under the broiler.

POTATO AND CELERY SALAD

Cut celery and cold, boiled potatoes in strips. Mix and chill. When ready to serve, toss lightly with mayonnaise dressing which has been thinned with French dressing to which a few chopped chives have been added. Serve surrounded with curled lettuce leaves.

FILLED ANGEL FOOD CAKE
(Ann's)

Cut the top off of an angel food cake and remove the center, leaving a 2-inch shell. Fill with the following cream mixture: Cook in the top of a double boiler 2 cups of milk, ¾ cup of sugar, and 4 beaten egg yolks, until it thickens. Dissolve 1 tablespoon of gelatine in ¼ cup of cold water and add to the hot custard. Stir occasionally until it thickens but is not stiff. Whip ½ pint of cream, flavor with rum or sherry, and add to the gelatine. Fill cavity in cake with this mixture. Replace top of cake and set in refrigerator all night. Just before serving, whip ½ pint of cream, spread over the cake, and sprinkle chopped nuts over the outside.

Menu

CHICKEN HASH PARMENTIER

MORNAY SAUCE

DUCHESS POTATOES

LIMA BEANS AND MUSHROOMS

ONION PUFFS

ARTICHOKES IN LEMON JELLY

ORANGE DESSERT

CHICKEN HASH PARMENTIER

Boil a hen until tender with a seasoning of onions and celery. Put the meat through a grinder, using the small blade. Heat ground chicken in a small amount of chicken stock and cook until reduced. (Prepare in the morning.)

Melt ½ cup of butter with ½ cup of flour and blend well. Gradually add 1 quart of strained chicken stock, stirring constantly until smooth. Place over a low fire and simmer slowly for 1 hour. Skim as needed, adding more stock to replace evaporation until sauce masks the spoon. Season with salt and pepper. Beat in 1 cup of cream. (Prepare in the morning.) Add chicken and reheat in top of double boiler. Remove to a heatproof serving dish, cover with Mornay Sauce and surround with a border of Duchess Potatoes. Serves 6.

Mornay Sauce. — Beat 4 slightly beaten egg yolks into 2 cups of white sauce. Cook in the top of a double boiler over hot, not boiling, water until the eggs are set. Season with salt and white pepper. Stir in 3 tablespoons of grated Swiss cheese. Pour over the chicken and sprinkle more grated cheese over the top.

Duchess Potatoes. — Whip seasoned, mashed potatoes, and for 6 potatoes add 2 beaten egg yolks. Arrange in a border around the chicken hash and brown under the broiler.

LIMA BEANS AND MUSHROOMS

Shell and cook 4 pounds of Lima beans. Slice 1 pound of mushrooms and fry in ½ cup of butter. Season the Lima beans, add the butter from the mushrooms, and arrange in a vegetable dish. Place the mushrooms over the top. Sprinkle with chopped parsley. (Cook the Lima beans in the morning and reheat in a double boiler.) Serves 6.

ONION PUFFS

Cut Bermuda onions in slices ¼ inch thick. Separate into single rings. Cover with milk and soak overnight. Drain and dredge well with salted flour. Dip in milk and dredge again. Fry in deep fat at 380° until pale brown. Drain well on brown paper and put aside. (Prepare ahead of time.) Just before serving, deep-fry again. The rings will puff up and have the appearance of small doughnuts.

ARTICHOKES IN LEMON JELLY

Dissolve 1 package of lemon gelatine in 1¾ cups of hot water. Add 2 tablespoons of tomato catsup and 2 tablespoons of tarragon vinegar. Season with salt and pepper. Rub a ring mold with a clove of garlic and then lightly with oil. Arrange halves of canned artichokes in the mold and pour in the lemon gelatine. Add 1 bottle stuffed olives, drained, and place in the refrigerator until firm. (Prepare the day before.) Unmold on a serving platter and surround with lettuce. Place a bowl of mayonnaise in the center. Serves 6.

ORANGE DESSERT
(Delphine's)

Soak 1½ envelopes of gelatine in ¼ cup of cold water for 5 minutes. Beat together 3 egg yolks and ⅓ cup of sugar. Heat 2 cups of milk and add the yolk mixture. Cook until thick in a double boiler. Remove from the fire and add the gelatine. Stir until the gelatine is dissolved; then let it cool. When it begins to thicken, fold in 1 cup of shredded cocoanut and the whites of the eggs, beaten stiff. Add a pinch of salt and 1 teaspoon of vanilla. Line a mold with sections of oranges and slowly pour in the mixture. Chill until firm. (Prepare the day before.) Unmold and serve with whipped cream flavored with grated orange rind. Serves 6.

Menu

LAMB CHOPS IN WINE EN CASSEROLE

BOILED CUCUMBERS WITH CURRIED CORN

POTATO CROQUETTES FILLED WITH JELLY

CREAMED SWEET AND SOUR BEETS

CALIFORNIA SALAD

STRAWBERRY TARTS

LAMB CHOPS IN WINE EN CASSEROLE

In an earthenware casserole brown 6 large loin lamb chops in butter with small, whole white onions and scraped baby carrots. Season with salt, pepper, and a pinch of mixed herbs. Add ½ cup of dry white wine and ½ pound of sliced mushrooms. Cover and let cook very slowly for 30 minutes. Serves 6.

BOILED CUCUMBERS WITH CURRIED CORN

Cut cucumbers in half lengthwise and scoop out the seeds. Boil in salted water until tender. Fill the center with fresh or canned kernel corn, mixed in a cream sauce flavored with curry. (Prepare in the morning and reheat in the oven in a covered dish, with a small amount of hot water to keep from sticking.)

POTATO CROQUETTES FILLED WITH JELLY

Beat 4 cups of mashed potatoes until light, adding hot milk, salt and pepper, and 1 egg. Cool. Shape the potatoes into 2-inch rounds, place a bit of currant jelly in the center, and fold over. Press the edges together. Dip in a beaten egg and then in sifted cracker crumbs. (Prepare in the morning.) Fry in deep fat. Drain on brown paper. Serves 6.

CREAMED SWEET AND SOUR BEETS
(Judy's)

Drain 1 can of tiny beets and save the juice. Melt 2 tablespoons of butter and add 2 tablespoons of sugar, mixed with 1½ tablespoons of flour. Add 2 tablespoons of lemon juice and gradually add ½ cup of beet juice. Let cook until thickened. (Prepare in the morning and reheat.)

Heat beets in double boiler and pour into a glass casserole. Add 1 cup of hot cream to the beet juice mixture and pour over the beets. Cover thickly with ground nut meats. Brown lightly under the broiler. Serves 4 to 6.

CALIFORNIA SALAD

Boil ⅔ cup of sugar and ⅔ cup of water for 5 minutes. Soak 2 tablespoons of gelatine in ½ cup of orange juice and dissolve in the hot syrup. Cool. Add 2 cups of grapefruit pulp and juice mixed. Pour into a ring mold and chill until firm. (Prepare the day before.) Unmold on a serving platter and surround with water cress. Place a bowl of Orange and Lemon Mayonnaise (p. 64) in the center. Serves 6.

STRAWBERRY TARTS

Mix 2 beaten eggs, ½ cup of sugar, ¼ teaspoon of salt, and 2 tablespoons of flour. Heat 1 cup of milk in the top of a double boiler and add the egg mixture. Cook until thick, stirring constantly. Flavor with ½ teaspoon of vanilla and, when cool, fold in ½ cup of cream, whipped. Make individual tart shells from pie dough the day before. Later fill with the cool custard and spread strawberry preserves over the top. Serves 6.

Menu

MILLBROOK RANCH ROAST PORK

CAULIFLOWER WITH PARMESAN CHEESE

HOMINY GRITS PUDDING

BEETS WITH ORANGE SAUCE

ASSORTED VEGETABLE RELISHES

LEMON FLUFF

MILLBROOK RANCH ROAST PORK

Use either pork leg or shoulder. Place in a large roasting pan and add 1 quart of dry white wine plus enough boiling water to cover. Add 12 whole black peppers, 2 onions, 2 mashed garlic beans, 2 carrots, 1 bay leaf, and 1 pinch each of thyme, rosemary, and sage. Let simmer on top of the stove, allowing ½ hour for each pound of meat. If you have a meat thermometer, test with that. (A meat thermometer is an excellent investment. It is inexpensive and eliminates the guess work in cooking meat.) Let the pork cool in its liquor. (This is best prepared the day before.) Remove from the liquor and roast in a moderate oven until brown and heated through — about 1 hour.

If you require the oven for other cooking, you may remove the roast when well browned, and keep it warm on top of the stove over a low fire. Put a lid on the pan but be sure there is enough liquid in the pan to keep the roast from burning.

CAULIFLOWER WITH PARMESAN CHEESE

Boil the cauliflower whole in salted water until tender, drain, and set on a large glass pie dish. Put 2 tablespoons of evaporated milk in the top of a double boiler. Add ¼ pound of grated Parmesan cheese, 2 tablespoons of butter, the beaten yolks of 4 eggs, ½ teaspoon of Worcestershire sauce, 1 teaspoon of lemon juice, and a pinch each of nutmeg, pepper, and salt.

Stir slowly over hot water, *without boiling*, until the sauce is well thickened. Spread it over the cauliflower, and sprinkle liberally with bread crumbs and grated Parmesan cheese. Reheat and brown in a medium oven. Serve on a round platter, surrounded with freshly cooked string beans. Serves 6.

HOMINY GRITS PUDDING

Pour boiling salted water over 1 cup of hominy grits until the consistency of thin mush. Boil for about 10 minutes, or until thick. Remove from the fire and slowly add 1 cup of milk, beating constantly to avoid lumps. Add the beaten yolks of 2 eggs, and last fold in carefully the stiffly beaten whites. Put in a buttered glass casserole and bake for half an hour in a 375° oven. Serves 4 to 6.

BEETS WITH ORANGE SAUCE

Melt 1 tablespoon of butter in a double boiler. Add 4 tablespoons of brown sugar mixed with 1½ tablespoons of flour. Stir in ¾ cup of orange juice and 2 tablespoons of grated orange peel. Cook until thick, stirring constantly. Season with ⅛ teaspoon of salt and a dash of paprika. (Prepare in the morning.) Add 2½ cups of cooked, diced beets and heat thoroughly. Serves 4.

LEMON FLUFF
(Muriel's)

¾ pound vanilla wafers or graham crackers
⅓ cup melted butter
2 tablespoons gelatine
¼ teaspoon salt

⅓ cup cold water
7 eggs, separated
2 cups sugar
3 lemons, juice and rind

Crush wafers or crackers; add butter. Line the sides and bottom of a spring mold with this mixture, reserving ½ cup. Soak the gelatine in the cold water. Beat the yolks of the eggs with 1 cup of sugar until light. Add the lemon juice, grated rind, and gelatine. Cook in a double boiler until thick. Cool. Add the salt to the egg whites; beat stiff, adding the other cup of sugar gradually. Fold in the cooled lemon mixture. Pour into the spring mold. Sprinkle the remaining crushed crumbs on top and place in the refrigerator until firm. (Prepare the day before.) Unmold and serve with whipped cream. Serves 6.

Menu

VEAL CHOPS WITH MUSHROOMS AND CHESTNUTS

BAKED HOMINY

CUCUMBERS IN LEMON SAUCE

BAKED PEARS

ROQUEFORT CHEESE MOLDS

COTTAGE PUDDING RING WITH COTTAGE PUDDING SAUCE

VEAL CHOPS WITH MUSHROOMS AND CHESTNUTS

Brown 6 veal chops in butter or bacon fat in an earthenware casserole and then add 1 cup of canned consommé and the juice from 1 large can of mushrooms. Chop 2 large onions very fine and add with 1 bay leaf to the casserole. Season with salt and pepper. Cover and bake in a slow oven (275°) for 1 hour. In the meantime, prick the shells of 1 pound of chestnuts and place in boiling water until the shells have softened. Remove the shells and the skin. Boil for 10 minutes, or until tender, and then cut into pieces. Remove the cover from the casserole and pour over the chops an additional cup of consommé blended with 1 tablespoon of flour and 2 tablespoons of sherry. Add the chestnuts, the canned mushrooms, and 2 tablespoons of butter. Cover again and cook slowly until all the ingredients are tender.

BAKED HOMINY

Drain 1 can of hominy and mix in 3 tablespoons of melted butter. Add 2 well-beaten eggs to 1 cup of scalded milk and stir into the hominy. Season with salt and pepper and mix well. Pour into a buttered casserole or baking dish and bake in a 300° oven until well browned. (Grated cheese may be added.) Serves 6.

CUCUMBERS IN LEMON SAUCE

Peel 6 cucumbers, cut in half lengthwise, and remove the seeds. Simmer until tender in boiling salted water to which a little lemon juice has been added. (Prepare in the morning.)

Melt 2 tablespoons of butter, add 2 tablespoons of flour, and stir until well blended. Add gradually 2 cups of the cucumber liquid and boil until it thickens. Beat in 4 egg yolks and keep hot, but do not boil. Season with salt, pepper, and lemon juice. Reheat the boiled cucumbers in a covered dish. Pour the sauce over them, sprinkle with chopped parsley and serve. Serves 6.

BAKED PEARS

Arrange large halves of canned Bartlett pears (No.-2½ can), core side up, in a greased baking pan. Dot with butter and sprinkle with a mixture of 1 tablespoon of cinnamon and ½ cup of granulated sugar. Add pear juice and bake in a hot oven (375°) for 15 minutes. Serve cold. (These may be baked the day before.) Serves 6.

ROQUEFORT CHEESE MOLDS

Soak ½ tablespoon of gelatine in ¼ cup of cold water and dissolve over hot water. Mash 3 packages of Roquefort cheese spread and mix with ½ cup of milk. Mix with the dissolved gelatine and add ¼ cup of chopped stuffed olives, ½ cup of finely chopped celery, and ½ teaspoon of lemon juice. Season with salt and pepper. Fold in 1 stiffly beaten egg white and, at the last, add ½ cup of cream, whipped. Place in individual molds in the refrigerator until firm. (Prepare the day before.) Place a bowl of French dressing in the center of a large platter and surround with the molds, alternating with peeled halves of ripe tomatoes covered with chopped chives. Around the edge of the platter arrange the curled leaves of endive and bunches of fresh or canned asparagus. Serves 6.

COTTAGE PUDDING RING

Cream together ¼ cup of butter and ½ cup of sugar. When smoothly blended, add 1 egg and 1 teaspoon of vanilla and beat again. Measure 1½ cups of sifted flour and resift with 2 teaspoons of baking powder and ¼ teaspoon of salt. Add to the batter alternately with ½ cup of milk and beat thoroughly. Pour into a greased ring mold and bake for about 25 minutes in a 400° oven. Serve hot with Cottage Pudding Sauce. Serves 6.

Cottage Pudding Sauce. — Cream 4 tablespoons of butter and stir in gradually 1 cup of powdered sugar. Beat until light. Add, while beating constantly, the whites of 2 eggs. (At this point the preparations may be discontinued until just before the sauce is to be served.) Set the bowl with the mixture in boiling water, and add ½ cup of brandy and ½ cup of boiling water. Stir until light. Serves 6.

Menu

CHICKEN SUPRÊME EN CASSEROLE

RICE BROWNED IN OLIVE OIL

ONION RING WITH PEAS AND CARROTS

SHREDDED BEETS

ROMAINE LETTUCE WITH HERB DRESSING

FROZEN APRICOTS

CHICKEN SUPRÊME EN CASSEROLE

Cut up a 5-pound stewing hen and place in a kettle. Cover with hot water and dry white wine in equal proportions. Add 1 chopped onion, 2 stalks of celery diced fine, 1 large bay leaf, a few sprigs of parsley, 3 whole cloves, and a pinch of thyme. Season with salt and add 3 whole black peppers. Cover and simmer gently until the chicken is tender. Let the chicken cool in the stock. Cut the meat in medium-sized pieces, discarding the skin and bones. (The chicken may be cooked the day before.) Place in the top of a double boiler to reheat.

Sauté 2 finely minced onions in 2 tablespoons of butter over a very slow fire, but do not brown. Add ½ cup of white wine and allow to simmer until the wine has cooked away. Scald 1½ cups of sour cream and stir into the onions. Mash through a purée sieve and then cook until blended. Season with salt and pepper. Pour over the chicken and keep hot in the double boiler. Serve in an earthenware casserole. Serves 6.

ONION RING WITH PEAS AND CARROTS
(Harriet's)

Purée boiled onions to make 1 cup. Melt 2 tablespoons of butter, add 2 tablespoons of flour, and blend in ½ cup of milk and the onion purée. Season with ¾ teaspoon of salt and ⅛ teaspoon of pepper. Add 3 beaten egg yolks and, lastly, fold in the stiffly beaten egg whites. Pour into a buttered ring mold, place in a pan of hot water in the oven, and bake 30 minutes in a moderate oven (350°). Unmold and fill the center with buttered peas and carrots. Serves 4 to 6.

SHREDDED BEETS

Peel and shred 1 bunch of raw beets. Boil 2 cups of water with 1 tablespoon of butter. Add the shredded beets and cover tightly. Cook over a hot fire for 10 minutes. (Prepare in the morning and reheat in a double boiler.) Add butter and season to taste. Serves 4 to 6.

ROMAINE LETTUCE WITH HERB DRESSING

Add chopped chives and water cress to French dressing. Break chilled romaine lettuce into 2-inch pieces and toss lightly with the dressing in a wooden salad bowl.

FROZEN APRICOTS

Pour 1 can of apricots into the freezing tray of the refrigerator and freeze. It will take a few hours. When frozen, but not too hard to cut, invert on a serving platter or serve in a bowl. Spread with whipped cream, sweetened, and flavored with brandy. Decorate with whole brandied apricots, if desired. Serves 6.

Menu

PORK CHOPS IN LOAF

MILLBROOK RANCH SAUERKRAUT

STRING BEANS WITH SOUR CREAM

SAUTÉED ZUCCHINI

APPLESAUCE SALAD RING

PRUNE SOUFFLÉ WITH BRANDY SAUCE

PORK CHOPS IN LOAF

To serve 6 people, prepare this amount of dressing: Simmer ¼ cup each of finely chopped celery and onions in 2 tablespoons of butter, but do not brown. Pour over 2 cups of bread crumbs and mix lightly. Season with ½ teaspoon of sage, 1 teaspoon of salt, and ⅛ teaspoon of pepper. Add 2 tablespoons of chopped parsley.

Place a pork chop in the end of a bread pan and place some of the dressing between that chop and the next one. Keep adding chops, with dressing packed between them, until the pan is full. Bake in a slow oven (275°) for 1½ hours. (For the loaf of 6 chops, you will need an extra chop to close off the last layer of dressing.)

MILLBROOK RANCH SAUERKRAUT

Put the contents of 1 can of sauerkraut in a colander and wash thoroughly. In a French earthenware casserole melt 3 tablespoons of butter. Chop fine 2 onions and 1 peeled apple and add with the sauerkraut to the casserole. Mix well with a fork. Pour in 1 cup of white wine and add a sprinkling of freshly ground black pepper. Put on the lid and cook slowly on top of the stove or in the oven for about 1 hour. Add more wine, if necessary. (Prepare in the morning and reheat.) Serves 6.

STRING BEANS WITH SOUR CREAM

Wash and cut diagonally 2 pounds of string beans. Cook in boiling salted water until tender. (Prepare in the morning.) Melt 4 tablespoons of butter and add 1 large onion chopped fine. Cook until tender but do not brown. Add 4 tablespoons of flour and stir until well blended. Add 2 cups of sour cream and cook for a few minutes. Drain the beans, add them to the sour cream, and cook a few minutes longer. Serves 6 to 8.

SAUTÉED ZUCCHINI

Slice thin the desired number of zucchini. Mash a clove of garlic and sauté in olive oil. Remove the garlic and then add the sliced zucchini. Keep turning the squash until it is tender and lightly browned. Season with salt and pepper.

APPLESAUCE SALAD RING
(Mabel's)

Heat 2½ cups of applesauce until it comes to a boil. Add 1 tablespoon of gelatine which has been soaked in 2 tablespoons of cold water. Stir until the gelatine is dissolved.

Add ¼ cup of sugar, 3 tablespoons of red cinnamon candies, and ¼ teaspoon of nutmeg. Stir until the candies and sugar are dissolved. Add 1 teaspoon of lemon juice. Pour into a ring mold rinsed in cold water. Chill until firm. Serve with a tart mayonnaise dressing. Serves 6.

PRUNE SOUFFLÉ

This recipe was given me by the cook of a well-known gourmet. He once invited members of my family for dinner and they were dismayed when faced with prunes for dessert. But they asked for second helpings!

Stew 25 large, or 30 small, prunes, and press through a sieve. Add ¾ cup of sugar, 1 teaspoon of vanilla, and 1 cup of nut meats chopped fine. Cool. (Prepare in the morning.) Fold in 4 stiffly beaten egg whites. Pour into the top of a double boiler, which has been buttered. Steam for 1½ hours and do not lift the lid! Invert on a dessert platter and surround with Brandy Sauce.

Brandy Sauce. — Beat 4 egg yolks with 1 cup of milk and add ¾ cup of sugar. Cook in a double boiler over a slow fire, stirring constantly until thick. When cool add 1 tablespoon of brandy.

Menu

COLD BOILED SALMON

GREEN MAYONNAISE

CARROTS ANNA

HAM AND SPINACH SOUFELÉ

CURRIED EGG SAUCE

BARLEY AND MUSHROOMS

HIDDEN STRAWBERRIES

BANANA CAKE

COLD BOILED SALMON

On the evening before your party, prepare the Court Bouillon and let it boil in the fish kettle for 15 minutes. Lay the fish on the rack and submerge in the hot liquid. (All fish kettles come equipped with a rack, which makes the lowering and raising of the fish very easy.) Be sure there is enough liquid to cover the fish. Let the bouillon boil up again after the fish has been added. Put the lid on the kettle and simmer for 5 minutes. Do not raise the lid again. *Turn off the heat* and leave the fish until morning. At that time, it will be perfectly cooked. Raise the rack from the kettle and slide the salmon onto a china serving platter. Remove the skin. Place the fish in the refrigerator. Chill thoroughly. Decorate with slices of hard-boiled egg and ribbons of mayonnaise. Serve with Green Mayonnaise (p. 40).

Court Bouillon. — To 6 quarts of water, add ½ cup of chopped carrots, 1 cup each of chopped celery and onions, 3 minced cloves of garlic, 1 tablespoon of whole peppers, 2 tablespoons of mixed dried herbs, 3 tablespoons of salt, and 1½ cups of vinegar.

CARROTS ANNA

Sauté 2 minced onions in 2 tablespoons of butter for 5 minutes. Peel 12 carrots, shred lengthwise, and roll in ¼ cup of flour. Add to onions and cook until flour is browned. Add 1 cup of bouillon, season with salt and pepper to taste, and simmer 20 minutes. Serves 4 to 6.

HAM AND SPINACH SOUFFLÉ
(Ada's)

Some of your guests may not care for salmon; so it is a good idea to offer another entree. This soufflé does double duty, inasmuch as it is partly a vegetable.

Make a cream sauce with 2 tablespoons of butter, 3 tablespoons of flour, and 1 cup of hot milk. Let cool and add ½ cup each of ground, cooked ham and finely chopped, cooked spinach. Season to taste. (Prepare in the morning.) Add the beaten yolks of 3 eggs, mix well, and then fold in gently the stiffly beaten whites. Pour into a well-buttered baking dish. Place the dish in a pan of water and bake in a moderate oven (350°) for about 40 minutes. Serve with a Curried Egg Sauce. Serves 4 to 6.

Curried Egg Sauce. — Make a cream sauce with 1 tablespoon of butter, 1 tablespoon of flour, and 1 cup of hot milk. Cook in the top of a double boiler. Add 1 diced hard-boiled egg and ½ tablespoon of curry powder blended with 3 tablespoons of cream. Season to taste.

BARLEY AND MUSHROOMS

Drop 1 cup of coarse barley, a little at a time, into plenty of rapidly boiling water. Add 1 teaspoon of salt and cook for about 1 hour, covered, until the kernels are tender. Drain. Season with salt, pepper to taste, and 4 tablespoons or more of butter. Cover and keep hot while you prepare the mushrooms. Stem, peel, and finely chop ½ pound of mushrooms (or use a 6-ounce can). Sauté in 2 tablespoons of butter. Mix lightly with the barley. Serves 6.

HIDDEN STRAWBERRIES

Wash and stem 1 quart of strawberries. Place in a serving bowl and sprinkle over them ½ cup of powdered sugar, the juice of 1 orange, and the grated rind of 2 oranges. Sprinkle ⅓ cup of curaçao liqueur over the berries. Cover the dish and store in the refrigerator for several hours. Make a boiled custard with 2 beaten egg yolks, 2 tablespoons of sugar, and 1 cup of milk. Flavor with 1 teaspoon of vanilla. Chill. Whip 1 cup of cream and fold in the custard. Serve the berries in the serving bowl with the cream and custard mixture poured over them, completely hiding the berries. Serves 6.

BANANA CAKE

This cake brings back the memory of my first and last case of hostess jitters when, as a young bride, I attempted to prepare the refreshments for my first afternoon bridge party. But all my jitters vanished when I saw the guest of honor, a European countess, literally gobbling down the cake and reaching for a second helping — a proceeding which, in our small town, was considered the height of bad manners.

Cream together ½ cup of shortening with ½ cup of sugar, and add 2 eggs beaten with 4 tablespoons of cream. Sift 1 cup of flour with 1 teaspoon of baking powder, 1 teaspoon of soda, and ½ teaspoon of salt. Mix in 1 cup of chopped English walnuts until well covered with the flour. Mash enough bananas to measure 1 cupful and add to the cake mixture. Stir in the flour. Bake in a tube baking pan and serve without frosting. This cake is better if made the day before it is to be served.

The Men Are Wearing Black Ties

There is no more complimentary way to entertain that "special guest" than with a formal dinner. Be sure to select your guests carefully. Invite only those who will be interested in him and those whom he will enjoy.

When the dinner is small, its tempo will depend largely on your guests, so be sure to include at least one genial talker who will add a gayness to your party and will draw the entire table into congenial conversation. If it is a large dinner, arrange your seating so that those who talk easily are next those who prefer to listen.

If you have invited guests who are not well acquainted, give each a word of explanation about his dinner partner. You may say to Mr. Brown, "You are sitting next to Mrs. Jones this evening. She has just returned from Alaska where she has been living for the past two years. Knowing how much pleasure you derived from your trip there last summer, I thought you would enjoy talking to her."

Then go to Mrs. Jones and say, "You are sitting next to our dear friend, Mr. Brown, who is much interested in Alaska, and I know you will enjoy exchanging experiences."

Or, if you have a guest who is shy and difficult to talk to, do give her partner a clue! Don't leave him floundering around trying to find something to talk about until, in desperation, he gives up and concentrates on eating his dinner, leaving the shy lady to do likewise.

Seating often spoils what otherwise would be a perfect party. Try writing out your place cards and while you sit at one end of the table, arrange them as you visualize your guests. If you have a couple and the wife is a little flirtatious, put an attractive man next to her. She will have a good time, and at least the man will not be bored. But don't seat her husband opposite her. Instead, seat him on the same side of the table as his wife, where it is impossible for him to check on her every word and smile. And watch the "noisy spots" at your table. Don't seat all your good conversationalists together for, if you do, the other guests will be envying the gayer group and perhaps wish they were there with them.

If you receive a telephone call from one of the wives you have invited, saying her husband will be out of town on the night of the dinner, don't worry if the seating at your table is unbalanced. Urge her to come anyway. If you *must* have an even number, surely you know an extra man whom you can call upon at the last moment. Ask him frankly, "Do you mind substituting for Mr. Jones, who has been called out of town?" And do remember to add flatteringly, "It is wonderful to have someone like you, whom I can always count on."

An efficient hostess will have everything ready the day before her dinner; the silver polished, the supply of china and crystal adequate, cigarettes and cigars on hand, and decorations ordered.

Whether you have a maid or not, it is wise if possible to set the table the evening before: silver, napkins, ash trays, even fresh candles — everything except the flowers.

While it is possible to prepare the formal dinner yourself, it is practically impossible to serve it without a maid. And remember, unless you have a very simple dinner, one maid can serve only four guests successfully.

Your dining room should not be too brilliantly lighted; neither should dinner be served in the gloom of an ancient cathedral. Walls and draperies should not be so definite in color that they limit the table decorations or possibly clash with the gowns of the guests. My own dining room is decorated in green and white which allows me to use any colors I choose for decorations and is also a flattering background for every woman. The walls are white, the rug a soft green, and at the windows are fluffy, wide-ruffled curtains. The sheen of the old walnut furniture, the glow of the Sheffield silver, and the sparkle of the crystal fixtures add that note of warmth that every room needs.

Use candles to light your room. There is something about the yellow glimmer of candlelight that makes a woman's eyes shine and her complexion look like peaches and cream. If your husband dislikes candlelight and insists that he wants to see what he is eating, persuade him to let you use candles at least on party nights. And use plenty of candles, especially on the table. The rest of the room may be left in shadows, allowing all the interest to center on your table — the stage set for the evening.

Plan something different for your decorations. Let them give your party a lift as well as giving your guests something to talk about. Had you ever thought of combining fruit and flowers of the same color? Such as white grapes with white flowers? One of the loveliest table decorations that I use in my green and white room is babies'-breath or gypsophila. I arrange huge quantities of it in a large glass bowl; the delicate sprays suggest a bride or a young girl making her first communion. Or Queen Anne's lace, which grows wild by the roadside, takes on great importance when it shares honor with pink geraniums and pink candles.

In winter combine red apples with red berries. This is a cheery combination and will brighten any dark day, especially if you use red candles.

You can even bring much of your vegetable garden into the room. Have you ever used the long stalks of onion top, left when the onions have gone to seed? The feathery pompoms on the ends give a lovely, light touch to any bouquet and are amusing in themselves. Or how about using Bibb lettuce, jars of ivy, and sprays of green leaves?

In the fall, bare your table of cloth or doilies and pile a profusion of assorted vegetables and fruit down the center of the table, and strew colorful autumn leaves around the edge.

You need never use a tablecloth or doilies unless you wish to. Instead I use round glass disks which any glass cutter will cut for you from heavy window glass. I find nine inches a convenient size, because I use mine only to rest the plate on and I place the waterglass and silver directly on the table. The advantage of using glass is that it requires no laundering and also makes the table appear larger. If you use the larger size and want them more decorative, you may gum flower or hunting prints underneath, or you may have your monogram cut in the glass or pasted on the under side. Mirrored glass may be used in place of the plain window glass, if preferred.

Don't have any hard and fast rules about serving the after-dinner coffee. I prefer having it brought to the drawing room, where I serve it myself, so that timid souls may feel free to ask for a second cup in case no one offers it to them. But many a time, I have found my guests having such a gay time at the table that I hesitated to break the spell. When you move people from one spot to another, the tempo of your party invariably changes.

Don't regiment your guests! Don't insist on everyone playing bridge or poker after dinner. Ask them if they would like to play, but never pounce on them with the order, "You are playing at table number five," or "You are to play poker in the library." A busy hostess is tiresome.

What I am really trying to advise you is — relax and let your guests do likewise! Let them feel they are at liberty to stand or sit, talk or listen, stay or go home. In other words, leave them alone as long as they seem to be having a good time.

Menu

CLEAR TOMATO SOUP

ASPIC OF FISH

CHICKEN ROASTED WITH TARRAGON

CELERY ROOT SOUFFLÉ

GRAPEFRUIT AND ROMAINE SALAD

ALMOND MOLD WITH CUSTARD SAUCE

CLEAR TOMATO SOUP

Mix 1 large can of tomatoes with 2 cans of bouillon and 2 cups of water. Season with 3 tablespoons of chopped onion, 1 bay leaf, 1 stalk of celery, 6 cloves, salt, and pepper. Simmer for about half an hour. Strain, taste for seasoning, and serve hot with puffed crackers. (Prepare the day before.)

ASPIC OF FISH

Place small boned trout or fillets of sole on the rack in a fish kettle. Put sufficient water in the kettle to make a stock that will cover the fish, and season with celery, onion, a little vinegar, salt, and pepper. Let it come to a good boil. Lower the rack into the water and leave for 10 minutes, or a little longer, depending on the size of the fish. Have the water simmering gently but not boiling. Remove the rack and let the fish cool. In the meantime, make an aspic. Soak 2 tablespoons of gelatine in ½ cup of cold water and dissolve in 2 cups of hot fish stock, strained. Add 1 cup of white wine and ¼ cup of tarragon vinegar. Chill until it begins to thicken.

Arrange the poached fish on a serving platter, and fill in the spaces between with white seedless grapes. Pour part of the aspic over gently, so as not to disarrange the grapes, adding more aspic as the first becomes firm. (Prepare in the morning.) Serve with mayonnaise flavored with grated cucumber.

CHICKEN ROASTED WITH TARRAGON

For a 5-pound roasting chicken use 6 branches of tarragon. Rub the chicken well inside and out with salt and pepper. Cut off a few of the tarragon leaves and put the rest inside the bird. Mix 2 tablespoons each of flour and butter and rub the legs and breast until well covered. Roast in a moderate oven (350°) until tender, basting every few minutes with melted butter. (The basting is very important!) Chop the reserved tarragon leaves and add them to the juice in the pan. Although dried tarragon may be used, the fresh is preferable.

CELERY ROOT SOUFFLÉ

Mash enough cooked celery root to make 3 cups. Add 1 cup of rich cream sauce and season with salt and pepper. Cool. (Prepare in the morning.) Fold in 2 stiffly beaten egg whites. Pile lightly in a baking dish and bake for about 30 minutes.

GRAPEFRUIT AND ROMAINE SALAD

Arrange romaine lettuce on a platter with segments of grapefruit. (Prepare grapefruit in the morning and chill in the refrigerator until ready.) Place a bowl of French dressing in the center of the platter and serve.

ALMOND MOLD

Soften 1 tablespoon of gelatine in ¼ cup of cold water. Pour over it 1 cup of boiling water and stir until the gelatine is dissolved. Add 1¼ cups of sugar and stir until the sugar is dissolved. Place in the refrigerator until the mixture begins to thicken; then beat until light and frothy. Whip 6 egg whites until stiff and add the beaten gelatine gradually, whipping all the time, until the two mixtures are thoroughly blended. Add ½ cup of sherry and ⅛ teaspoon of almond extract and stir well. Pour a layer of the gelatine mixture into a melon mold and sprinkle chopped almonds over it; then add more gelatine and almonds alternately until all the gelatine and 1 cup of the chopped nuts have been used. Chill until firm. (Prepare the day before.) Unmold on a serving platter decorated with green leaves or white roses. Serve with a Custard Sauce (p. 31) flavored with sherry. Serves 6.

Menu

LOBSTER COCKTAIL

COCKTAIL SAUCE

CONSOMMÉ SUPRÊME

LAMB COOKED IN WHITE WINE

MIXED GREEN AND WHITE VEGETABLES

BAKED PEACHES WITH SHERRY SAUCE

LOBSTER COCKTAIL

Cube fresh lobster meat and mix with Jim's Cocktail Sauce. Serve with a sprig of parsley on top.

COCKTAIL SAUCE
(Jim's)

Season mayonnaise dressing with tomato catsup, Worcestershire sauce, and a little lemon juice. Add some cream whipped stiff and, last of all, the surprise — a dash of gin!

CONSOMMÉ SUPRÊME

Boil 6 cups of water with 6 chicken broth cubes, adding a pinch of mixed herbs (which can be bought packaged at any store selling herbs), 1 onion, and some whole black peppers. Let boil for ½ hour, adding more water to keep the amount 6 cups. Strain, and add 2 cans of consommé. Season with celery salt. Add sherry to taste. (Prepare the day before.) Serves 6.

LAMB COOKED IN WHITE WINE

Mix a marinade of 1 cup of olive oil, ½ cup of vinegar, mixed spices, mixed dried herbs, and 2 cups of white wine. Soak a leg of lamb in this mixture for 24 hours, turning the lamb from time to time so that all parts of the meat come in contact with the marinade. Drain and thoroughly dry the lamb and put in a roasting pan in a hot oven (425°). Roast for ½ hour. Strain the marinade, add 1 cup of it to the lamb, and reduce the oven heat to 350°. Baste the lamb every 10 minutes until it is cooked through. In the meantime, add to the rest of the marinade 1 can of mushrooms, 2 tomatoes diced, and a few chicken livers (or some chopped calf liver) browned in butter. Let this simmer slowly until reduced and thoroughly blended. Taste for seasoning. Carve the lamb into slices, but send the roast to the table with the slices replaced and covered with chopped walnuts browned in butter. Serve the sauce in a separate bowl. Serves 6.

MIXED GREEN AND WHITE VEGETABLES

Cook separately: green peas, string beans which have been cut diagonally in small pieces, and potato balls. (Baby Lima beans may be used also.) Drain. (Prepare vegetables in the morning.) Melt butter in the top of a double boiler and gently mix in the vegetables. Add a large handful of tiny sprigs of parsley.

BAKED PEACHES

Drain 1 large can of halved peaches. Place in a baking pan, with the cut sides up. Put a dab of butter and a little sugar in each hollow. Crumb one half of a macaroon over each peach and press down into the butter. (Prepare in the morning.) Bake in a moderate oven (350°) for ½ hour. Serve with Sherry Sauce.

Sherry Sauce. — Add 1½ tablespoons of sugar to 3 egg yolks. Beat until light, adding gradually ½ cup of sherry. Cook in the top of a double boiler over water which is hot, not boiling. Stir constantly until thick and smooth. Place in the refrigerator until ice-cold. (Prepare in the morning.) Serve the peaches hot, right out of the oven, and the sauce very cold. Serves 6.

Menu

CREAM OF CRAB SOUP

CALIFORNIA FRIED CHICKEN

DELICIOUS CORN

BISCUITS

COOKED CELERY HEART SALAD

ORANGES IN SYRUP

CREAM OF CRAB SOUP

Mix 1 can each of crab meat (flaked and with bones removed), tomato soup, pea soup, and consommé. Add 1 large can of evaporated milk and thin to the right consistency with fresh milk. Bring to a boil and serve piping hot with 1 tablespoon of sherry added to each serving.

CALIFORNIA FRIED CHICKEN

Have 2 fryers cut into serving pieces. Place in a baking pan and cover with salt water for 10 minutes. Remove the chicken and dry thoroughly. Dust all over with salt, pepper, and flour, with a pinch of ginger. (This may be done very easily by placing the ingredients in a paper bag and shaking the pieces of chicken in the mixture until well coated.) Heat half lard and half butter in a skillet, put in the chicken, and cook until brown on all sides. Turn the flame very low, and flick a little water over the chicken, using the tips of your fingers. Put the lid on tight and cook until the chicken is tender. Then remove the chicken and, if you want gravy, add water or cream to the juice in the pan and thicken. Serves 6.

DELICIOUS CORN

Run a sharp knife through the center of each row of kernels on 2 dozen ears of corn. Then scrape the inside paste out of the kernel with the back of a knife. Put in a double boiler with ½ cup of butter. (Prepare in the morning.) Cook 1 hour. Serves 6.

COOKED CELERY HEART SALAD

Cook celery hearts in diluted canned consommé until tender. (Consommé may be used later for soup.) Remove from the broth and when cool cut lengthwise. Marinate in sharp French dressing. Place in refrigerator for several hours. (Prepare the day before.) Serve on a large glass platter with romaine lettuce leaves. Sprinkle chopped, hard-boiled eggs and chopped fried bacon over the celery.

ORANGES IN SYRUP
(Margaret's)

Peel 12 small navel oranges very thin with a sharp knife. (Be careful to remove only the yellow part of the skin.) Cut this yellow peel in as thin shreds as possible. (It may take a little time, but it is worth it.) Place these shreds in boiling water and cook for 15 minutes. Drain and pour more boiling water over the orange peel, and boil again for 15 minutes. Drain. Peel all the white skin off the oranges, cut them in half and remove the core. Place in a large bowl. Make a syrup by boiling together 2 cups of sugar with 1 cup of water for 10 minutes. Tint with a few drops of red coloring. Pour this hot syrup over the orange halves and let stand until cool. Pour the syrup off and boil it again for 15 minutes. Add the shreds of orange peel and pour back over the halves of oranges. Place in the refrigerator until thoroughly cold, basting the syrup over the oranges from time to time. This dish may be prepared the day before you wish to serve it. Serves 8.

Menu

MINTED STRAWBERRIES

STUFFED DOUBLE LAMB CHOPS

CAULIFLOWER FRIED IN BATTER

PEAS WITH BACON CRUMBS

GRAPE SALAD

NEVER-FAIL CHOCOLATE SOUFFLÉ

MINTED STRAWBERRIES

Use large, perfect, whole strawberries. Clean and hull. Pour over the berries orange juice to which a little chopped mint has been added. Sprinkle with powdered sugar and chill thoroughly. Serve in cocktail glasses.

STUFFED DOUBLE LAMB CHOPS

Have a pocket cut in a double, small loin lamb chop. Fill this with mushroom garlic dressing: Chop fine 6 mushrooms and cook in 1 tablespoon of butter. Remove from the fire and add 2 tablespoons of bread crumbs, a pinch of salt and pepper, 1 teaspoon of chopped parsley, and a clove of garlic, finely minced. Stir the mixture well, and when cool add 1 beaten egg yolk. If not moist enough, add a very little cream. Fill the pocket of the chop, close the opening with a toothpick, and place in the roasting pan with a little water. Cover and bake in the oven for 1 hour. This recipe gives the proportions for 1 chop.

CAULIFLOWER FRIED IN BATTER

Separate a head of cauliflower into florets and parboil until almost tender. Drain. (Prepare in the morning.)

Make a batter by beating together 2 egg yolks, ¼ cup of water, ¼ cup of cream or evaporated milk, and 1 tablespoon each of lemon juice and melted butter. Add 1 cup of sifted flour, mixed with a pinch of salt. Beat the 2 egg whites with a pinch of salt and fold into the batter. Dip the florets in the batter and fry in deep fat.

PEAS WITH BACON CRUMBS

Mince 6 slices of bacon very, very fine. Fry until crisp, stirring all the time so that it does not burn. Remove the bacon and drain on brown paper. Pour off all but 1 tablespoon of fat and add ¾ cup of bread crumbs. Sauté until brown. Mix the bacon with the bread crumbs and sprinkle over green peas.

GRAPE SALAD

Remove the seeds from red, black, and white grapes. Marinate in port wine. (Prepare in the morning.) Serve thoroughly chilled on lettuce leaves with French dressing.

NEVER–FAIL CHOCOLATE SOUFFLÉ

Beat 10 egg whites until stiff and dry. Fold in gently 1 cup of sugar, and when blended fold in 4 ounces of melted bitter chocolate. Add 1 cup of finely ground nuts, such as almonds, walnuts, or Brazil nuts. Put the mixture in the well-greased top of a double boiler. Cover and cook over hot water for 45 minutes. Turn onto a platter and serve with Orange Soufflé Sauce (p. 280).

Menu

AVOCADO COCKTAIL

SPINACH SOUP

FRIED CHICKEN WITH WHITE WINE AND
BRANDY

CARROT RING FILLED WITH GREEN PEAS

STRAWBERRIES WITH PURÉED APRICOTS

AVOCADO COCKTAIL

Cut avocado in cubes and serve with cocktail sauce. For the sauce mix ½ cup each of mayonnaise and tomato catsup, and add ¼ cup of whipped cream. Arrange the cubes in individual glasses and pour the sauce over. Garnish with a sprig of water cress.

SPINACH SOUP

Grind 3 pounds of spinach fine, being careful to save all the juice. Add 2 cups of water and cook for 10 minutes. Press through a purée sieve and add 8 cups of canned consommé. Heat slowly for 15 minutes. Season with salt, pepper, ½ teaspoon of mace, and a little lemon juice. Put through a fine wire sieve and, if necessary, add a little green vegetable coloring. (Prepare the day before and reheat.) Serve hot, garnished with a slice of lemon. Serves 6.

FRIED CHICKEN WITH WHITE WINE AND BRANDY

Disjoint a young fryer and place all except wing tips and back in an iron skillet. Add plenty of butter and cook over a quick fire, turning frequently to brown all sides. Add ¼ pound of mushrooms and 2 peeled ripe tomatoes cut in quarters. Cook a few minutes more and then add ½ cup of white wine and ½ cup of canned consommé. Season with salt and pepper and cook slowly for 20 minutes. Remove the pieces of chicken and keep hot. To the sauce add finely chopped parsley and 1 tablespoon of minced onion. Cook for about 10 minutes longer. Remove from fire and add brandy to taste. Pour the sauce over the chicken and serve. This amount is for 1 chicken and will serve 2 or 3 people. Multiply ingredients when additional chicken is used.

CARROT RING FILLED WITH GREEN PEAS

Add 1 cup of cream sauce and 3 egg yolks to 1 cup of cooked, mashed carrots. Cool. Beat the whites of the eggs stiff and fold into the mixture. Place in a greased ring mold and bake in a pan of hot water in a moderate oven (350°). Fill the center with green peas. Serves 4.

STRAWBERRIES WITH PURÉED APRICOTS

Wash ½ pound of dried apricots and soak overnight in cold water. Drain. Add ½ cup of sugar and 3½ cups of water. Boil slowly for 35 minutes. Rub the apricots through a purée sieve. Shred in fine slivers the thin yellow rind of 2 oranges and cook slowly for 15 minutes in ½ cup of water and ½ cup of sugar. Add to the apricots. (Prepare in the morning.) In a large serving bowl put 3 pints of strawberries, washed and hulled, and pour over them ¼ cup of honey. Chill. When ready to serve, cover with 1 pint of whipped cream, sweetened with 1 tablespoon of powdered sugar and 2 tablespoons of rum. Carefully pour over the apricot purée until the entire surface is covered. Serves 6.

Menu

TOMATO SOUP DE LUXE

LEG OF LAMB WITH OLIVE SAUCE

CARROTS GLAZED WITH MINT JELLY

RAW ZUCCHINI SALAD

COCOANUT MOLD WITH
HOT BUTTERSCOTCH SAUCE

TOMATO SOUP DE LUXE

Combine 3½ cups of tomato juice with 2⅔ cups of consommé and heat well. Add 2 teaspoons of angostura bitters and ½ teaspoon of sugar. Season with salt and pepper and serve. Serves 6.

LEG OF LAMB WITH OLIVE SAUCE

Rub a leg of lamb with a clove of garlic and stuff another one between the bone and the end of the leg. Melt 2 tablespoons of butter or bacon fat in a roasting pan and brown the lamb on top of the stove. Add 1 chopped onion, 1 bay leaf, a sprinkling of thyme, a few sprigs of parsley, and 2 cans of consommé. Put the lid on and simmer slowly on top of the stove or in a slow oven (275°) for 3 hours. Do not remove the lid during that time.

In the meantime, brown 2 tablespoons of butter in a stew pan, add slowly 2 heaping tablespoons of flour, and brown again. Add 1 can of consommé and stir until smooth and thick. When the lamb is cooked, add the strained juice from the pan and cook together 5 minutes. Add 1 tablespoon of Worcestershire sauce and taste for seasoning. Stir in 2 cups of chopped green olives and cook until well heated. Carve the lamb and replace the slices. Pour the sauce over the lamb and serve. Serves 6.

CARROTS GLAZED WITH MINT JELLY

Scrape and cut in julienne strips as many carrots as desired. Boil in salted water and drain. (Prepare in the morning.) Add butter and reheat in top of double boiler. Place in a serving dish and pour over them mint jelly melted over hot water.

RAW ZUCCHINI SALAD

Shred raw, peeled zucchini into long match-like strips. Chill. Arrange on a serving platter in bunches with a strip of bell pepper across each bunch. Decorate the platter with romaine lettuce and place a bowl of French dressing in the center.

COCOANUT MOLD

Dissolve 2 tablespoons of gelatine in ½ cup of cold milk. Heat 1 cup of sugar with 1½ cups of milk and ¼ teaspoon of salt. Stir into the gelatine. Put in the refrigerator until the mixture starts to thicken; then beat until light and fluffy. Fold in 1 pint of cream, whipped stiff, 2 cups of grated fresh cocoanut, and 1 teaspoon of vanilla. Pour into a melon mold and place in the refrigerator until firm. (Prepare the day before.) Unmold in center of a glass platter and decorate with white flowers. Serve with Hot Butterscotch Sauce (p. 33).

Menu

BAYOU RIPE TOMATO COCKTAIL

CREAM OF SALMON SOUP

CHICKEN IN LIQUORS

HOT CAULIFLOWER MOLD

PEACH SOUFFLÉ

BAYOU RIPE TOMATO COCKTAIL

Peel ripe tomatoes and chop fine. Season with onion juice, salt, pepper, and celery salt. Add enough Tabasco sauce to give the mixture a bite. Chill in freezing tray of the refrigerator but do not freeze. Heap in mounds in cocktail glasses and top with a spoonful of stiff mayonnaise seasoned with curry powder.

CREAM OF SALMON SOUP

Pour off the oil, and remove the bones and skin from 1 can of salmon. Grind or mash the salmon as fine as possible. Heat 1 quart of rich milk or cream, and thicken with 2 tablespoons of flour blended with 1 tablespoon of butter. Add salmon and cook for 10 minutes. Press through a purée sieve. (Prepare in the morning.) Serve hot with chopped parsley sprinkled on top. Serves 6.

CHICKEN IN LIQUORS

Cut up 3 fryers and brown in butter in a casserole. Bake in a slow oven until tender. Remove the chicken to a serving platter and keep warm. Add ⅓ cup each of whiskey, brandy, and port to the casserole and cook on top of the stove until blended. Remove from the fire, and add 2 egg yolks beaten with ½ cup of cream. Stir well and pour over the chicken. Serves 6.

HOT CAULIFLOWER MOLD

Cook a head of cauliflower in boiling salted water until tender. Drain and mash fine with a fork. Make a cream sauce with 2 tablespoons of butter, 2 tablespoons of flour, ½ teaspoon of salt, and 1 cup of rich milk. Cook until thick. Stir in the cauliflower. Add ⅛ teaspoon pepper and stir in 2 beaten egg yolks. Mix 1 cupful of dried bread crumbs with melted butter and sprinkle thickly over the bottom and sides of a buttered glass baking dish. Pour in the cauliflower mixture and set the baking dish in a pan half filled with boiling water. Bake for 1 hour, starting at 325° and increasing the heat to 375° during the last 15 minutes. Turn out on a platter and surround with buttered Lima beans and whole tiny crooked-neck squashes. Serves 6.

PEACH SOUFFLÉ
(Maud's)

Wash ½ pound of dried peaches and soak overnight. Cook the peaches in the same water in which they were soaked until all the liquid is absorbed. Rub through a purée sieve. (Prepare in the morning.) Beat the whites of 5 eggs stiff with ⅛ teaspoon of salt. Fold in gently ¾ cup of sugar, 1 cup of peach pulp, the juice of ½ lemon, 1 teaspoon of vanilla, and ½ cup of finely chopped nuts. Pour into a buttered baking dish and place in a pan of hot water. Bake in a moderate oven (350°) for about 1 hour. Serve with sweetened whipped cream. Serves 6.

Menu

CREAM OF SHRIMP SOUP

CROWN ROAST OF LAMB

BRUSSELS SPROUTS AND CHESTNUTS

BAKED CUCUMBERS WITH BANANAS

LEMON BUTTER

CHINESE GINGER ICE CREAM

CUP CAKES

CREAM OF SHRIMP SOUP

Clean 2 cups of cooked shrimps and put through the food chopper. Put in the top of a double boiler over direct heat and add 2 tablespoons of butter, 1 onion grated, and a dash of black pepper. Simmer for 5 minutes. Place the pan over hot water and add 1 quart of milk and 1 cup of cream. Season with salt to taste. Cook for ½ hour, stirring occasionally. Serves 6.

CROWN ROAST OF LAMB

Have your butcher prepare a crown roast of lamb. Wrap the exposed bones in salt pork to keep them from burning. Rub the meat with a clove of garlic, season with salt and pepper, and dredge with flour. Fill the center of the roast with well-seasoned sausage meat. Place the roast in a pan in a hot oven (400°) and brown well. Add ½ cup of water and 1 tablespoon of vinegar and baste often. Cook about 2 hours. Remove the roast. To make gravy, remove all the grease from the pan except 3 tablespoons and blend with 2 tablespoons of flour. Add 2 cups of water and cook until thick. Serve separately. Serves 4 to 6.

BRUSSELS SPROUTS AND CHESTNUTS

Use equal amounts of chestnuts and brussels sprouts. Parboil and shell the chestnuts. Wash and remove any dried leaves from the brussels sprouts. Place with the chestnuts in a covered casserole, cover with chicken stock, and let cook in a slow oven for 2 hours. When ready to serve, thicken the stock with 2 tablespoons of butter and 1½ tablespoons of flour.

BAKED CUCUMBERS WITH BANANAS

Remove the skins from 3 bananas and peel 3 cucumbers. Cut them in half lengthwise, then crosswise. Place the cucumbers in a baking dish with the cut side up and place a piece of banana over each. Slip each pair inside a slice of lemon to hold them in place. Bake in a moderate oven (350°) until tender. Serve on a platter with a bowl of Lemon Butter in the center.

Lemon Butter. — Heat 3 tablespoons of lemon juice and 4 tablespoons of orange juice with ½ cup of water. Add 2 tablespoons of butter.

CHINESE GINGER ICE CREAM

In the top of a double boiler heat 1 cup of milk. Then add 18 marshmallows and heat until the marshmallows are dissolved. Stir until smooth. Let cool. Beat 1 cup of cream until thick and add to the marshmallows. Fold in ¾ cup of finely chopped preserved ginger, drained of all syrup. Freeze without stirring. (Prepare the day before.) Serves 4 to 6.

CUP CAKES

Cream together ⅓ cup of butter and ⅔ cup of sugar. Beat in the yolks of 2 eggs. Sift together 1½ cups of sifted flour, 2 teaspoons of baking powder, and ¼ teaspoon of salt. Add the flour mixture alternately with ½ cup of milk. Fold in the stiffly beaten whites of the 2 eggs. Flavor with 1 teaspoon of vanilla. Grease and flour muffin tins and pour in the cake mixture. Bake in a moderate oven (350°) until brown.

Menu

CHICKEN AND CLAM BROTH

BOILED CUCUMBERS WITH SHAD ROE

NEVER-FAIL HOLLANDAISE SAUCE

LAMB ROASTED WITH COFFEE AND CREAM

PEAS AND CARROTS IN WHITE STOCK

CORN MEAL WAFERS

WINE GELATINE

GRAHAM COCOANUT SNAPS

CHICKEN AND CLAM BROTH

Mix half and half canned chicken broth and clam broth. Serve very hot.

BOILED CUCUMBERS WITH SHAD ROE

Cut cucumbers in half lengthwise and remove the seeds. Cook in boiling salted water until tender. Brown canned shad roe in a little butter and place one in each cucumber half. Pour Never-Fail Hollandaise Sauce (p. 89) over the cucumber. Serve hot.

LAMB ROASTED WITH COFFEE AND CREAM

First skin the leg of lamb, as the skin is the cause of the strong flavor. Rub the roast with garlic and then season well with salt, pepper, and dry mustard. Place thin slices of salt pork over the lamb and roast in a hot oven (400°) for ½ hour until the lamb is well browned. Remove the pork. Pour over the lamb 2 cups of strong coffee with cream and turn the heat low. For the next 2 hours baste as often as possible, for the more you baste the more delicious is the flavor of the meat. Add 1 cup of port wine and continue basting for ½ hour more. Carve the lamb, but replace the slices. Serve the gravy separately. Serves 6.

PEAS AND CARROTS IN WHITE STOCK

Shell 3 pounds of peas and dice 1 bunch of carrots very, very fine. Melt 3 tablespoons of butter in a saucepan and add the carrots. Cook gently for 15 minutes but do not brown. Season with salt and pepper. Add the peas and 1 cup of chicken broth. (This may be made by adding 2 chicken broth cubes to 1 cup of hot water.) Simmer until the vegetables are tender. (Prepare in the morning and reheat in a double boiler.) Cover with chopped parsley and serve in a heated vegetable dish. Serves 6.

CORN MEAL WAFERS

Beat together 4 eggs and 2 cups of milk. Add a scant ½ cup of butter, which has been melted and clarified. (Discard the milk substance which sinks to the bottom when butter is melted.) Sift together 1½ cups of corn meal, 3 cups of white flour, 1 cup of sugar, 2 teaspoons of baking powder, and ¼ teaspoon of salt. Add to the egg mixture. Turn a baking pan upside down and spread this mixture on the bottom very, very thin. Put into a moderate oven (350°) until it dries enough to cut. Remove and cut into oblongs 2 × 3 inches. Put back in a 450° oven to brown. If these wafers are stored in a tin box, they will keep for about a week.

WINE GELATINE

Soak the contents of 1 envelope of gelatine in ¼ cup of cold water. Dissolve in ½ cup of boiling water. Add ¼ teaspoon of salt, ½ cup of sugar, and ¼ cup of orange juice. Stir until dissolved. Add ¾ cup of sherry and 1 tablespoon of lemon juice. Rinse a mold in cold water and pour in the gelatine. Serve with whipped cream. Serves 4. (Prepare the day before.)

GRAHAM COCOANUT SNAPS

Beat ⅓ cup of butter until soft and slowly add 1¼ cups of brown sugar sifted to remove all lumps. Beat well together until creamy. Beat in 2 eggs. Add ½ teaspoon of vanilla and beat again. Add 1 cup of sifted all-purpose flour and ½ cup each of crushed corn flakes and graham crackers sifted after they were measured. Beat well. Stir in ½ cup each of chopped nut meats and shredded cocoanut. Spread on a greased cookie sheet and bake in a hot oven (400°) for ½ hour. Cut into small squares while warm.

Menu

BORSCH WITH SOUR CREAM

COMBINATION OF FISH IN MOLD

CUCUMBER AND WATER CRESS SANDWICHES

FRIED CHICKEN WITH BING CHERRIES

STRING BEANS WITH FRIED WALNUTS

ROMAINE LETTUCE WITH EGG DRESSING

CRÈME BRÛLÉ

LACE COOKIES

BORSCH WITH SOUR CREAM

Peel and put through a coarse grinder 1 cup of beets, 1 cup of carrots, and ½ cup of onions. Cover with water and boil gently for about 20 minutes with the pan covered. Add 2 cans of consommé, 1 cup of canned tomatoes, and 1 cup of shredded cabbage. Cook for 15 minutes. Strain and taste for seasoning. Add 1 tablespoon of lemon juice. If the soup is not a clear red, tint slightly with red vegetable coloring. Serve with a dab of sour cream on the top. Serves 4.

COMBINATION OF FISH IN MOLD

Pour a little cooled aspic in the bottom of a fish mold. Place a slice of stuffed green olive in the position for the eye. Use curved slices of hard-boiled white of egg for the scales and matchlike shreds of green pepper for the fins. Pour a little more aspic over to hold them in place. Chill until firm. Fill the mold with alternate layers of fresh crab meat, cleaned shrimps, and pieces of lobster meat. Pour the aspic over the fish and set in the refrigerator until firm. Serve with Green Mayonnaise (p. 40). Serves 6.

Aspic. — Soak 1 tablespoon of gelatine in ¼ cup of cold water. Add 2 tablespoons of vinegar. Heat 1 can of consommé and pour over the gelatine. Stir until dissolved.

CUCUMBER AND WATER CRESS SANDWICHES

Cut thin rounds of bread the size of a slice of cucumber. Spread with mayonnaise and place a slice of cucumber on the bread and then a sprig of water cress, so that the water cress projects over the side. Place another round of bread on top.

FRIED CHICKEN WITH BING CHERRIES

Fry 2 chickens until tender (California Fried Chicken, p. 222).

Remove chickens to a platter and keep warm. Add 2 table-spoons of butter and 2 finely minced onions to the skillet in which the chicken was cooked. Add 1 can of consommé and 1 cup of hot water. Simmer gently while you drain the juice from 1 can of pitted Bing cherries. Mix the juice with 2 tablespoons of corn-starch and add to the consommé mixture. Strain into a stewpan; add cherries and ½ cup of sherry. Taste for seasoning and heat. Place a bowl of the sauce in the center of the platter of chicken and pour the rest of the sauce over the chicken. Serves 6 to 8.

STRING BEANS WITH FRIED WALNUTS

Shred string beans and boil until tender. Drain and season with salt and pepper. Melt butter in a frying pan and cook until browned. Add chopped walnut meats and pour over the string beans. (Shredded almonds may be used.)

ROMAINE LETTUCE WITH EGG DRESSING

Hard-boil 4 eggs. Mash the yolks and add to a tart French dressing. Break romaine lettuce into short pieces and toss in a salad bowl with egg dressing. Sprinkle the chopped egg whites over the top.

CRÈME BRÛLÉ

For 4 people, heat 2 cups of cream in the top of a double boiler until warm. Stir in 2 tablespoons of brown sugar and 2 tablespoons of brandy. Beat 4 egg yolks and stir into the cream. Pour into a glass baking dish of the right size so that the pudding is about 1½ to 2 inches deep. Place the dish in a pan of hot water in a 250° oven and bake until set. It will take about 1½ hours. Remove from the oven to cool and then place in the refrigerator to chill thoroughly. (May be prepared the day before.)

About 2 hours before the dessert is to be served, cover the surface with a ¼- to ½-inch layer of sifted brown sugar and place under a hot broiler. Watch it constantly! The top of the brown sugar will melt and form a hard glaze, while the part underneath will remain soft. Put back in the refrigerator until ready to serve.

This dessert should be accompanied by a tart canned fruit such as canned green gage plums, apricots, or cherries. The fruit may or may not be soaked in brandy.

Crème Brûlé Made with Evaporated Milk. — Use the same recipe as the one using cream, substituting ¾ cup of evaporated milk mixed with 1¼ cups of fresh milk in place of 2 cups of cream. Cover while baking; otherwise the evaporated milk forms a tough skin over the top. (I like to add ⅛ teaspoon of salt to either recipe.)

LACE COOKIES

Beat 2 eggs well and add 1 cup of sugar, ½ teaspoon of salt, and 1 teaspoon of baking powder. Mix in 1½ cups of oatmeal and let the batter stand for 1 hour. Drop by spoonfuls onto a buttered cookie sheet and bake in a moderate oven (350°). Take cookies off the sheet as soon as they finish baking.

Menu

CONSOMMÉ MADRILÈNE

LIME RING FILLED WITH CRAB MEAT

FRIED CHICKEN

SPINACH IN BROTH

POTATO SOUFFLÉ

CHOCOLATE POTS DE CRÈME

LIME RING FILLED WITH CRAB MEAT

Dissolve 2 packages of lime gelatine in 2 cups of boiling water. Cool and add 1 cup of cold water. Stir in the contents of 1 large bottle of horse-radish, 2 tablespoons of vinegar, and season with salt and pepper. Pour into a ring mold and place in the refrigerator until firm. Unmold on a platter and fill the center with fresh or canned crab meat with Thousand Island Dressing (p. 103). Surround with water cress.

FRIED CHICKEN
(Margaret's)

Cut 3 frying chickens in serving pieces. Boil the backs, wing tips, and necks for stock. Rub the rest of the pieces with salt, pepper, and ginger. Sauté until brown and then flick with a little water. Put the lid on the pan and cook over a slow fire until tender. Remove from the pan and keep warm.

In the pan blend 2 tablespoons of flour. Add 2 cups of the chicken stock. Cook until thick. Add 1 large can of mushrooms and 1 bottle of pitted green olives chopped fine. Mix in 2 tablespoons of chopped chives. Flavor with sherry and taste for seasoning. Arrange the chicken on a large platter and pour the sauce over it. Garnish with canned artichoke hearts, which have been well heated, alternating with broiled zucchini halves.

SPINACH IN BROTH

Wash 6 bunches, or 3 pounds, of spinach thoroughly. Sauté 1 sliced onion and 3 strips of chopped bacon in a pan; simmer for 10 minutes with 2 cups of water, strongly flavored with chicken soup cubes. Strain the broth and add to the spinach. Cook for 15 minutes. Drain and chop fine. Season with melted butter, salt, and pepper. (May be prepared in the morning and reheated in the top of a double boiler.)

POTATO SOUFFLÉ

To 4 cups of mashed potatoes add the yolks of 2 eggs, ½ cup of cream, and 2 tablespoons of butter. Beat until light and creamy. Fold in the stiffly beaten egg whites and heap in a buttered casserole. Brush with melted butter and bake in a 325° oven for 30 minutes.

CHOCOLATE POTS DE CRÈME

Break into pieces a 1-pound bar of sweet chocolate. Place it in the top of a double boiler to melt and gradually add ¼ cup of milk. Stir with a wooden spoon until well mixed and absolutely smooth. Beat the yolks of 4 eggs and add to the chocolate mixture. Cook for about 10 minutes, stirring constantly until the mixture thickens. Remove from the stove and let cool. Beat 3 egg whites until stiff and add to the cool chocolate mixture. Add 1 pint of cream, beaten stiff, and pour the mixture into little cups. Put in the refrigerator overnight.

This dessert should be served in the little French custard cups. You can buy them in this country in any large city. After-dinner coffee cups may be used.

Menu

MUSHROOMS SAUTÉED IN BUTTER AND
SHERRY

FILLET OF SOLE WITH EGG SAUCE

MALLARD DUCKS STUFFED WITH BROWN RICE

SMOTHERED PEAS

STRAWBERRIES IN WINE WITH
FROZEN CREAM

FILLET OF SOLE WITH EGG SAUCE

Melt 1 tablespoon of butter in a saucepan and add 1 small, minced onion. Stir for a moment but do not brown. Soak ½ cup of bread crumbs in as much milk as they will absorb. Squeeze out superfluous milk and add the bread crumbs to the mixture in the saucepan. Add 16 cooked shrimps, finely minced, 1 teaspoon of chopped parsley, 1 hard-boiled egg mashed fine, ½ teaspoon of salt and pepper. Cook gently for 3 minutes; remove from the fire and cool. Add 1 egg white beaten stiff.

Rub 6 equal-sized fillets of sole with salt and pepper. Fill with the shrimp mixture, roll, and fasten with toothpicks. (Prepare in the morning.) Bake 20 to 30 minutes in a moderate oven (350°). Remove toothpicks. Serve with Egg Sauce.

Egg Sauce. — Melt 2 tablespoons of butter in a saucepan. Add 2 tablespoons of flour, ¼ teaspoon of salt, and ¼ teaspoon of white pepper. Stir until smooth. Add, while whipping with a wire whisk, 1 cup of hot stock or diluted consommé. Simmer 5 minutes, whisking constantly. Add 5 hard-boiled eggs, chopped fine, and 2 tablespoons of heavy cream and bring to the boil once. Remove from the stove and add 1 teaspoon of Worcestershire sauce, 3 drops of Tabasco sauce, 1½ teaspoons of minced parsley, and 1 teaspoon of capers. Serve hot. (Prepare in the morning and reheat in a double boiler.) Serves 6.

MALLARD DUCKS WITH BROWN RICE

For enough stuffing for 4 mallard ducks, boil 1 cup of brown rice in 1 quart of boiling salted water for 30 minutes. Drain. Crumble enough stale bread to fill 1 cup and mix lightly with the rice. Sauté 1 minced onion and ⅓ cup of chopped celery in 3 table-spoons of butter until soft, not brown. Mix with the rice and bread. Season with 1 teaspoon of poultry seasoning, 1 teaspoon of salt, and ½ teaspoon of pepper. Add 2 tablespoons chopped parsley. Stuff the ducks lightly so that the stuffing has room to swell. Sew the opening. Place them in a pan with 1 cup of water and cover. Cook in a very hot oven (425°) for about 1 hour. Reduce the heat to 350° and cook another hour. Remove the lid of the roaster and cook for about ½ hour more. Baste every few minutes during the entire cooking time. The more you baste, the more flavor the ducks will have. Remove to a hot platter.

Add 1 cup of orange juice, 1 tablespoon of grated orange rind, 1 glass of currant jelly, and 2 tablespoons of sherry to the fat in the roasting pan. Stir well, bring to a boil, and pour over the ducks. Serves 6 to 8.

STRAWBERRIES IN WINE

Clean strawberries and cover with dry white wine. Sprinkle heavily with sugar — 1 cup to a quart of berries. Allow the berries to stand in the refrigerator for 2 hours. Drain off the juice and put the berries in a serving bowl. Bring the juice to a boil. Chill and then pour back over the berries. Serve with Frozen Cream (p. 62).

Menu

JELLIED TOMATO JUICE

HALLIWAY OYSTERS

NEVER-FAIL HOLLANDAISE SAUCE

RACK OF LAMB

ZUCCHINI AND MUSHROOMS WITH
BROWNED CRUMBS

CHERRIES BAKED IN BRANDY

JELLIED TOMATO JUICE

Soften 1 package of gelatine in ½ cup of cold water. Season 2 cups of tomato juice with Worcestershire sauce, lemon and onion juice, salt and pepper. Bring to a boil and pour over the gelatine. Stir until dissolved. Chill thoroughly. Serve very cold with a dab of sour cream on top. (Prepare the day before.) Serves 4.

HALLIWAY OYSTERS

Chop 1 onion fine and sauté in 4 tablespoons of butter. Add 1 quart of chopped oysters. Season with ½ teaspoon of salt, a dash of cayenne, and 1 teaspoon of Worcestershire sauce. Cook for about a minute; then add 2 beaten eggs and ¾ cup of fine bread crumbs, mixed with 4 tablespoons of melted butter. Add 2 tablespoons of finely chopped parsley. Stir lightly and place in a glass pie dish. Bake for ½ hour in a moderate oven (350°) until firm and brown. Serve with Never-Fail Hollandaise Sauce (p. 89). This dish may also be served for a Sunday night supper. Serves 6.

RACK OF LAMB

A rack of lamb weighing 7 pounds should be enough for 8 people. Season and brush with butter. Place in a roasting pan and add 2 onions and 2 carrots, sliced. Cook with the lid off in a medium oven, allowing 25 minutes per pound. Remove roast from pan, skim off the fat, then add 1 can of consommé. Boil the mixture up once and strain. Cut the lamb in 16 pieces, and arrange on a round platter with water cress in the center. Pour sauce from the roaster over the meat.

ZUCCHINI AND MUSHROOMS WITH BROWNED CRUMBS

Slice zucchini and add half the amount of mushrooms. Brown in an iron skillet with melted butter. Lower the fire, put on a lid, and simmer slowly until the squash is tender. Season with salt and pepper. Sprinkle with dried bread crumbs browned lightly in butter.

CHERRIES BAKED IN BRANDY

Drain 2 cans of pitted Black Bing cherries. Add 1 teaspoon of lemon juice, 2 tablespoons of sugar, and a few grains of cinnamon to the cherries. Put in a glass pie plate, cover with a glass of currant jelly, sprinkle with shredded walnuts, and bake for 10 minutes. Pour a wine glass of brandy over the cherries and serve lighted. Serve with a bowl of Frozen Cream (p. 62). Serves 6 to 8.

Menu

QUICK VICHYSSOISE

BROOK TROUT FILLED WITH SPINACH

SQUABS STUFFED WITH WILD RICE

GREEN SUMMER SQUASH AND TINY ONIONS

ASPARAGUS WITH VINAIGRETTE DRESSING

TOASTED CHEESE CRACKERS

RUM PUDDING

QUICK VICHYSSOISE

Cook 8 sliced onions in a little water until tender. Add 2 cans of potato soup and 4 cans of chicken rice soup. Heat thoroughly and mash through a purée sieve. Add 1 cup of cream and season to taste. Chill thoroughly and serve ice-cold, with mixed chopped chives and parsley sprinkled over the top. (May be prepared the day before.) Serves 6 to 8.

BROOK TROUT FILLED WITH SPINACH

Have your fish dealer clean and bone the desired number of trout. Stuff the trout with chopped, cooked spinach, which has been seasoned with butter, salt, and pepper. Sauté fish in butter on both sides until brown and cooked through. Squeeze a few drops of lemon juice on each fish, pour browned melted butter over them, and sprinkle with finely chopped parsley. Serve.

SQUABS STUFFED WITH WILD RICE

For 8 squabs, use 4 cups of cooked wild rice. Then cook and mash the livers from the birds and mix with 1 teaspoon each of chopped fried bacon, chopped parsley, and chives. Sauté ½ cup of mushrooms, either canned or fresh, and chop fine. Add the liver mixture and chopped mushrooms to the rice, with enough canned consommé to moisten.

Stuff the squabs and close the openings with skewers. (Prepare in the morning.) Place in a pan in a 425° oven and add butter and a little water. Baste continually, for the more the birds are basted, the better the flavor. When the birds are brown, reduce the heat and add 1 glass of currant jelly to the liquid. Continue basting until the birds are tender. Remove the skewers and place the birds on a serving platter. Pour the gravy over them. It will take about 30 minutes to cook the squabs, or perhaps a little longer if they are large. Serves 8.

GREEN SUMMER SQUASH AND TINY ONIONS

Boil or steam whole round summer squash (the patty-pan variety), and scoop out the inside from the stem end. Cook tiny onions (little seed onions) in boiling salted water until tender. Make a rich cream sauce and add the onions. Fill the squash with the creamed onions and put grated cheese and butter on the top. (Prepare in the morning.) Place squash in a pan with a little boiling water and set in a moderate oven until reheated. Place under the broiler until brown.

TOASTED CHEESE CRACKERS

These are good served as a quick canapé or with the salad course.

Mix equal parts of butter and fresh grated cheese. Work well together and add salt, pepper, and quite a bit of cayenne. (Prepare in the morning.) Spread on saltines and bake in the oven until brown.

RUM PUDDING

Soak 1½ tablespoons of gelatine in 2 tablespoons of cold water. Dissolve in 6 tablespoons of boiling water. Add 1 cup of sugar, ⅔ cup of rum, and 4 tablespoons of bourbon. Stir until the sugar dissolves. Cool until it begins to thicken; then add 2 egg whites beaten stiff. Beat 1 pint of cream stiff and add to the gelatine mixture, 2 tablespoons at a time, beating after each addition. Beat until light and pour into a melon mold rinsed in cold water. Chill until firm. (Prepare the day before.)

Unmold on a platter and cover with chopped nuts. Surround with Custard Sauce (p. 31) flavored with rum and sift a little nutmeg over the top. Serves 4 to 6.

The Lilac Tea

For thirty years our great purple lilac bush had been steadily growing until at last it stretched twelve feet into the air. From its sheltered corner in the ell of the old ranch house, it waited for the first signs of the spring thaw.

At Easter time we announced the engagements of two of our daughters. Never before in all its years had the lilac bush put forth such an abundance of bloom! So we gave a Lilac Tea to honor the two young girls.

You may not have lilacs and you may not be announcing the engagements of two daughters, but you may sometime wish to give a special tea. And what could be more delightful than a flower tea?

Many other flowers would be just as effective and spectacular as the lilacs. In California we have a brown-eyed yellow daisy that grows in great abundance by the roadside. If the colors in your rooms harmonize with yellow, you can make a gorgeous display with no expense but the effort of picking them. For an autumn tea, rooms banked with brilliant autumn leaves would be striking, or you might have a hollyhock tea, with tall branches in jars of water concealed in baskets, and short-stemmed blossoms floating in low bowls on tables. Delphinium, lupine, and syringa are ideal for such decoration.

Keep the food simple and delicious and be sure that the tea is of a good blend and served piping hot. The recipes I give for the food served at our Lilac Tea have been used innumerable times in my own home for all kinds of teas — when the girls were very young, when they were in college, and when their engage-

ments were announced. Later, when they married, they took
copies of these recipes with them to use in their new homes.
Some of the recipes are simple, some are more difficult, but
nearly all can be prepared far enough ahead of time to eliminate
any last-moment worry.

OPEN SANDWICHES

STRAWBERRY JAM SANDWICHES

Cut sliced white bread in a diamond shape and decorate the
edge with a fluting of cream cheese. Place a bit of jam or jelly in
the center.

EGG CIRCLES

Slice hard-boiled eggs and place the slices on buttered rounds
of bread the same size. Dot with mayonnaise and sprinkle with a
dash of paprika.

OPEN CUCUMBER SANDWICHES

Peel and slice cucumbers thin; let stand in salted water for 20
minutes. Drain well. Slice white bread thin and cut in rounds the
size of the cucumber. Butter the bread, cover with a slice of cucumber, sprinkle lightly with celery salt, top with mayonnaise,
and add a dash of paprika.

TOMATO JELLY SANDWICHES

Heat 3 cups of tomato juice with 1 slice of onion and boil 3
minutes. Remove the onion and add 2 tablespoons of gelatine
soaked in a little cold tomato juice. Season with 1 teaspoon of
celery salt and 2 teaspoons of Worcestershire sauce. Fill a flat pan
¼ inch deep and place in the refrigerator until firm. Cut the tomato
jelly in shapes the same size as slices of white bread. Spread the
bread with butter, place the tomato jelly on top and decorate with
mayonnaise.

PIMIENTO CHEESE CRESCENTS

Cut white bread in the shape of crescents, spread with pimiento
cheese, and top with sliced, stuffed olives.

EGG AND ANCHOVY SANDWICHES

Cut white bread in small rounds. Spread with a mixture of anchovy paste and mayonnaise, cover with a slice of hard-boiled egg, and place a curled anchovy on top.

PECAN AND CREAM CHEESE

Spread white bread with cream cheese and top with pecans.

SCOTCH–HAM FINGERS

Spread slices of square, whole-wheat sandwich bread with butter mixed with mustard. Cover with pressed ham or Scotch ham, then cut in 4 fingers. Decorate with slices of baby gherkins, held in place with some of the butter mixture.

SHRIMP AND PEANUT BUTTER

Cream together 2 tablespoons of peanut butter and 2 tablespoons of butter. Add 1 teaspoon of curry powder and ⅛ teaspoon of salt. Spread on rounds of white bread. Split 6 shrimps lengthwise and place half a shrimp on each round of bread. Sprinkle with paprika and serve very cold.

TOASTED ORANGE MARMALADE AND PECAN SANDWICHES

Cut slices of white bread into fingers. Spread with orange marmalade and arrange pecan meats down the center. Toast under the broiler.

CLOSED SANDWICHES

CHICKEN SALAD SANDWICHES

Combine 1 cup of chopped, cooked chicken with ½ cup of chopped nut meats and 3 tablespoons of finely diced celery. Moisten with enough mayonnaise to spread. Season to taste, adding a little lemon juice.

RIPE OLIVE SANDWICHES

Combine ½ cup of chopped ripe olives with 1 cream cheese, mashed. Add 2 tablespoons of chopped green pepper and enough mayonnaise for spreading. Season with a little onion juice, salt, and pepper.

LOBSTER SANDWICHES

Chop canned lobster meat fine and add to chopped hard-boiled eggs and cucumber. Flavor with lemon juice and mix with sufficient mayonnaise to spread.

PECAN AND OLIVE SANDWICHES

Chop fine 4 hard-boiled eggs, 1 cup of stuffed green olives, and 1 cup of pecans. Add enough mayonnaise to moisten, and season to taste.

ROLLED ASPARAGUS SANDWICHES

Remove crust from a loaf of bread and slice thin. Wrap in a damp napkin and keep in a cool place for a few hours so that the bread will roll without breaking. Before time to serve, spread each slice with soft butter, dip a canned asparagus stalk in highly seasoned mayonnaise, and roll in a slice of bread. Fasten with a toothpick and cover with a damp cloth until ready to serve.

COOKIES AND TEA CAKES

DATE–NUT BARS

Cut in small pieces 1 cup of dates and 1 cup of nuts. Mix ¾ cup of brown sugar with 3½ tablespoons of flour and 1 teaspoon of baking powder. Add nuts and dates; then add 2 egg yolks which have been beaten with 1 teaspoon of vanilla. Fold in 2 stiffly beaten egg whites. Smooth in a buttered pan and bake in a moderate oven (350°) 20 minutes. Cut in bars and dust with powdered sugar.

CORN FLAKE MACAROONS
(Emma's)

2 egg whites	1 cup cocoanut
1 cup brown sugar	½ cup chopped nut meats
2 tablespoons melted butter	½ teaspoon salt
1 tablespoon vanilla	4 cups corn flakes

Beat egg whites until stiff and dry; then add sugar. Add the remaining ingredients and mix thoroughly. Drop by teaspoonfuls onto a greased cookie sheet and bake in a moderately hot oven (350°).

CINNAMON CRISPS

Sift together 2 cups of flour, 1 teaspoon of cinnamon, and 3 teaspoons of baking powder. Cream ½ cup of butter and add 1 cup of sugar. Add the flour alternately with ½ cup of milk. (Add more flour, if necessary.) Chill the dough until firm. Roll the dough very thin and cut into fancy shapes. Bake on a greased tin in a moderate oven (375°) for about 7 minutes.

CHOCOLATE SQUARES

Cream 2 cups of brown sugar with 1 cup of butter and beat until light and creamy. Add ⅓ cup of melted Baker's chocolate. Beat 1 whole egg with 3 egg yolks and stir into the mixture. Add alternately 1 cup of sour milk and 2 cups of sifted flour, and at the last add 1 teaspoon of soda dissolved in a little milk. Pour into a baking pan to a depth of about ½ inch. Bake in a moderate oven (350°). When cool, cut in squares and ice with Easy Chocolate Frosting.

Easy Chocolate Frosting. — Beat 4 egg whites stiff, add 2 teaspoons of vanilla, and gradually beat in 3 cups of confectioner's sugar. Lastly beat in 4 squares of melted chocolate.

ORANGE MARMALADE DROP CAKES

Cream ⅓ cup of butter and add gradually ⅔ cup of sugar. Add 1 beaten egg and 6 tablespoons of marmalade; then stir in 1½ cups of flour sifted with 2 teaspoons of baking powder. Drop the dough by spoonfuls, far apart, onto a greased cookie sheet. Bake in oven (275°) for 10 minutes.

DATE COOKIES

Mix 1 cup of flour, 1 cup of sugar, 1 cup of rolled oats, and 1 teaspoon of soda. Add a pinch of salt and mix in lightly ¾ cup of butter. Divide this mixture in half. Place ½ in the bottom of a baking pan and cover with Date Filling. Put the rest of the flour mixture on top and bake in a 350° oven until a golden brown. Cut in 2-inch squares.

Date Filling. — Mix in top of a double boiler 1 large cup of chopped, pitted dates, 1 cup of chopped walnuts, and ½ cup of sugar. Cook until smooth and let cool.

JAM PUFFS
(Kay's)

Mix ½ cup of butter with 1½ cups of sugar. Add 1 cup of finely chopped nuts, 1 teaspoon of vanilla, and ½ teaspoon of grated lemon rind. Mix thoroughly. Stir in 1½ cups of sifted flour and place the bowl containing the dough over hot water until the dough softens enough to roll into 1-inch balls. Make a depression in the top of each ball and place a bit of jam in it. Bake on a greased cookie sheet for 10 minutes in a 400° oven. Dust with powdered sugar.

DRINKS

McCARTHY'S ICED TEA

Iced tea, when combined with this syrup, has a most unexpected and refreshing flavor.

Put in a saucepan 1 cup of sugar and 1 cup of water. Squeeze the juice of 1 lemon over the sugar and drop the lemon in the pan. Boil for 15 minutes and pour over 6 large sprigs of crushed mint. Cool. Strain the syrup and add enough to sweeten the iced tea.

HOT CHOCOLATE

Melt 2 squares of chocolate over hot water and add gradually ¼ cup of boiling water and ⅛ teaspoon of salt. Mix 1 teaspoon of cornstarch and ½ cup of sugar with a little cold water. Add 1 quart of scalded milk and stir until it thickens. Add to the chocolate and beat with an egg beater until foam forms on top.

FROSTED EGGNOG
(Margaret's)

Beat 10 egg yolks until lemon-colored. Gradually beat in ¾ cup of sugar, beating well after each addition. Gradually add 1 bottle of sherry, beating all the time. Fold in 1 quart of cream beaten stiff. Pour into freezing trays in the refrigerator and chill for 3 hours. Serve topped with a dash of nutmeg.

~~~~~~

Having "The Girls" for Luncheon

~~~~~~

The next time you are having the girls for luncheon, add some touch to make your party different, perhaps in the table decorations or in your choice of menu. The luncheon may be served formally, requiring the services of a maid, or, if you plan to serve it yourself, the food may be arranged on the buffet and the guests help themselves.

Carry the same color scheme through the entire luncheon. Gold and green, for instance, is a combination easily adapted to decorations as well as to food. Use yellow or orange flowers with their green leaves, and candles to match either color. Carry your color scheme into your drinks. Orange juice will appeal to those who prefer a non-alcoholic beverage, or a stinger made with green instead of white crème de menthe for those who wish it. The two colors make a beautiful contrast when served together on the same tray.

If this luncheon is formal, the first course will probably be soup, say Bordelais, which is an attractive pale green in color. The entree could be chicken. You might serve half a broiler stuffed with a highly seasoned dressing and then baked. Vegetables that may be cooked early should be selected, as they may be rewarmed at the last minute. To continue the orange and green motive, I suggest baby summer squash stuffed with Golden Bantam corn that has been mixed with a cream sauce.

And now, last but not least, the dessert! An apricot gelatine mold surrounded with whole brandied apricots, decorated with green leaves, and with a bowl of whipped cream in the center.

If you have no maid to serve the luncheon, select a menu that you can prepare easily and serve informally. You may still wish to serve soup; if so, pour it into cups and serve it to your guests while they are still in the living room. Arrange the entree on the buffet. It may be a ring mold, prepared the evening before and served cold, or a combination of food served hot from a casserole. To simplify the menu, the salad may be arranged on individual plates and served at the table, or it may be waiting on the sideboard with the entree.

Menu

(A Green and Gold Luncheon)

STINGERS *or* ORANGE JUICE

BORDELAIS SOUP

WATER CRESS SANDWICHES

STUFFED BROILERS

GREEN SUMMER SQUASHES FILLED WITH
GOLDEN BANTAM CORN

ORANGE BISCUITS

GOLDEN JELLY WITH BRANDIED APRICOTS

WHIPPING CREAM CAKE

STINGER

Mix ⅓ glass of white crème de menthe with ⅔ glass of brandy. Add plenty of shaved ice and shake well. (To carry out the color scheme, green crème de menthe may be used.)

BORDELAIS SOUP

2 pounds green peas	3 egg yolks
1 head lettuce	1 cup cream
2 cups chicken stock	Salt and pepper
2 tablespoons white chicken meat, diced	

Cut pea pods at each end, cook in salted water. Add chopped lettuce. When cooked to a good green color (about 20 or 25 minutes), drain. Remove peas from pods, crush pea pods, peas, and lettuce and put through a sieve. Pour chicken stock into the mixture and cook for 10 minutes. Skim and strain. (Prepare the day before.) Add cream and heat in top of double boiler. Just before serving add beaten egg yolks and stir over hot, but not boiling, water until thickened. When ready to serve, add a little diced chicken to each cup. The soup should be a light emerald green color. Serves 4.

I have made a passable substitute for this soup by putting 3 cans of chicken soup with rice through a sieve and adding 1 can of pea soup. Add 1 pint of cream and tint a pale green with vegetable coloring.

STUFFED BROILERS

Serve ½ broiler for each person. Split the broilers in half and rub, inside and out, with a mixture of salt, pepper, and a little ginger. Fill the cavity of the broiler with dressing. Place, skin-side down, in a roasting pan with melted butter. Cover. Roast for 1½ hours at 300°.

Dressing Enough for 1 Broiler. — Chop 6 mushrooms fine. Moisten 4 tablespoons of bread crumbs with 4 tablespoons of butter. Add 1 beaten egg yolk, 1 teaspoon of chopped parsley, ⅛ teaspoon of salt, and pepper. Mince 1 slice of raw bacon and 1 clove of garlic very fine. Mix all together and fill the cavities. (Prepare in the morning and roast when ready.)

GREEN SUMMER SQUASHES FILLED WITH GOLDEN BANTAM CORN

Cook round summer squashes in boiling salted water until tender, but not too soft. Cut off stem end and scoop out center. Heat canned whole kernel Golden Bantam corn with butter, and season. Fill squash shells. (Prepare in the morning.) Reheat in a moderate oven.

ORANGE BISCUITS

Sift together 2 cups of flour, 4 teaspoons of baking powder, and ½ teaspoon of salt. Mix in lightly with the fingers 2 tablespoons of shortening and add enough milk to make the right consistency to roll. Roll about 1 inch thick. Cut out. Soak a small-sized lump of sugar in orange juice and press in the top of each biscuit. Bake in a hot oven (475°) for about 12 minutes. Serves 6.

GOLDEN JELLY WITH BRANDIED APRICOTS

Soak 4 tablespoons of gelatine in 1 cup of water; then stir in 2 cups of boiling water. To the juice of 4 oranges and 2 lemons add 1 cup of granulated sugar. Drain 2 large cans of peeled apricots and put through a purée sieve. Mix everything and put through a wire sieve. Pour into a decorative ring mold and place in refrigerator until firm. (This dessert may be made the day before.) Unmold on a large glass platter. In the center of the mold place a bowl of sweetened whipped cream, flavored with brandy. Surround with whole brandied apricots, decorated with fresh green leaves. Serve with white cake. Serves 8.

WHIPPING CREAM CAKE

2 eggs	2 cups sifted flour
1 cup sugar	2 teaspoons baking powder
½ pint whipping cream	1 teaspoon vanilla

Beat eggs and add sugar. Sift flour and baking powder together. Add to first mixture alternately with cream. (Do not whip cream.) Stir in vanilla. Makes 2 layers. (For the luncheon, bake in 1 layer and cut in squares.) This cake may be baked the day before.

Menu

BOTTLED APPLE JUICE

BAKED EGGPLANT STUFFED WITH
SHRIMPS AND MUSHROOMS

BROWN BREAD SANDWICHES

MOLDED OLIVE, CHERRY, AND NUT SALAD

ANGEL FOOD CAKE COATED WITH
PECAN BRITTLE

Pass the ice-cold apple juice in the drawing room, and serve the rest of the luncheon from the buffet.

BAKED EGGPLANT STUFFED WITH SHRIMPS AND MUSHROOMS
(Peg's)

Cut eggplant in half lengthwise. Scoop out the pulp, leaving a shell ½ inch thick. Cube the pulp of the eggplant and cook in boiling salted water until tender. Drain the cooked eggplant and add 1 can of shrimps, cleaned, and 1 can of mushrooms Mix with a little mayonnaise and fill the 2 eggplant halves. Place in a casserole with a little water, put on the lid, and bake in the oven until well heated through and the shells have softened. Serve with buttered brown bread sandwiches. Serves 6.

MOLDED OLIVE, CHERRY, AND NUT SALAD

Drain 1 can of pitted Bing cherries and mix the cherry juice with the juice of 1 lemon and enough water to make 2 cups. Bring to a boil and pour over 1 package of lemon gelatine. Chill until it begins to stiffen; then add the cherries, with 1 small bottle of stuffed olives and ½ cup of chopped almonds or walnuts. Pour into a ring mold and chill until firm. Invert on a platter, surround with lettuce, and place a bowl of Orange and Lemon Mayonnaise (p. 64) in the center. Serves 6.

ANGEL FOOD CAKE COATED WITH PECAN BRITTLE

1 angel food cake	8 egg yolks
1 tablespoon gelatine	1 cup powdered sugar
¼ cup cold water	1 pint whipping cream
2 tablespoons bourbon	½ pound pecan brittle

Soak gelatine in cold water. Place over boiling water to dissolve; then add the bourbon. Beat egg yolks until thick, beating in the sugar gradually. Add gelatine mixture and mix thoroughly. Let cool but do not let stiffen. Fold in the whipped cream. Chill until it begins to stiffen. Cut angel food cake in two, just a little above the center (which prevents the top layer from slipping). Spread cream mixture between layers and over top and sides. Place in refrigerator for several hours. When ready to serve, sprinkle thickly with the crushed pecan brittle. Use the egg whites to make the cake, or for Orange Soufflé (p. 279).

Menu

GRAPEFRUIT WITH RUM

SHRIMPS IN WHITE WINE

CUCUMBERS IN SOUR CREAM

ROLLED TOAST

ANGEL PIE

GRAPEFRUIT WITH RUM

4 grapefruit	2½ cups peeled white grapes
⅓ cup rum	1½ cups powdered sugar

Cut the grapefruit in halves and loosen the segments. Remove the pithy center and fill with the grapes. Sprinkle with the sugar dissolved in the rum. Chill thoroughly and serve very cold. Serves 8.

SHRIMPS IN WHITE WINE

Clean 3 pounds of boiled shrimps. Cream ¾ cup of butter and mix in 1 teaspoon of salt and 1 minced clove of garlic, also a dash of cayenne and paprika. Stir ½ cup of white wine into 1 cup of bread crumbs and mix with the butter. Add 4 tablespoons of minced parsley. Place in a buttered casserole alternate layers of boiled shrimps and the bread crumb mixture. Bake in a hot oven (400°) for 25 minutes. Serves 6.

CUCUMBERS IN SOUR CREAM

Chill 2 cups of sliced cucumbers in ice water. Season 1 cup of sour cream with vinegar, salt, and pepper. Add 1 teaspoon each of chopped chives and parsley. Drain the cucumbers and mix lightly with the sour cream. Serves 4.

ROLLED TOAST

Slice sandwich bread wafer-thin. Remove crusts and brush lightly with creamed butter. Roll on the diagonal. Toast slowly, turning until crisp and brown.

ANGEL PIE

Beat 3 egg whites stiff. Add ¼ teaspoon of cream of tartar and 1 cup of sugar. Beat until stiff and glossy. Shape as a pie crust in a 9-inch pie pan. Bake 20 minutes at 275° and then 40 minutes at 300°. Cool. Fill with custard and whipped cream.

Custard Filling. — Mix ¾ cup of sugar with 2 tablespoons of cornstarch and ¼ teaspoon of salt. Moisten with 3 egg yolks beaten with 1 tablespoon of lemon juice. Add ¾ cup of boiling water, 1½ teaspoons of grated lemon rind, and 5 tablespoons of lemon juice. Cook until thick, stirring all the time. Cool. Whip ½ pint of cream stiff and spread half of it over the cooled meringue shell. Add all of the cooled custard and top with the remaining cream. Leave in the refrigerator 24 hours.

```
Menu

LETTUCE SOUP

MOLDS OF RED CAVIAR SURROUNDED WITH
VEGETABLES

QUICK RAISED ROLLS

COFFEE CREAM CHIFFON PIE
```

LETTUCE SOUP

Melt 1 tablespoon of butter in a frying pan and blend in 1 teaspoon of flour. Add 1 teaspoon of tarragon vinegar and 1 teaspoon of sugar. Chop 2 heads of lettuce very fine and add to first mixture. Simmer slowly for 15 minutes. Add 6 cups of canned consommé. Season with salt and pepper. Add 1 cup of cream and serve. Serves 6.

MOLDS OF RED CAVIAR SURROUNDED WITH VEGETABLES

The first time I ate these delicious molds was at a ladies' luncheon. My hostess had arranged the platter most attractively. A bowl of dressing in the center was surrounded with the caviar molds alternating with hearts of artichoke filled with celery and peas, which had been marinated with French dressing. The edge of the platter was decorated with water cress and halves of peeled small tomatoes covered with chopped egg.

Dissolve 1 tablespoon of gelatine in ¼ cup of cold water. Add 1 cup of boiling water, 1 grated onion, and season with ½ teaspoon each of salt and pepper. Stir until gelatine is dissolved and then put it in the refrigerator until it starts to thicken. Beat ½ cup of cream and mix with ½ cup of mayonnaise and the juice of ½ lemon. Add the thickened gelatine and gently fold in a large jar of domestic red caviar. Fill 6 timbale molds which have been greased with salad oil. Keep in the refrigerator until firm. (Prepare the day before.) Serve with a piquant dressing made with ¾ cup of mayonnaise chopped chives and parsley, and 2 tablespoons of lemon juice. Season with 1 teaspoon of A–1 sauce, 2 tablespoons of tomato catsup, and salt and pepper. Thin with a little cream. Serves 6.

QUICK RAISED ROLLS
(1 hour)

Heat 1 cup of milk to room temperature and add 2 teaspoons of sugar, 1 egg, 1 teaspoon of salt, 4 teaspoons of shortening, and 1 yeast cake. Mix all together; then add enough flour to make a soft dough. Roll out and cut in small circles. Let rise until twice their size and bake in a moderate oven.

COFFEE CREAM CHIFFON PIE

Soak 2 tablespoons of gelatine in ½ cup of cold water. Dissolve in 2 cups of strong, hot coffee with ½ cup of sugar. Pour into 2 beaten egg yolks. Beat thoroughly; then place in the top of a double boiler and cook until the mixture thickens. Let cool until gelatine stiffens. Whip with a wire whisk until it is fluffy; then add 1 teaspoon of vanilla. Beat 1 cup of cream until stiff and add 1 tablespoon of sugar. Add ⅛ teaspoon of salt to 2 egg whites and beat until stiff. Fold the whipped cream into the coffee mixture and then fold in the egg whites. Pour into the shell of Zwieback Crumb Crust (p. 80) and chill before serving. (Prepare the day before.) Serves 6.

Menu

ORANGE AND RASPBERRY NECTAR

STUFFED HAM SLICES

MIXED GREEN SALAD

MOLDED BING CHERRIES

ORANGE AND RASPBERRY NECTAR

Chill 1 quart of orange juice very cold. Just before luncheon, beat in 1 pint of raspberry sherbet. Serve in glasses with a sprig of mint on top. Serves 6.

STUFFED HAM SLICES

Have your butcher slice boiled ham (which comes in oblong loaf), using slicer No. 7. Make a stuffing of 2 cups of fresh bread crumbs and season with a dash of pepper and ¼ teaspoon curry powder. Add ½ cup melted butter or margarine and ¾ cup of whole kernel corn. Mix thoroughly. Bind together with the white of 1 egg.

Butter each slice of ham lightly, cover with stuffing, roll, and fasten with toothpicks. Place in a roasting pan, not too close together. Pour over ½ cup of melted butter or margarine. Bake in a moderate oven (350°) about half an hour, basting often. Remove ham rolls and add ⅓ cup of cream to the sauce in the pan. Mix well and pour over ham rolls.

MOLDED BING CHERRIES

Soak 3 tablespoons of gelatine in ½ cup of orange juice. Drain 1 can of pitted Bing cherries and mix the juice with 1½ cups of orange juice and 1 cup of sherry. Heat to the boiling point, add the gelatine mixture, and stir until dissolved. Put in the refrigerator until it begins to stiffen and then pour into a fancy ring mold. Add the Bing cherries, which have been stuffed with any kind of nut meat. (Prepare the day before.) Unmold and serve with a bowl of whipped cream in the center and surround with assorted canned fruit and green leaves. Serves 6.

Menu

EGGS IN ASPIC WITH GREEN MAYONNAISE

CHICKEN FRIED WITH ALMONDS

CASSEROLE OF EGGPLANT AND CORN

PEARS IN WINE SYRUP

CHOCOLATE MACAROONS

EGGS IN ASPIC WITH GREEN MAYONNAISE

Poach in metal poaching rings the desired number of eggs. Leave in the rings and pour over each canned, jellied consommé. Place in the refrigerator until the consommé has stiffened. (Prepare the day before.) Unmold on slices of tomato covered with a thin slice of liverwurst. Serve with Green Mayonnaise (p. 40).

CHICKEN FRIED WITH ALMONDS
(Henri's)

Cut 2 young frying chickens into serving pieces (discard backs, necks and tips of wings). Dip the chicken in milk and then roll them in finely ground almonds. Dredge with flour, well seasoned with salt and pepper, and sauté in butter until well browned and tender. Place the chicken in an earthenware casserole, cover with 1½ cups of cream or evaporated milk, and continue cooking for about 10 minutes. Sprinkle with chopped almonds and serve in the casserole. Serves 6.

CASSEROLE OF EGGPLANT AND CORN
(Emma's)

Sauté 1 sliced onion and 1 minced clove of garlic in 2 table-spoons of olive oil until tender but not brown. Peel 3 large to-matoes, cut into pieces, and remove the seeds. Season with salt, pepper, and cayenne. Simmer in a stewpan until thickened. Peel 1 large eggplant and cut into cubes. Season with salt and pepper and dredge with flour. Brown in 2 tablespoons of olive oil. Ar-range in a casserole with the onion and garlic and pour the to-mato mixture over it. Cover and bake in a slow oven for 15 minutes. Meanwhile mix 2 cups of canned corn (cream style) with 2 beaten egg yolks and 2 tablespoons of melted butter. Beat the egg whites stiff and fold into the corn. Remove the casserole from the oven and pour the corn mixture over the eggplant. Replace in the oven and bake without a cover until the corn mixture is set and brown. Serves 6.

PEARS IN WINE SYRUP

Boil together for 10 minutes 1 cup of brown sugar, 2 cups of red wine, and 2 cloves. Peel 8 firm pears, leaving the stems on. Place in the syrup and boil until done, turning the pears from time to time so that all sides reach the syrup. Remove the pears, boil the juice down to a thick syrup, and pour back over the fruit. Chill until ice-cold and serve with sour cream. (Prepare the day before.) Serves 8.

CHOCOLATE MACAROONS

Beat 2 egg whites stiff. Add 1 cup of sugar and ⅛ teaspoon of salt and beat again. Add ½ teaspoon of vanilla. Melt and mix in 1½ squares of chocolate (or 1½ ounces), and add 1½ cups of dry cocoanut. Drop by teaspoonfuls onto a greased cookie sheet and bake in a slow oven (275°) for ½ hour. (Prepare the day before.)

Menu

SOUP SUPERB

LOBSTER IN ASPIC

BUTTERY MELBA TOAST

STRAWBERRIES ROMANOFF

SOUP SUPERB
(Peggy's)

Dilute 2 cans of real turtle soup with 1 can of consommé and 1 can of water. Add 2 cans of pea soup. Heat in a French earthenware casserole. Cover with 1 cup of cream, whipped. Sprinkle thickly with grated Parmesan cheese. Brown under the broiler. Serve the soup in the casserole. Serves 6.

LOBSTER IN ASPIC

Soak 2 tablespoons of gelatine in ¼ cup of cold water. Dissolve in 2 cups of diluted, hot, canned bouillon. Add 1 cup of dry white wine.

Fill a fish mold almost full with either canned or fresh boiled lobster and pour in the aspic. Chill in the refrigerator until firm. (Prepare the day before.) Unmold on a serving platter. Surround with hard-boiled eggs, peeled tomato halves, and sliced cucumbers seasoned with French dressing. Decorate the platter with lettuce leaves. Serve with Green Mayonnaise (p. 40). Serves 6.

STRAWBERRIES ROMANOFF

Clean and hull 2 quarts of strawberries. Sweeten with sugar. Whip 1 pint of vanilla ice cream and fold in ½ pint of cream, whipped. Add the juice of 1 lemon, 1 ounce of rum, and 2 ounces of Cointreau. Pour the cream over the strawberries. Serves 8.

Menu

TOMATO JUICE COCKTAIL

CHICKEN BREASTS IN ASPIC À LA STUART

MUFFINS

DATE TORTE WITH BRANDY BUTTER SAUCE

TOMATO JUICE COCKTAIL

Simmer together for 30 minutes 1 large can of tomatoes, 1 bay leaf, 1 clove of garlic, ½ onion, and a few whole black peppers. Strain and season with salt, celery salt, pepper, and Worcestershire sauce. A dash of Tabasco may be added, also lemon juice. Chill and serve very cold. (Prepare the day before.) Serves 6.

CHICKEN BREASTS IN ASPIC À LA STUART

Fry 4 chicken breasts in fat with a clove of garlic until very brown. Chop fine 1 onion, 1 clove of garlic, a few sprigs of parsley, and 2 raw carrots. Sauté in 3 tablespoons of butter but do not brown. Add to the chicken; then add 2 cups of water, 2 chicken bouillon cubes, and 1½ cups of white wine. If you have a pressure cooker, place the chicken in it and cook for ½ hour; otherwise simmer in a covered kettle until the chicken is tender. Discard the bones and arrange the chicken in a mold. Strain and measure the stock and, if necessary, add more water to make 3 cups. Soak 2 tablespoons of gelatine in ½ cup of cold water. Heat the stock and add the gelatine, stirring until dissolved. Pour over the chicken. Place in the refrigerator until firm. (Prepare the day before.)

Unmold on a platter and surround with hard-boiled eggs split lengthwise, the yolks removed, and the whites refilled with red caviar. Decorate the platter with water cress. Serve with Sour Cream Dressing. Serves 6.

Sour Cream Dressing. —

1½ cups mayonnaise	1 tablespoon chopped chives
¾ cup sour cream	¼ teaspoon dry mustard
2 tablespoons chopped parsley	2 teaspoons horse-radish

Mix well and place in the refrigerator until needed. (Prepare in the morning.)

DATE TORTE

Beat the yolks of 4 eggs and add 1 cup of sugar gradually. Add ¼ cup of cracker crumbs and 1 teaspoon of baking powder. Mix in 1 package of dates, pitted and sliced, and ½ cup of walnut meats cut in pieces. Place in a square pan and bake about 1 hour in a 300° oven. Cut in squares and serve with Brandy Butter Sauce. (Prepare the day before.) Serves 6.

Brandy Butter Sauce. — Blend 4 tablespoons of butter with 2 tablespoons of flour. While stirring, add slowly 1 cup of water and 2 tablespoons of sugar. Let come to a boil and then continue cooking over hot water for 10 minutes. Flavor with brandy. Serve hot.

Menu

CREAM OF CARROT SOUP

FRIED SHRIMPS WITH ALMONDS

GREEN PEAS COOKED WITH BUTTER

COFFEE NUT FLUFF WITH
COFFEE CUSTARD SAUCE

CREAM OF CARROT SOUP

Cook enough carrots to measure 1 cupful when mashed. Rub through a purée sieve. Melt 3 tablespoons of butter in the top of a double boiler and add 2 tablespoons of flour. Stir until well blended. Add gradually 2 cups of hot milk and cook until thick. Stir constantly. Add the carrot purée and 1 can of consommé and taste for seasoning. (Prepare the day before and reheat in a double boiler.) Serve hot with chopped parsley sprinkled over the top. Serves **6**.

FRIED SHRIMPS WITH ALMONDS

Cut into slivers ½ cup of blanched almonds. Melt ½ cup of butter in an iron skillet and sauté the almonds until a light brown. Remove from the butter and keep warm. Add 2 cans of shrimps, drained and cleaned. Sauté until a light brown. Remove to a serving platter and sprinkle with the almonds. Add 3 tablespoons of lemon juice to the butter in which the shrimps were cooked and pour over the shrimps and almonds. Decorate the platter with parsley and serve at once. Serves **4**.

GREEN PEAS COOKED WITH BUTTER

Shell 3 pounds of peas. Place in a pan with 3 tablespoons of butter and ¼ cup of water. Season with salt and sugar. Cover the pan tightly and cook until tender, shaking the pan frequently. Serves **6**.

COFFEE NUT FLUFF

Prepare 2 cups of very strong coffee. Soak 2 tablespoons of gelatine in 4 tablespoons of cold water. Dissolve in the hot coffee and chill. Whip 1 cup of cream until stiff and add ¾ cup of powdered sugar and 1 teaspoon of vanilla. When the gelatine starts to thicken, whip until light and fluffy. Fold in the whipped cream and add 1 cup of ground walnut meats. Pour into a mold rinsed in cold water. Place in the refrigerator until firm. (Prepare the day before.) Unmold and serve with Coffee Custard Sauce (p. 85). Serves 6.

Menu

MELON CUP

CUSTARD MOLD WITH MUSHROOMS

GREEN CORN FRITTERS

MINTED PEAR DESSERT

MELON CUP

Scoop out balls from the ripe flesh of a honeydew melon, a cantaloupe, and a watermelon. Place the melon balls in a bowl and add, for each person to be served, the juice of 1 lemon and 1 orange, 2 tablespoons of preserved ginger, and a little ground ginger. Place in the refrigerator for half an hour and serve in individual glasses decorated with sprigs of mint.

CUSTARD MOLD WITH MUSHROOMS

Beat 8 eggs and add to 1 quart of milk seasoned with salt and pepper. Add dry mustard and Worcestershire sauce to taste. Pour into a buttered ring mold, place in a pan of hot water, and bake in a moderate oven (350°). When firm, unmold on a platter, fill with canned mushroom soup, and surround with broiled mushrooms. Serves 8.

GREEN CORN FRITTERS

Scrape enough kernels from fresh corn to make 4 cupfuls. Add 4 beaten egg yolks. Sift 1 cup of flour with ½ teaspoon of baking powder and 1 teaspoon of salt, and add to the corn. If necessary add enough milk to make a soft batter. Fold in the stiffly beaten whites. Drop by spoonfuls on a well-buttered griddle and sauté until crisp and brown. Serves 8.

MINTED PEAR DESSERT

Remove mint jelly from 2 large glasses and whip it with a fork until broken into small pieces. Soften 2 teaspoons of gelatine in 4 tablespoons of cold water and then melt over hot water.

Add the juice of 2 lemons and then fold in 2 cups of cream, whipped. Lastly add the jelly.

Drain a can of Bartlett pears and place in a serving dish. Pour green mint syrup or crème de menthe over them. Lightly cover the pears with the mint gelatine, leaving it uneven and ruffled in peaks. Set in the refrigerator until the gelatine is firm. (Prepare the day before.) Serves 8.

Menu

CHINESE CHICKEN SOUP

CRAB MEAT WITH MUSTARD DRESSING

SPOON BREAD SOUFFLÉ

STRAWBERRIES WITH COFFEE ICE CREAM

CHINESE CHICKEN SOUP

Thin canned chicken and noodle soup with water but add enough chicken bouillon cubes for a good flavor. For each can of soup, slice thin 1 stalk of celery and 1 green onion (use both green and white parts). Add to the soup and cook for 15 minutes. (The celery and onion should not be soft.) Sprinkle chopped hard-boiled egg over the top.

CRAB MEAT WITH MUSTARD DRESSING

Pick over canned crab meat, lobster, or shrimp. Mix with Mustard Dressing (p. 75). Pile in the center of a platter, sprinkle with capers, and surround with artichoke hearts and halves of hard-boiled eggs. (Prepare ahead of time and chill in the refrigerator.)

SPOON BREAD SOUFFLÉ

Heat 2 cups of milk until boiling. Stir in gradually ½ cup of corn meal and continue stirring until the mixture is the consistency of mush. Add 1 teaspoon of salt and 2 tablespoons of butter. Beat 3 egg yolks with ½ cup of milk and stir into the batter. Add 1 teaspoon of baking powder and fold in the stiffly beaten whites of 3 eggs. Pour into a greased baking dish and bake for 30 minutes in a 400° oven. Serve at once.

STRAWBERRIES WITH COFFEE ICE CREAM

Wash and hull 1 quart of strawberries. Sprinkle with powdered sugar. (Prepare in the morning.) Pour a glass of port wine over them and let boil for 5 minutes. Pour brandy over them. Light and bring to the table burning. To be served over coffee ice cream. These strawberries may be prepared in a chafing dish at the table. Serves 4.

Menu

SCALLOPED SEA FOOD WITH WINE

LIMA BEANS FLAVORED WITH MINT

GRAPES WITH GINGER ALE AND
PINEAPPLE SALAD RING

ORANGE AND LEMON MAYONNAISE

COFFEE FLUFF

SCALLOPED SEA FOOD WITH WINE

Heat 1 can of mushroom soup with ¼ cup of cream. Add 4 tablespoons of dry white wine and 2 tablespoons of sherry. Fold in 1 medium-sized can of shredded tuna, salmon, or shrimps. Pour into buttered fish shells and cover with bread crumbs with or without grated cheese. (Prepare in the morning.) Dot with butter and bake in a hot oven (400°) until crumbs are brown. Serves 4.

LIMA BEANS FLAVORED WITH MINT

Cook fresh Lima beans until tender. Melt butter in a separate dish and add sprigs of fresh mint leaves. Let stand while beans are cooking. Drain beans, add the mint-flavored butter (minus the mint), and serve.

GRAPES WITH GINGER ALE AND PINEAPPLE SALAD RING

Soak 2 tablespoons of gelatine in 2 tablespoons of cold water. Drain a No.-2½ can of grated pineapple and heat the juice. Stir the gelatine into the hot pineapple juice; when dissolved, add 2 cups of ginger ale, ¼ cup of lemon juice, 2 tablespoons of sugar, and a pinch of salt. Place gelatine in a cool place until it begins to set; then stir in the grated pineapple. Pour into a decorative ring mold and place in the refrigerator until firm. (Prepare the day before.) Unmold on a platter and fill the center with Orange and Lemon Mayonnaise (p. 64). Serves 6.

Seed green grapes and red grapes and soak in port wine. Arrange in bunches around the outside of the platter. Decorate with fresh grape leaves.

COFFEE FLUFF

Melt 20 to 25 marshmallows in 1 cup of hot, very strong coffee. This must be stirred often while cooling, as the gelatine in marshmallows does not mix well. When smooth and cold, add ½ pint of whipped cream and let stand in the dish in which it is to be served. Keep in the refrigerator until time to serve. (Prepare the day before.)

Serve with Hot Chocolate Sauce (p. 43).

Menu

STUFFED BEET SALAD

HAM AND CUSTARD PIE

QUICK BISCUITS

BING CHERRIES WITH
WHIPPED CREAM SAUCE

STUFFED BEET SALAD

Boil large beets until tender. Peel and chill. Hollow out the center and squeeze a small amount of lemon juice inside the cavity. Fill with finely chopped celery and green peas mixed with tart mayonnaise. Serve on lettuce leaves. Pour over French dressing just before serving.

HAM AND CUSTARD PIE

Make a rich pastry and line a pie tin. Fill with dried beans to hold the crust in shape and bake until the crust is nearly cooked; then remove the beans and finish baking. (Prepare in the morning.)

Mince 1 onion fine and cook in a little butter until soft, but do not brown.

Heat 2 cups of cream and pour over 4 beaten eggs. Season with salt and pepper. Add the minced, cooked onion and 1 tablespoon each of chopped chives and parsley.

Sprinkle the bottom of the pie crust with 4 slices of shredded boiled ham and pour the custard over it. Bake in a 325° oven until the custard is set. Serves 6.

BING CHERRIES WITH WHIPPED CREAM SAUCE

Heat canned Bing cherries. Flavor with sherry or brandy. Serve hot with Whipped Cream Sauce. Other canned fruits may be used in place of the cherries.

Whipped Cream Sauce. — Beat 2 egg yolks and add gradually 1 cup of powdered sugar. Fold in 1 cup of cream, whipped, and ½ cup of brandy or sherry.

Menu

JELLIED CHICKEN SALAD

MACARONI AND MUSHROOM SOUP CASSEROLE

FLUFFY CORN MEAL DROPS

BAKED LEMON PUDDING

JELLIED CHICKEN SALAD

Dissolve 1 package of lemon gelatine in 1 cup of boiling water. Add ½ cup of cold water and the juice and grated rind of 1 lemon. Mix in ½ cup of diced, cooked chicken (canned will do), and ¼ cup each of chopped celery, canned peas, chopped nuts, and stuffed olives. Pour into a ring mold and place in the refrigerator until firm. (Prepare the day before.) Unmold and fill the center with mayonnaise and surround with bunches of canned asparagus. Serves 6.

MACARONI AND MUSHROOM SOUP CASSEROLE

Boil 1 small package of macaroni; drain and add 2 cans of mushroom soup mixed with ½ cup of grated cheese. Bake in a casserole with strips of bacon over the top until bacon is brown. Serves 6.

FLUFFY CORN MEAL DROPS
(Peggy's)

Pour 7 tablespoons of boiling water over 5 tablespoons of white corn meal. Mix and cool. Beat 4 egg whites with ¼ teaspoon of salt until stiff. Fold into the corn meal. Drop by spoonfuls onto a greased cookie sheet and bake in a 325° oven for about half an hour. Serves 6.

BAKED LEMON PUDDING
(Helen's)

Cream 1 cup of sugar with 1 tablespoon of butter. Add a pinch of salt and the juice and grated rind of 1 lemon. Beat together 2 egg yolks, 2 tablespoons of flour, and 1 cup of milk. Add to the first mixture. Lastly fold in the 2 stiffly beaten egg whites. Place in a buttered glass casserole and put in a pan of hot water. Bake in a slow oven (275°) 30 minutes. Serves 4.

If a larger quantity is desired, make 2 puddings instead of a double recipe.

Menu

SWEETBREADS AND BLACK WALNUTS

CREAMED SPINACH RING WITH
BROILED MUSHROOMS

FLAMING PEARS WITH SABAYON SAUCE

THIN BUTTER COOKIES

SWEETBREADS AND BLACK WALNUTS

Soak sweetbreads in salted water for half an hour. Place them in a saucepan and just cover with water to which 1 tablespoon of vinegar has been added. Let simmer 20 minutes. Remove and place in cold water for 15 minutes. Drain. Remove the membrane and season with salt and black pepper. Dip sweetbreads in white of egg and roll in finely ground black walnuts. (Prepare in the morning.) Sauté slowly in butter in a covered pan.

CREAMED SPINACH RING WITH BROILED MUSHROOMS

Wash spinach and cook in a very small quantity of water. When cooked, drain and press out as much water as possible with your hands. Chop fine, season, and mix with enough thick cream sauce to hold together. Place in a buttered ring mold, cover with paper, and place in the refrigerator. Reheat by placing mold in a pan of hot water in a medium oven. Invert ring on a platter and serve filled with broiled mushrooms.

FLAMING PEARS WITH SABAYON SAUCE

Heat canned pears, whole ones, if possible. Drain off the syrup. Place the pears in a chafing dish and bring them into the dining room. Pour ½ cup of brandy over them and light. Serve with Sabayon Sauce.

Sabayon Sauce. — Beat 8 egg yolks, a pinch of salt, 1 cup of sugar, and the juice of ½ lemon. Cook in the top of a double boiler until thick, stirring constantly. Cool. (Prepare the day before.) Add gradually 2 teaspoons of brandy and 1 cup of cream, whipped. Serve.

THIN BUTTER COOKIES

Cream 1 cup of butter. Add 1 cup of sugar and continue creaming. Mix in 4 beaten egg yolks until smooth. Add enough flour to roll out thin. Cut with small-sized, fancy cutter. Paint each cookie with egg yolk and sprinkle with sugar and chopped nuts. Bake in a hot oven (400°).

Menu

ARTICHOKES STUFFED WITH SHRIMPS

LUNCHEON GELATINE SALAD

CHEESE BISCUITS

ORANGE SOUFFLÉ

ARTICHOKES STUFFED WITH SHRIMPS

Boil 8 artichokes in water to which 2 tablespoons of vinegar have been added for about 45 minutes, or until tender. Turn upside down until drained and cool. Cut off stem end and spread leaves apart. Remove choke. Fill with the following mixture and place in the refrigerator until cold and ready to serve: 3 cups of shrimps, cleaned, 1½ cups celery, diced, and 4 hard-boiled eggs, chopped fine. Blend with mayonnaise — about ¾ cup, or enough to hold the mixture together. When ready to serve, put 1 tablespoon of mayonnaise on top of each artichoke. (Prepare ahead of time.) Serves 8.

LUNCHEON GELATINE SALAD

Slice 1 small bottle stuffed olives. Add to 1 package of lime gelatine (prepared according to the recipe on the package). Add 1 cup of chopped nuts. Put in a ring mold and place in the refrigerator until firm. (Prepare the day before.) Unmold on a platter and fill the center with cottage cheese flavored with onion juice and thinned with mayonnaise. Serves 6.

CHEESE BISCUITS

Sift together 2 cups of flour, 2 teaspoons of baking powder, and ½ teaspoon of salt. Mix in 2 tablespoons of shortening lightly with the fingers and add enough milk to make the right consistency for rolling. Roll out to about 1 inch thick. Cut out and place biscuits in a pan, close together. Mash ½ cup of butter with 1 cake of pimiento cheese and spread it over the biscuits. Bake in a hot oven (475°) for about 12 minutes. (Cheese mixture may be prepared ahead of time.)

ORANGE SOUFFLÉ
(Mary's)

Use 1 egg white for each person and 1 for the double boiler, and 1 tablespoon of sugar for each egg white. First beat the egg whites stiff; then beat in the sugar gradually. Add orange marmalade in the proportion of 5 tablespoons of marmalade to 6 egg whites. (Increase the marmalade with the number of whites, but always have 1 tablespoon less of marmalade than the number of egg whites.) Butter the top of a double boiler, put in the soufflé, and put the lid on. For 6 to 8 eggs steam for 1 hour. Serve with Soufflé Sauce.

If your guests are late, don't worry, just turn down the flame and keep the water under the soufflé hot. It won't fall!

Soufflé Sauce. — Beat 2 egg yolks and add powdered sugar until the mixture is too stiff to beat. Beat two thirds of a half pint of cream and just before serving mix the two together. Flavor with brandy. This amount of sauce will serve 4.

Menu

CHICKEN, MUSHROOMS, AND SPINACH
EN CASSEROLE

DELICIOUS MUFFINS

MOLDED ALMOND AND RASPBERRY SALAD

CHOCOLATE STEAMED PUDDING

CHICKEN, MUSHROOMS, AND SPINACH EN CASSEROLE

This is a good way to use what is left of a holiday bird:

Make a rich cream sauce, using 3 cups of whole milk and 3 tablespoons each of flour and butter. (Put aside 1 cup of the white sauce to be used later.) Sauté 2 large onions, chopped fine, in 2 tablespoons of butter, but do not brown. Add 1 pound of mushrooms, either fresh or canned, and let simmer with onion for a few minutes. Save a few of the mushrooms to put on the top layer and add the rest to the cream sauce. Boil enough spinach for 6 people, drain, put through the food chopper, and mix with the additional cup of cream sauce. Season to taste. Put in the casserole and cover with the mushroom mixture. Arrange pieces of chicken or turkey on top, adding the remaining mushrooms last. Put the cover on and warm in the oven.

This dish may be made early in the day and reheated in time for luncheon. The spinach and cream sauce may be cooked the day before. Canned chicken may be used and the chicken may be sliced or shredded. Mushroom soup may be used also, instead of mushrooms. Serves 6.

MOLDED ALMOND AND RASPBERRY SALAD

Drain and heat the juice from 1 large can of red raspberries. Soak 1 tablespoon of gelatine in ¼ cup of cold water and dissolve in the heated fruit juice. Add the juice of 1 large lemon and ¼ cup of sugar. Stir until dissolved. Place in the refrigerator to chill, and when it begins to congeal, fold in ⅔ cup of slivered celery, ½ cup of shredded almonds, and then the drained raspberries. Pour into a rinsed ring mold and allow to set in the refrigerator. (Prepare the day before.) Unmold on hearts of lettuce and serve with a mayonnaise dressing. This salad can also be used as a dessert, using whipped cream instead of mayonnaise. Serves 6.

CHOCOLATE STEAMED PUDDING

Pour ½ cup of port wine over ¾ cup of bread crumbs. Cut 2 tablespoons of almonds in slivers and combine with 1 square of melted chocolate, 3 tablespoons of sugar, ⅛ teaspoon of ground cloves, and ⅛ cup of dried currants. Mix with bread crumbs and add the beaten yolks of 4 eggs. Fold in the stiffly beaten whites. Butter a covered mold and fill two-thirds full. Steam for 2 hours and serve with whipped cream or Hot Chocolate Sauce (p. 43). Serves 4.

Menu

CRAB WITH SHERRY IN SHELLS

PURÉED PEAS IN RING

BUTTERED CARROTS

MOLDED PINEAPPLE AND CABBAGE SALAD

CHOCOLATE RING WITH BING CHERRY SAUCE

CRAB WITH SHERRY IN SHELLS

2 cups crab meat	2 teaspoons lemon juice
2 hard-boiled eggs, chopped	½ teaspoon Worcestershire sauce
1 cup mayonnaise	½ teaspoon prepared mustard
1 teaspoon grated onion	3 tablespoons sherry
1 teaspoon chopped parsley	1 cup buttered bread crumbs

Mix all the ingredients, saving out ½ cup of bread crumbs for the top. Place in scallop shells or ramekins and cover with the remainder of the crumbs. (This may be prepared in the morning and stored in the refrigerator. Take out ahead of time, to remove the chill.) Bake in a 400° oven for 15 minutes. Serves 6.

PURÉED PEAS IN RING

Shell and cook 5 pounds of peas in enough boiling water to cover. Season with ½ teaspoon of salt and 1 teaspoon of sugar. When cooked, drain and press through a purée sieve. Add 3 tablespoons of melted butter and pack in a buttered ring mold. (This part of the recipe may be prepared the day before.) Cover the mold and place in a pan of water. Bake in a moderate oven for 20 minutes. Serves 8. (Canned puréed pea soup may be used.)

BUTTERED CARROTS

Dice fine 2 bunches of carrots and boil until tender. Mix with melted butter and fill the center of the ring of puréed peas.

MOLDED PINEAPPLE AND CABBAGE SALAD

Dissolve 1 package of lime gelatine in 1 cup of boiling water. Let cool. In the meantime place the contents of 1 small can of crushed pineapple in a sieve, pressing the pineapple with a spoon to drain off as much juice as possible. Add enough water to the juice to make ¾ cup of liquid. Flavor with ⅛ teaspoon of peppermint extract and add to the lime gelatine. Place in refrigerator until the mixture starts to thicken. Add the crushed pineapple and 1 cup of shredded cabbage. Pour into a decorative mold and chill until firm. Serves 6. (Prepare the day before your party.) Unmold on a serving platter and serve with mayonnaise.

CHOCOLATE RING WITH BING CHERRY SAUCE

Melt 1½ squares of Baker's chocolate and mix with 1 cup of sugar and 2 tablespoons of butter. Beat in 2 eggs, 1 at a time, and add 1 cup of milk. Sift together 1 cup of flour and 2 teaspoons of baking powder. Stir into the chocolate mixture. Flavor with 1 teaspoon of vanilla. Pour into a buttered ring mold and bake in a moderate oven (325°) for 20 minutes. Unmold and fill the center with a bowl of the Bing Cherry Sauce.

Bing Cherry Sauce. — Heat 2 cans of pitted Bing cherries in the top of a double boiler. Add 2 tablespoons of cornstarch mixed with a little cold water. Add ½ cup of granulated sugar and the juice of ½ lemon. Cook until thick. Add 1 cup of broken walnut meats. (Prepare ahead of time and reheat.)

Dessert Bridge

The idea of dessert bridge was born of the desire of brides or young mothers to entertain easily and inexpensively. Having neither the money nor the time to prepare the elaborate bridge luncheons that their mothers give, they have devised the dessert bridge. Instead of hours spent in concocting delicious and tempting foods, they serve only the crowning glory of a luncheon or dinner — in other words, the dessert.

The dessert bridge allows the guests as well as the hostess to feed the babies and tuck them safely in bed before the party. The time usually set for the afternoon dessert bridge is one-thirty, but, naturally, it can be earlier or later, as long as the girls are prompt and don't delay the start of the bridge game.

The dessert itself should be delicious as well as glamorous. But be sure it can be made the day before or else very early in the morning, for no matter how hard you try or how carefully you may have laid your plans, an emergency may interfere with the success of the party.

The dessert may be served at the dining-room table or be passed by the hostess to the guests seated at the bridge tables. If it is a mold and has been attractively arranged on a platter, display it on a sideboard with plates and coffee cups and let each guest help herself.

Nothing is more unattractive than a woman struggling with a bridge table while her guests stand around making futile efforts to help; so, as long as relaxation is our goal, why not have the tables all ready with their decks of cards? Or, if you are planning to serve dessert on them, then cover each one with a cloth and place a tiny bouquet of flowers in the center.

Numerous desserts may be used, one of the easiest to serve being individual sponge cakes, which may be bought at the bakery, topped with a scoop of vanilla ice cream and covered with Hot Butterscotch Sauce (p. 33), which you have undoubtedly made the day before the party. Or a sponge cake may be hollowed out and filled with a cream and gelatine mixture and later coated with whipped cream. Do you like Angel Pie, or would you rather have Pots de Crème? Any dessert made with a gelatine base, or any frozen dessert, may be made the day before, giving you time to relax on the day of your party.

So all you brides or young mothers may look over the many dessert recipes that are in this chapter as well as elsewhere in the book and select something that you feel will be easy to prepare.

CARAMEL ALMOND SPONGE

Soak 1 tablespoon of gelatine in ¼ cup of cold water. Heat ½ cup of sugar until caramelized. Pour in very slowly ¾ cup of milk and stir until the sugar is dissolved. Add the gelatine with 3 tablespoons of sugar and ¼ teaspoon of salt. Stir until the sugar and gelatine are dissolved. Pour into a bowl and chill until the mixture starts to thicken. Beat until light and fluffy; then fold in ¾ cup of cream, whipped. Add ½ cup of chopped almonds and ¾ teaspoon of vanilla. Pour into a mold and chill until firm. Serves 4.

PEANUT BRITTLE BISQUE

Scald 2 cups of milk in the top of a double boiler and add 3 tablespoons of quick-cooking tapioca. Cook over hot water until the mixture is thick and the tapioca transparent. Stir, but do not rub, the mixture through a very fine sieve. Add ¼ teaspoon of salt and 4 tablespoons of light corn syrup and mix well. Cool. Beat 2 egg whites stiff and add slowly 2 tablespoons of sugar. Fold into the cold tapioca mixture. Beat 1 cup of cream stiff and add with 1 teaspoon of vanilla. Grind ½ pound of peanut brittle and add to the cream. Turn into the freezing tray of the refrigerator and set the control at the coldest point. Serves 6.

CHOCOLATE CHARLOTTE

Line 6 glasses with ladyfingers split in half. In the top of a double boiler melt 1 pound of sweet chocolate with 2 cups of milk. Stir in the well-beaten yolks of 6 eggs. Cook until thickened. Strain, pour into the glasses, and chill. Top with unsweetened whipped cream. Serves 6.

RUM CAKE

Sprinkle a sponge cake as evenly as possible with rum, using about 1 cup. Cut in sections for serving but leave intact. Spread with sweetened whipped cream and serve.

MAPLE SYRUP MOLD
(Grace's)

Soak 1 tablespoon of gelatine in ½ cup of milk. Heat 1 cup of maple syrup in the top of a double boiler and add 5 beaten egg yolks. Add the gelatine and continue beating until thick. Cool. Add 1½ cups of cream, whipped. Pour into a melon mold and place in the refrigerator until firm. Serves 4.

LIME ICE WITH RUM

Boil together for 5 minutes 3 cups of sugar and 3 cups of water. Cool and add 2 cups of strained lime juice. Pour into the freezing tray of the refrigerator and as soon as freezing begins, remove and beat with a wooden spoon. Return to refrigerator and when half frozen, beat again. Continue freezing. Serve in chilled champagne glasses, pour over each a generous spoonful of white rum, and serve at once. Serves 8.

ICE CREAM MOLD

Line a melon mold with vanilla ice cream and fill the center with orange ice. Pack in an ice and salt mixture until ready to serve. Turn out on a platter and coat thickly with freshly grated cocoanut. Surround with peeled orange sections.

MERINGUE SHELLS

Beat 3 egg whites until stiff, adding gradually 1 cup of sugar and 1 teaspoon of vinegar. Put in well-greased muffin tins and bake in a 275° oven for 5 minutes, increasing the temperature to 300° for 15 minutes. Remove from the oven. Cool and fill with vanilla ice cream. Serve with Hot Butterscotch Sauce (p. 33).

The meringue may also be baked in a pie pan and filled with any fresh fruit mixture. (The shell will crack, so do not be alarmed.) Serves 6.

ZWIEBACK TORTE
(Peggy's)

Mix thoroughly 1 package of zwieback (ground to crumbs), ½ cup of butter, ⅔ cup of sugar, and 1 tablespoon of cinnamon. Save 1 cup of the crumbs for the top, and use the rest to line the bottom and sides of a buttered oblong pan. Fill with Cream Filling.

Cream Filling. — Cook in the top of a double boiler 2 cups of milk, ½ cup of sugar, ½ teaspoon of salt, and 3 tablespoons of flour. Add 4 egg yolks and cook until thick. Cool. Stir in 1 teaspoon of vanilla. Fold in the stiffly beaten whites of 4 eggs and pour into the zwieback crust. Cover with the remaining crumb mixture and bake for 25 minutes in a 350° oven. Chill. When ready to serve, sprinkle thickly with chopped salted almonds. Serves 8.

PINEAPPLE ICE CREAM
(Edna's)

Melt ½ pound of marshmallows in ⅔ cup of milk in the top of a double boiler. Chill. When it begins to thicken, add ½ cup of drained, crushed, canned pineapple. Stir in ⅛ teaspoon of salt and ½ cup of sherry. Beat 1 cup of cream until stiff and stir into the pineapple mixture. Pour into the freezing tray of the refrigerator and freeze without stirring. Serves 6.

BAKED MACAROON SOUFFLÉ

Line a buttered mold with 18 large macaroons, which have been dipped in 1 cup of sherry. Beat 4 eggs until light, add 4 tablespoons of light brown sugar and 1 cup of blanched, ground almonds. Mix 1 cup of stale sponge cake (or toasted bread crumbs) with 2 cups of milk and flavor with 1 teaspoon of almond extract. Add to the egg mixture and pour into the macaroon-lined mold. Place additional macaroons on the top. Set in a pan of hot water and bake until firm. Unmold and serve with whipped cream flavored with sherry. Serves 6.

DATE PUDDING

Cream ½ cup of butter with 1 cup of brown sugar. Add ⅛ teaspoon of salt, ½ teaspoon of baking powder, and 1 cup of raw rolled oats.

Cut into pieces 1 package of pitted dates. Mix with 1 cup of sugar and ½ cup of water and cook to a paste. (Add more water, if necessary.)

Place half of the oatmeal mixture in the bottom of a buttered baking pan. Cover with the date mixture and top with the rest of the oatmeal mixture. Bake in a slow oven (275°) for about 30 minutes. Turn out of the pan and cool. Serve with flavored whipped cream. Serves 6.

RUM MOLD

Beat 5 egg yolks with ½ cup of sugar until light. Heat 2 cups of milk until boiling and pour over the egg mixture. Cook in the top of a double boiler until thick, stirring constantly.

Soak 2 tablespoons of gelatine in ¼ cup of cold water and dissolve in the hot mixture. Chill and when it starts to thicken, whip in 1 cup of light rum. Beat 1 cup of cream until stiff and fold into the mixture. Pour into a melon mold, which has been rinsed with cold water, and place in the refrigerator until firm. Unmold and serve with Raspberry Sauce.

Raspberry Sauce. — Melt 2 glasses of raspberry jelly over hot water. Serve slightly warm. Serves 8.

CHOCOLATE CHIP ICE CREAM

Roll 16 chocolate wafers fine. Crush 12 pieces of chocolate chip candy and stir into 1 quart of vanilla ice cream. Line the tray of the refrigerator with waxed paper and spread half of the wafer crumbs on the bottom. Fill with the ice cream mixture and cover with the remaining crumbs. Freeze. Serves 8.

RASPBERRY FREEZE

Pour 1 can of raspberries into the freezing tray of the refrigerator. When frozen, cover with 1 quart of vanilla ice cream and freeze for 1 hour longer. Serves 8.

ORANGE–DATE FROZEN MOUSSE

Chop ½ cup of pitted dates, add ¾ cup of water, and cook for 10 minutes, stirring constantly. Press through a purée sieve. Add 3 well-beaten egg yolks and stir vigorously. Put in the top of a double boiler and cook until thick. Cool. Stir in ½ cup of orange juice and mix thoroughly. Whip 1 cup of cream and fold in a little at a time, until well blended. Pour into the freezing tray of the refrigerator. Serves 6.

ORANGE CREAM

In the top of a double boiler put the beaten yolks of 2 eggs, the grated rind of 1½ oranges, the juice of 1 orange, 1 teaspoon of lemon juice, and 2 teaspoons of sugar. Cook slowly, stirring constantly, until thickened. Strain and cool.

Soak 2 teaspoons of gelatine in 2 tablespoons of water and dissolve over hot water. Beat 1 cup of cream, add the dissolved gelatine, and stir into the orange mixture. Pour into a mold and place in the refrigerator until ready to serve. Serve with Orange Fruit Sauce. Serves 4.

Orange Fruit Sauce. — Peel 3 oranges, removing all the white skin. Cut the oranges into small pieces, eliminating any tough fiber. Make a syrup by cooking 1 cup of sugar with 1 cup of orange juice. Pour hot over the oranges and chill.

BEIGNET'S SOUFFLÉS
(Jetta Grieve's)

½ cup cold water	4 eggs
1 cup flour	2 tablespoons sugar
4 tablespoons butter	⅛ teaspoon of salt
Vanilla or orange flower flavoring	

Boil together, water, butter, sugar, and salt. Add flour slowly and stir until the mixture forms a ball in the center of the pan. Cool. Add eggs one by one. Beat, beat, and beat after each egg is added. Add the flavoring.

Shape in small balls and fry in deep fat. They will more than double their size. Roll in powdered sugar and serve with Chocolate Sauce (p. 43).

PINEAPPLE DESSERT
(Lillyon's)

Peel and shred 1 fresh pineapple, or use 8 slices of canned pineapple, shredded. Cut ½ pound (2 boxes) of marshmallows into small pieces (using a pair of scissors) and stir into the pineapple. Add a little pineapple juice and leave in the refrigerator for 2 hours. Whip 1 cup of cream and add 2 tablespoons of sugar. When ready to serve, add 1½ teaspoons of lemon juice to the pineapple and fold in the whipped cream. Serve immediately. Serves 8.

APRICOT BAVARIAN CREAM

Juice of ½ lemon	1 tablespoon gelatine
½ cup apricot juice	⅓ cup cold water
½ cup sugar	1 cup canned apricots
⅛ teaspoon salt	½ cup whipping cream
3 egg yolks	3 egg whites

Mix the fruit juices, sugar, salt, and the beaten egg yolks in the top of a double boiler. Stir constantly until the mixture thickens; then remove from the fire. Add the gelatine, that has been soaked in the cold water, and the apricots, rubbed through a sieve. Chill until the mixture begins to thicken; then fold in the stiffly beaten cream and egg whites. Pour into a wet mold and chill. Serves 6. (This may be prepared the day before.)

Index

DATE DUE

MAY 2 1 1984